Let Me Be a Refugee

Let Me Be a Refugee

Administrative Justice and the Politics
of Asylum in the United States,
Canada, and Australia

REBECCA HAMLIN

OXFORD
UNIVERSITY PRESS

OXFORD
UNIVERSITY PRESS

Oxford University Press is a department of the University of Oxford.
It furthers the University's objective of excellence in research, scholarship,
and education by publishing worldwide.

Oxford   New York
Auckland   Cape Town   Dar es Salaam   Hong Kong   Karachi
Kuala Lumpur   Madrid   Melbourne   Mexico City   Nairobi
New Delhi   Shanghai   Taipei   Toronto

With offices in
Argentina   Austria   Brazil   Chile   Czech Republic   France   Greece
Guatemala   Hungary   Italy   Japan   Poland   Portugal   Singapore
South Korea   Switzerland   Thailand   Turkey   Ukraine   Vietnam

Oxford is a registered trademark of Oxford University Press
in the UK and certain other countries.

Published in the United States of America by
Oxford University Press
198 Madison Avenue, New York, NY 10016

Library of Congress Cataloging-in-Publication Data
Hamlin, Rebecca, author.
Let me be a refugee : administrative justice and the politics of asylum in the United States, Canada, and
Australia / Rebecca Hamlin.
pages cm
Summary: "This book compares the refugee status determination (RSD) regimes of three popular asylum
seeker destinations. Despite similarly high levels of political resistance to accepting asylum seekers, because
administrative justice is conceptualized and organized differently in every state, they vary in how they draw
the line between refugee and non-refugee"—Provided by publisher.
ISBN 978-0-19-937330-7 (hardback) — ISBN 978-0-19-937331-4 (paperback)   1. Asylum,
Right of—United States.   2. Asylum, Right of—Canada.   3. Asylum, Right of—Australia.
4. Refugees—Legal status, laws, etc.—United States.   5. Refugees—Legal status, laws, etc.—Canada.
6. Refugees—Legal status, laws, etc.—Australia.   7. Administrative procedure—United States.
8. Administrative procedure—Canada.   9. Administrative procedure—Australia.   I. Title.
K3268.3.H36
2014 325'.21—dc23
2014003746

9 8 7 6 5 4 3 2 1
Printed in the United States of America
on acid-free paper

To Rev. Harry J. Almond
(1918–2007)
He cared deeply about the world's conflicts and worked to heal wounds.

He never questioned his granddaughter's desire to get a PhD,
and always read my work with a pencil in hand.

CONTENTS

ACKNOWLEDGMENTS

I became forever fascinated by the refugee experience during my first post-college job, working with a consortium of Mutual Assistance Associations in the refugee resettlement neighborhood of Uptown, Chicago. I got to know families from China, Vietnam, Cambodia, Laos, Ethiopia, Iraq, Bosnia, and El Salvador, many of which had escaped war, persecution, and terrible traumas. My admiration for those with the resilience and bravery to start over in a new place, regardless of whether or not they are labeled as *refugees*, motivates and inspires all my work.

My interest in refugees and asylum seekers propelled me to Berkeley, California, for graduate school, where it was a delightful surprise to discover I not only respected and admired the intellectual capabilities of the people I met, I found friendship of the finest caliber again and again. I am grateful to the Institute of Governmental Studies for housing me, and for the camaraderie of Boris Barkanov, Naazneen Barma, Jennifer Bussell, Rebecca Chen, Thad Dunning, Brent Durbin, John Hanley, Dave Hopkins, Amy Lerman, Manoj Mate, Michael Murakami, Jessica Rich, and Regine Spector. I also cannot imagine my years at Berkeley without the intellectual support and collegiality of the Interdisciplinary Immigration Workshop, the members of which have read many iterations of my work as it progressed. I thank them all, but I am most indebted to Ming Hsu Chen, Els de Graauw, Shannon Gleeson, Ken Haig, and Phil Wolgin for their insightful feedback as well their ongoing friendship.

Of course, it is not just the graduate students that make Berkeley a special place. The faculty, too, are people of extraordinary capabilities and great warmth. As dissertation co-chairs, I could not imagine a better combination than Robert Kagan and Gordon Silverstein. Although they have different styles, Bob and Gordon share a generosity of spirit for which I have been grateful many times over the years, and both of them have been present with advice, insight, and encouragement throughout the life of this project. Bob's attention to detail, knack for practical advice, and penchant for parsing out complex concepts is the perfect match for Gordon's love of big ideas, his ability to see larger implications and ask important questions, and his regular reminders to go to the Marin Headlands and think it over. Together, they have helped me see the forest *and* the trees.

Irene Bloemraad rounded out my dissertation committee with her migration expertise, her sociological perspective, and lots of good humor. She is the founder of the beloved Interdisciplinary Immigration Workshop, and works tirelessly to bring together students and faculty from across a dispersed campus to talk about migration scholarship and share their work on a regular basis. I am so very grateful for her insightful comments, her support, and the opportunities for collaboration she has given me over the years. Beyond my dissertation committee, I particularly thank Berkeley faculty members Bruce Cain, Taeku Lee, Paul Pierson, Sarah Song, Laura Stoker, and Margaret Weir, as well as two professors who have passed away, but who were extremely influential during my early graduate school years: Judith Gruber and Nelson Polsby.

As a faculty member, I have found an incredibly supportive and generous institutional home in Grinnell College. I am very thankful for my department colleagues, as well as the friendship of many other Grinnellians, especially P. Albert Lacson, Jonathan Larson, Kelly Maynard, Angelo Mercado, and Deborah Michaels. I also thank De Dudley for academic support, and Elisabeth Rennick and Peter Sullivan for research assistance. The undergraduate students I have taught and mentored at both Grinnell and Berkeley are far too numerous to name, but I thank them wholeheartedly for helping me learn how to teach, and for helping me think through some complex questions about law, courts, justice, and migration.

I am extremely grateful for the feedback I received on this project from scholars at various conferences and symposia. In particular, I thank Chantal Berman, Alexander Betts, Joe Carens, Jim Hollifield, Leila Kawar, Anna Law, Susan Martin, Dagmar Soennecken, Steve Teles, Rachel Vansickle-Ward, and Yang-Yang Zhou for comments on various portions of this manuscript. I also thank members of Northwestern University's Center for Forced Migration Studies, Johns Hopkins University's Department of Political Science, the Southern California Law and Social Sciences Forum, and participants in the Ethics and Politics of the Global Refugee Regime Workshop at Princeton University's Bobst Center for Peace and Justice for their feedback. I will also be forever grateful to Steve Wasby for his thoughtful, kind, and much-needed mentoring through the publication stage.

Because the research for this book took me across three different countries and inside many government agencies, I relied on the generosity of hundreds of strangers to meet and speak with me about their job. In particular, I am grateful to the officials at the U.S. Department of Homeland Security, U.S. State Department, and U.S. Department of Justice; as well as the Canadian

Department of Citizenship and Immigration, and the Immigration and Refuge Board of Canada; and Australia's Department of Immigration and Citizenship, and Refugee Review Tribunal. I am also indebted to the judges, hearing officers, and asylum seekers who allowed me to observe their refugee status determinations, and to all of the advocates, lawyers, and asylum seekers who spoke to me about their experiences. I am extremely grateful to the Canadian Embassy in Washington, DC; the Pacific Rim Research Program; and the Institute for International Studies and Department of Political Science at Berkeley for generously funding portions of my research.

Book writing is not always compatible with sanity, and there are a few friends who feel like family that I must thank for keeping me afloat during this process. In particular, I owe a very special debt of gratitude to Kerri Berkowitz, who was my roommate for three long graduate school years and has miraculously remained a friend and confidante ever since. Other friends without whom I could not possibly have kept a sense of perspective, not to mention a sense of humor, during the life of this book are Alison Mckleroy, Jesse Noonan, Ben Hurwitz, Jeff Houze, and the "Cambridge Girls": Emma Berndt, Rachel Deutsch, Chloe Drew, Emily Gregory, Elise Lawson, and Alison Watkins. I thank each one of them for being inspirational people and unconditionally supportive friends.

Last, I thank my family, both old and new. My late grandfather, Harry J. Almond (to whom this book is dedicated), and my grandmother, Beverly Almond, have taught me that curiosity about the world and compassion for its people are keys to happiness. My parents, Bryan and Anne Hamlin, have made me into the person I am today. They taught me how much fun learning can be, and never to be afraid to ask questions. My in-laws, Drewcilla and Tom Annese, are similar parents, and I am thrilled to count them as family. My brother, John Hamlin, and his wife, Christina, have been incredibly supportive throughout, as have my aunt Elizabeth, my uncle Robert, and my cousins Jennifer and Christopher Lancaster. I am grateful to my brand-new daughter Althea for allowing me to slip away and complete the finals edits while she napped. And, I give my eternal gratitude and love to my husband, Tom Annese, for his patience, humor, and all he has taught me about nurturing as this book has grown.

Rebecca Hamlin
Los Angeles, California
December 2013

LIST OF ABBREVIATIONS

ADJR   Administrative Decisions (Judicial Review) Act (1977)—Australia
AWO   Affirmance Without Opinion—United States
BIA   Board of Immigration Appeals—United States
BRRA   Balanced Refugee Reform Act (2010)—Canada
CAT   Convention Against Torture (1984)
CIC   Department of Citizenship and Immigration—Canada
DCO   Designated Country of Origin—Canada
DED   Deferred Enforced Departure—United States
DIAC   Department of Immigration and Citizenship—Australia
EOIR   Executive Office of Immigration Review—United States
EVD   Extended Voluntary Departure—United States
H&C   Humanitarian and Compassionate (visa)—Canada
ICCPR   International Covenant on Civil and Political Rights (1976)
ICE   Immigration and Customs Enforcement—United States
IIRIRA   Illegal Immigration Reform and Immigrant Responsibility Act (1996)—United States
IJ   Immigration Judge—United States
INLA   Irish National Liberation Army
INS   Immigration and Naturalization Service—United States
IRB   Immigration and Refugee Board—Canada
IRPA   Immigration and Refugee Protection Act (2002)—Canada
OAU   Organization of African Unity
PRRA   Pre-removal Risk Assessment—Canada
RAD   Refugee Appeals Division—Canada
RPD   Refugee Protection Division—Canada

RRT   Refugee Review Tribunal—Australia
RSD   Refugee Status Determination
TPS   Temporary Protected Status—United States
UN   United Nations
UNHCR   United Nations High Commissioner for Refugees

PART

THE PUZZLE OF ASYLUM POLITICS

Once we had a country and we thought it fair,
Look in the atlas and you'll find it there:
We cannot go there now, my dear, we cannot go there now…
The consul banged the table and said:
"If you've got no passport you're officially dead";
But we are still alive, my dear, but we are still alive.
Refugee Blues, W.H. Auden (1939)

CHAPTER 1

Let Me Be a Refugee

The waiting room at the Toronto office of the Canadian Immigration and Refugee Board (IRB) is a space filled with muted tension. A sleepy-looking security guard glances periodically over the rows of airport-style chairs, all placed facing a bank of television screens listing the cases of the day and the hearing rooms to which they have been assigned. Potential refugees sit quietly, staring up at these screens in anticipation, not because they will reveal any new information, but for lack of an alternative distraction. As I sit there one spring morning, the activities of a family awaiting the start of their refugee status determination hearing catch my attention. The oldest daughter is amusing her younger siblings with a game she constructed out of a sheet of folded paper, a game I often played on the schoolyard as a child. She holds out the contraption with her fingertips and instructs them in Spanish to ask a question and then pick a number, so that she can use the paper to tell them their fortune. Under the circumstances, it is not difficult for the children to come up with a question. One of them asks, "Will we get to stay in Canada?" and the others nod in somber agreement. The girl looks at them and begins to count, "Uno, dos, tres, cuatro, . . ." finally unfolding a flap in the paper and reading aloud with obvious relief, "Sí." The other children erupt into cheers, momentarily breaking the anxiety-induced silence that characterizes the room.

Asylum seekers are migrants in search of a category. They arrive at the borders of states all over the world, hoping to resettle and start a new life. Yet, they often do not fall into one of the standard categories that states use to process immigrants, and thus their relationship with potential host countries is uncertain. Because many asylum seekers arrive without invitation, warning, or identification papers, they are often viewed as an undesirable and burdensome immigration problem. Policymakers worry that asylum seekers are, at best, economically motivated voluntary migrants who are skipping the extensive lines for entering developed states. At worst, they are potential terrorists attempting to enter undetected. Even if they are truly fleeing the poverty, violence, and despair that is a reality in much of the global south, there are far more people seeking refuge from those forms of oppression than host countries are able to accommodate. There are few incentives for states to welcome asylum seekers with open arms, yet states frequently allow asylum seekers to make a case for why they should be able to enter and stay. States allow them to make their case because, consciously or not, asylum seekers are asking to be officially categorized as refugees.

The modern refugee concept was conceived of by a group of European diplomats who met in Geneva, Switzerland, in 1951, while the cloud of the Second World War still hung low over their heads. These plenipotentiaries were tasked with codifying the obligations states had to protect the victims of persecution who abounded in Europe at that time. Their efforts were focused on aiding those who had already been persecuted by the Nazis or by members of the newly formed Soviet bloc. They did not anticipate the degree to which humans would continue to invent and inflict horrors upon each other in the decades to come. In fact, when the United Nations (UN) High Commissioner for Refugees (UNHCR) was appointed by the UN General Assembly in 1951, it was envisioned that the position would last three years (UN General Assembly Resolution 428(v), December 14th, 1950: Statute of the Office of the UNHCR). Instead, displacement caused by persecution has become an ongoing global phenomenon of massive proportions. The UNHCR still exists, and its office estimates that it assisted more than 28 million forcibly displaced people in 2012 alone (UNHCR 2013).[1]

Despite the historically contingent and specific vision shared by the framers of the 1951 Convention Relating to the Status of Refugees, that treaty (as updated by the Protocol to the Convention in 1967) still governs international refugee law today. One hundred forty-seven countries have signed on to these international agreements, which means that when an asylum seeker arrives at their borders, these states have pledged to determine his or her eligibility for a refugee visa. This process of evaluation is called *refugee status determination* (RSD). RSD is based on the definition written by the delegates to the 1951 Refugee Convention, which describes a refugee as someone who, because of a

> well-founded fear of being persecuted for reasons of race, religion, nationality, membership of a particular social group, or political opinion, is outside the country of his nationality and is unable, or owing to such fear, is unwilling to avail himself of the protection of that country. (Convention Relating to the Status of Refugees, Article 1, Section 1)

Wherever asylum seekers land, their stories are held up against this definition and are evaluated for compatibility with it.

States that sign on to the Convention and Protocol pledge not to return any asylum seekers to a county where their "life or freedom would be threatened" (Convention Relating to the Status of Refugees, Article 33). This principle (called *non-refoulement*, or *non-return*) is the central feature of international refugee law, obligating nations to willingly suspend their sovereignty and offer protection to people with no other claim to be present in their territory (Goodwin-Gill and McAdam 2007:1). Further, international refugee law does not require asylum seekers to follow traditional immigration channels to have their claims considered. Article 31 of the Convention states that host nations "shall not impose penalties, on account of their illegal entry or presence, on refugees who ... are present in their territory without authorization, provided they present themselves without delay to the authorities and show good cause for their illegal entry or presence." This aspect of the Refugee Convention is another test of nations' willingness to overlook the sovereign right of nations to protect and police their borders.

Although asylum seekers are a relatively small proportion of the world's total migrant population,[2] during the post-Cold War era, they have become a visible and controversial subsection of people seeking access to western democracies. Despite the active efforts of these states to deter asylum seekers, it is clear that the phenomenon of seeking refuge can no longer be contained within the developing world to the degree it was during the days of communist travel bars and prohibitively expensive global travel. Throughout the entire decade of the 1980s, there were 2.3 million applications for asylum lodged worldwide, mostly in western Europe, the United States, and Canada. During the 1990s, there were 6.1 million applications filed, almost three times as many, and the list of receiving nations grew to include Australia, New Zealand, Scandinavia, and southern Europe. During the 2000s, there were 5.5 million new applications filled worldwide, and countries such as Ireland, Greece, Poland, and South Africa became popular new destinations. In just the three years between 2010 and 2012, more than 2.6 million people went through the process of RSD worldwide, suggesting that the current decade may witness more asylum seeking than any other before it (UNHCR 2013).

Today, refugee protection is the most commonly invoked and interpreted area of international law. However, every time RSD is conducted, a shift occurs from the global to the particular, as the lofty ideals of international law take the more mundane form of bureaucratic decision making. The individual claims of asylum seekers are processed and adjudicated at the domestic level by the immigration officials of a particular state with its own conception and practices of procedural justice. For example, asylum seekers might be detained in a prison-like institution or they might be allowed to live free in the host country until their RSD hearing date. Asylum seekers might be required to hire an attorney to prove their case or they might find the necessary evidence is collected by the host country as part of their process of discovery. A refugee claim might be evaluated purely on paper or it might take place in person. A hearing might take the form of a casual conversation or it might be held in a courtroom and feel like a trial. Beyond these differences, in some countries, particular types of claims—such as a woman fleeing an abusive spouse—may be excluded from consideration by official precedent, whereas in other countries the same claim is very commonly accepted.

RSD is also fast becoming the largest area of administrative law in many destination states, and it is a particularly thorny example of bureaucratic decision making. RSD adjudicators are tasked with the distribution of an extremely valuable and coveted benefit, and the stakes of the decisions are high. A positive decision gives asylum seekers the ability to remain lawfully in the country where they seek refuge and, in most cases, eventually naturalize as citizens. In contrast, a rejection can mean deportation to a home country situation in which they could be jailed, tortured, or killed. Differentiating among potential refugees can be incredibly challenging, because the life experiences that lead people to seek refuge fall onto a wide continuum, ranging from those who are truly escaping certain death to those who are looking for economic opportunity. RSD requires decision makers to turn this continuum into a binary, and decide who among a wide spectrum of suffering deserves to be in, and who is out. In many instances, asylum decisions can often seem not much more reliable than a child's game of chance, flipping back and forth between yes and no.

In this book, I compare three popular asylum seeker destinations: the United States, Canada, and Australia. I examine the dynamic interactions among immigration politics, administrative procedures, constitutionally based rights, and international norms that shape the way RSD is conducted in each state. I find that, although the purpose of RSD is universal—to identify people who are truly in need of protection from persecution—in practice, RSD can differ greatly depending on the country where it takes place.

These cross-national differences are perhaps best illustrated by a direct comparison of the acceptance rates for asylum claims made by people originating from the same sending country. The People's Republic of China has long been a dominant source of asylum seekers in the United States, Canada, and Australia,[3] but the acceptance rates in the three states run on three remarkably distinct tracks. For example, in 2011, Australia accepted 18% of Chinese applicants, whereas the United States accepted Chinese claims more than twice as frequently, with an acceptance rate of 41%. Even more puzzling is the fact that Canada's acceptance rate for Chinese applicants was 53%, a proportion almost three times as high as Australia (UNHCR Statistical Online Population Database). These differences are apparent over a period of years; Australia's acceptance rates are consistently low, Canada's are consistently more than 50%, and the American rate has remained in between the two, but with a fair amount of variation over time.

All three states have adopted the 1967 Protocol to the 1951 Convention—the UN's treaty outlining the refugee definition in international law—and thus RSD decision makers in all three countries are interpreting an identical text to determine the validity of asylum claims. So, why do they frequently come to different conclusions, even in similar cases? Why are so many more Chinese asylum seekers categorized as refugees in Canada? Or, to put it another way, why are so few given refugee status in Australia? Furthermore, why are rates in Canada and Australia more stable, whereas they fluctuate more sharply from year to year in the United States?

Instead of answering these questions, previous research has focused almost exclusively on trying to explain the variation in refugee status grant rates *within* national contexts. For example, in the United States, Ramji-Nogales et al. (2007, 2009) extensively documented the ways in which RSD outcomes vary wildly based on who the randomly assigned decision maker is, even within the same regional office, and even among asylum applications from the same country of origin. Researchers for the Transactional Records Access Clearinghouse (TRAC) project at Syracuse University have confirmed the annual refugee status grant rates for Immigration Judges in the United States have an astonishingly wide range; judges vary between accepting 10% to 98% of asylum applications (TRAC 2012). Both studies have found that decision makers with backgrounds in immigration enforcement had lower grant rates; those who worked previously as immigration attorneys had higher grant rates. Women decision makers and those appointed by Democratic presidents also tended to grant asylum more often than others.

Similarly, in the Canadian context, Rehaag (2008:342) found that decision makers with high caseloads in Canada's administrative agency, the IRB, ranged in their grant rates from more than 95% to less than 7%.[4] Another recent study found that judges in the Federal Court of Canada were more likely to find in favor of refugee applicants if they had a liberal ideological reputation based on their previous decisions (Gould et al. 2010). No systematic analysis of acceptance rates in Australia has been done, but my interviews with advocates who regularly represent asylum seekers in RSD proceedings revealed widespread concern that, all else being equal, some Australian decision makers are far more likely to grant refugee status than others.

The fact that, no matter where asylum seekers land, RSD outcomes depend heavily on the individual characteristics of the decision maker certainly raises troubling questions about the effectiveness of the international protection regime. However, beyond this individual-level variation, there also seem to be systematic national differences that make some destinations more susceptible to individual bias and inconsistency than others. For instance, Macklin (2009b:136) wisely points out that the Canadian discrepancies are more "benign" than the American ones, because Canadian decision makers work in area-specific teams, so some may regularly hear cases from a particular refugee-producing country with violent on-the-ground conditions, whereas others regularly hear cases from places that are much more stable and less likely to produce refugees. When controlled for country of origin, the variation among RSD adjudicators is actually far more narrow in Canada than in the United States (Macklin 2009b). No existing studies have dedicated themselves to explaining this kind of cross-national difference.

In trying to understand why such cross-national variation exists, I consider several possible explanations. First, some might suggest that disparate RSD outcomes are the result of varying levels of public support for generous asylum policies. However, public support for asylum seekers is very difficult to measure, because asylum is not consistently a high-salience political issue in all three countries and there are no reliable public opinion data.[5] Especially in the United States, asylum is eclipsed by the much larger and politically contentious issue of undocumented migration, mostly from Mexico. Instead of assuming that public opinion drives outcomes, and that some countries are just "nicer" or "more welcoming" to asylum seekers, my book suggests mechanisms by which inclusive or exclusive public sentiment might translate into politics, and subsequently affect individual asylum decisions. It also considers ways in which refugee status decision making may become insulated from the battles between exclusive and inclusive interests that often drive migration politics.

Second, scholars of international relations focused on global governance and the diffusion of norms might assume that disparate outcomes are the result of judicial activism. By this logic, activist high courts can choose to enforce international norms, which then trickle down to lower levels of decision making. However, I find no empirical evidence for this theory. Of the three countries I examine in this study, Canada's Supreme Court is the least involved in asylum issues, yet the Canadian system is the most in line with international guidance. In contrast, Australia's High Court is very involved in asylum policy and frequently accused of activism by lawmakers, but it is not necessarily interested in enforcing international law, and its decisions do not trickle down to affect lower levels of decision making. Thus, I find that judicial activism does not equal internationalism.

Third, I consider whether differences in interest group activity could explain the range of RSD outcomes across countries. It is certainly the case that Canada has an established refugee and asylum seeker advocacy community with strong ties to government, and Australia has a burgeoning movement with very tense government relations. In the United States, there is strong activism led by immigration lawyers. I argue that these three styles of interest group activity are significant differences, but that they themselves need to be explained.

Finding these alternative explanations to be lacking, I develop the concept of a *refugee status determination regime.* I view an RSD regime as (1) the set of institutions that are responsible for conducting RSD and (2) the relationships and power dynamics among those institutions. The concept of a regime highlights the fact that RSD outcomes are the result of a large, complex system that must be studied holistically. A holistic approach is important because it allows for meaningful cross-national comparison that would be missed if equivalent cases on high-profile issues from each of the three countries were compared out of context or if the rhetoric of policymakers were compared without regard to outcomes. The regime approach helps us to understand why some particular issues are noncontroversial in one country, yet become contentious jurisprudential conundrums in another, and why asylum seeker advocacy takes such different forms in each place.

My comparison of RSD regimes provides a unique window into the different ways in which state actors, ranging from low-level administrators to high court judges, manage the competing pressures of sovereignty and international obligation. This study illustrates that international norms may have multiple entry points, not just via judges, for example, but also through the administrative agencies and the advocates who represent clients at those agencies. In this way, international norms can bubble up; they need not always trickle down. But beyond that insight, a systemic institutional approach also identifies additional influences on decision makers that are not related to international norms *or* migration politics. These pressures often stem from the institutional identity and professional obligations of decision makers or their place in a larger interbranch turf battle. Thus, I argue that it is a mistake to place an overemphasis on asylum policymaking when explaining RSD outcomes. Even when policymakers are openly hostile to asylum seeker claims, much of the politics is focused on the border. Once asylum seekers are inside the border, each state determines its own RSD process according to domestic patterns of administrative justice. Conceptions of due process, bureaucratic fairness, and judicial review are debated and resolved differently in each country, leading to some interesting cross-national divergences despite many observable similarities.

I conclude that the most important variable in explaining divergent RSD outcomes is the degree of insulation and independence enjoyed by the administrative agencies conducting frontline RSD decision making. Despite many political, cultural, and historic commonalities, and despite surprisingly parallel asylum policymaking, the United States, Canada, and Australia have varying traditions of procedural justice and administrative independence. Structural differences resulting from these traditions allow for differing levels of insulation from the exclusionary politics of deterrence, which in turn affects the role of courts in each RSD regime. When administrative agencies are insulated, they can weather political storms more easily, and policy is more stable over time. However, when RSD decision making tends to be driven by administrative concerns for efficiency and cost saving, there is less room for drawn out vetting of individual cases. When administrative insulation is low, courts tend to take on a much bigger role, as they try to limit legislative and executive interference in the policy area. Thus, RSD outcomes depend on the institutional players that end up dominating the process, the level of contention among actors, and the degree of centralization within the decision making processes. In other words, to understand why RSD regimes differ from one another so dramatically after asylum seekers are inside the border, we need a better understanding of the nature of bureaucratic decision making in each country.

Ultimately, this book explores not just the ways in which asylum policy is influenced by national conceptions of due process and individual rights, but also the ways in which asylum policy has come to influence these values. I argue that the process of interpreting and applying refugee rights, and the battles over what constitutes a fair refugee status determination, impact domestic structures in ways that have ramifications for procedural justice more generally. In all three countries, asylum policy has become a lynchpin in interbranch struggles over not just admissions policy, but also the establishment of institutional power. By examining the ways in which RSD regimes are connected to the development of national conceptions of administrative justice, this book provides insights into both the globalization of law and its limits.

In the next chapter, I set out an agenda for cross-national comparison. I discuss how the two dominant and opposing theories in the migration studies literature—one that sees convergence between receiving state policies and one that sees divergence between them—have together left us with an inadequate sense of the circumstances under which some state policies might be converging while others diverge. After arguing for a fruitful linkage between migration studies and the public law literatures on administrative decision making and comparative judicial politics, I explain why the United States, Canada, and Australia are perfect cases for a cross-national comparison of RSD regimes that can bring these literatures together. All three are historic "nations of immigrants" and popular asylum seeker destinations that conduct RSD on a large scale. They also share a common law system and a reputation for strong courts.

Chapter 3 is a careful account of the evolution of asylum politics in the United States, Canada, and Australia since the end of the Cold War. I illustrate that all three countries have dramatically increased their efforts to divert asylum seekers from reaching their shores and lodging claims that must be processed. I take the time to detail the rise of this regime of deterrence because many histories of asylum policy predate this trend, and so it has not yet been laid out comprehensively in the literature. It is also important for illustrating that the politics of asylum can essentially be held constant across the three country cases because they are so universally oriented toward deterrence. All three countries have become reluctant asylum seeker hosts and have put policies in place that reflect this reluctance. Thus, in order to understand divergent outcomes, we must look beyond asylum politics to the RSD regime.

Part II (Chapters 4, 5, and 6) gives an overview of the RSD regimes of the United States, Canada, and Australia in turn. For each destination, I discuss first the process and the key institutional players that are involved in RSD. I then describe the level of administrative insulation and the tenor of interactions between the administrative agency and the other players. Finally, I explain the most significant impacts of each RSD regime. Because each regime has a different character, a different institutional actor has become the focal point. In the United States, a culture of adversarial legalism, politicized interactions, and fragmentation has led to an increased judicial role in migration policy over time, particularly involving the federal Courts of Appeals. In Canada, bureaucratic centralization and high levels of agency insulation from both politics and judicial review have led to consistent and innovative policy development, but growing pressure on the administrative agency over time. In Australia, the highly uninsulated and politicized RSD regime combined with a constitutionally entrenched right for the High Court to review all decisions has led to high-profile turf battles over asylum policy between the High Court and Parliament.

Part III (Chapters 7–9) introduces several in-depth case studies that illustrate and further explain the differences between the three RSD regimes under study. In Chapter 7, I examine gender-based asylum claims in all three countries. The framers of the Convention did not anticipate claims of this nature, and the early jurisprudence was not built to incorporate them. The UNHCR has pressured receiving states to adapt to these types of claims, but each country has done so in a different manner. The Canadian administrative agency has developed innovative jurisprudence to incorporate these new types of claims within the refugee definition. The various players of the American RSD regime have battled over whether gender claims can be accepted and have made some incremental progress. In Australia, the High Court has issued some generous decisions on gender, which have inspired regressive legislation in Parliament. Thus, Chapter 7 illustrates the wide range of responses RSD regimes can have in the face of new developments on the ground.

In Chapter 8, I compare the reaction of the United States, Canada, and Australia to the large and challenging body of cases based on China's One-Child policy. As mentioned earlier, the People's Republic of China is a major source country for asylum seekers in all three destinations. However, the Chinese claims based on coercive population control do not fit naturally within the definition of a refugee. By looking at applications from the same country of origin in each place, I show how even similar claims are treated differently across receiving countries. I also show that RSD regime differences do not just matter at the margins; they can play out in ways that affect vast numbers of asylum seekers. In Canada, Chinese coercive population control claims have been subsumed under the general policy of generosity for gender-related claims. In the United States, a complex and contradictory web of jurisprudence has emerged such that it depends on which part of the country a person with a coercive population control claim lands and files their asylum application. In Australia, the High Court is engaged in a delicate interpretive dance with Parliament and has extended protection to a small subset of Chinese claimants via a strict textual reading of the refugee definition.

In Chapter 9, I move beyond the RSD process to examine the effect of RSD regimes on other related areas of migration policy. I compare the availability of complementary protection for those people who are not eligible for refugee visas but who may still be in need of protection. I find that the features of each RSD regime extend to these nontraditional asylum-seeking processes as well. In Canada, complementary protection is well integrated into the RSD regime; in the United States, it is unpredictable and highly fragmented; and in Australia, complementary protection is a highly politicized discretionary power of the Immigration Minister. This chapter illustrates that a comparative, critical understanding of a state's RSD regime can shed light on other aspects of migration decision making.

Together, the three case studies in Part III show that the impact of the cross-national differences described in Part II is more acute for the increasing number of asylum seekers whose claims do not fit naturally within the traditional concept of a refugee laid out in the 1951 Convention Relating to the Status of Refugees. Thus, Part IV consists of a single concluding chapter (Chapter 10) in which I discuss the future of international refugee protection, considering the political opposition and practical difficulties it faces. With so many asylum seekers falling into the gray area between obvious refugee and economic migrant, the significance of cross-national differences in how their claims are handled will only continue to grow. In other words, as asylum seekers' stories become more diverse, RSD regimes may come to matter more, and states will diverge further in their treatment of asylum seekers, even while ostensibly trying to crack down on asylum seeking. In sum, this book illustrates that the international law protecting refugees is generally under great strain, but that cross-national differences have large-scale consequences for the level of protection that vulnerable migrants receive.

CHAPTER 2

Building a Cross-National Comparison of RSD Regimes

Given the deep and obvious connection between refugees and concepts such as citizenship, national sovereignty, and war, the field of political science has displayed surprisingly little interest in the study of forced migration. Even international relations, which has paid vastly more attention to refugee issues than any other political science subfield, has left the area remarkably understudied (Betts 2009:15, Betts and Loescher 2010:3). Further, because international relations has been dominated by theories of realism and liberal institutionalism, both of which tend to treat states like a unitary black box, that subfield has not engaged much with the domestic politics that may influence state behavior in response to refugee movements (Betts 2009:23, 26). Instead, it has tended to assume, especially during the Cold War, that states make refugee policy based solely on their strategic geopolitical interests (Teitelbaum 1984, Zolberg 2009). Even constructivist and other theories within international relations that are more concerned with domestic politics assume that political decisions are influenced predominantly by international power dynamics, norms, and pressure from global governance institutions.

In contrast to the assumptions of international relations, I suggest that refugee status determination outcomes may often have more to do with domestic concepts of administrative justice than any influence coming from the global refugee regime. Explaining these dynamics requires bringing in the insights of the public law subfields related to comparative constitutional law and the role of courts, as well as administrative law and the role of bureaucracies. By taking a domestic politics approach informed by public law, this book engages in a new way with a longstanding debate about the status of universal human rights and the potential for a globalization of law.

Many comparative migration scholars point to the existence of a common international refugee definition and the widespread practice of RSD as evidence of a globalization of law. These scholars argue that the proliferation of international human rights has shifted the locus of power away from the state in defining the boundaries of membership, giving otherwise vulnerable people a new stake for their rights claims (Soysal 1994, Jacobson 1996, Sassen 1996, Guiraudon 2000, Jacobson and Ruffer 2003, Spiro 2007). For example, Jacobson (1996:10) argues that immigrants are increasingly "becoming the object of international law and institutions," suggesting that international law enables noncitizens to assert rights they would not otherwise have.

This line of scholarship implies that international human rights norms can trump the exclusionary tendencies of states, making it difficult for courts to distinguish between citizens and noncitizens when protecting rights. This proposition of *international convergence* helps to explain why there are 147 countries that have adopted international refugee protection treaties and have pledged to consider the claims of asylum seekers who arrive uninvited at their borders. But, recent scholarship in international relations has cast doubt on the strength of international convergence theory by demonstrating what happens to RSD outcomes in instances when humanitarian norms and strategic interests are in conflict with one another. For example, Salehyan and Rosenblum (2004) compared RSD outcomes in the United States for applicants from countries with good and bad human rights records, and for applicants from countries with friendly and adversarial relationships with the United States. They found that "both normative and instrumental factors influence outcomes" (Salehyan and Rosenblum 2004:689) and concluded that "the importance of instrumental state goals in shaping policy outcomes in the quintessentially humanitarian arena of asylum policy highlights the limited progress norm-based international regimes have made as constraints on state behavior" (2004:694).[1] In other words, a focus on international convergence ignores the many state practices that run counter to this trend, and thus paints an overly rosy picture of the globalization of law.

In contrast to the international convergence school, a line of more pessimistic scholarship has emerged recently that points to a different kind of cross-national merger: *exclusionary convergence*. These scholars observe "broadly similar patterns in the response of…receiving countries to asylum seekers and refugees over the last decade" and the development of "a similar legal doctrine, namely the sovereign right to exclude" (Kneebone 2009:281, 292; see also Gibney 2006). Pellerin (2008:190) suggests that this "global agenda on migration" is the result of a "new consensus among industrialized states" reacting against internationalism.

Exclusionary convergence theorists are correct in noting that, since the end of the Cold War, the asylum policies of the United States, Canada, and Australia (among many other, mostly European states) have converged on a politics of deterrence. States have become more focused on keeping asylum seekers out with more rigorous border control measures, interdiction at sea, visa requirements, multinational collaboration, and widespread use of detention (for a detailed discussion of this trend, see Gammeltoft-Hansen 2011). In many destination countries, asylum policymaking is dominated by an awareness of the cost of conducting RSD and concerns about border security. This shift is fairly well documented and it explains why it is increasingly difficult for asylum seekers to access the RSD programs of the United States, Canada, and Australia. However, it does not explain the divergence in outcomes when they do. If states were simply converging on an exclusionary approach to asylum policy, and that approach were dictating RSD, we would see acceptance rates converging and declining. Instead, we see considerable variation by receiving state.

Both types of convergence theory are concerned with the degree to which states are embracing the tenets of international law, but they come to opposite, even contradictory conclusions about how much international protection norms are influencing domestic politics. Thus, they cannot both be telling the whole story. Both types of convergence theory also tend to locate noncitizen rights outside the state by assuming that when such rights are protected, it is despite opposition from the exclusionary state, and the rights have no domestic source.

Other migration scholars make the argument that both exclusionary and inclusive forces are at play within states. For example, Joppke (1998a:110) suggests that "conflicts over asylum policy are...domestic conflicts over the dual mandate of liberal nation-states" (see also Schuck 1998). States must balance majoritarian, exclusionary forces against internal, often constitutional, pressures to protect the rights of vulnerable minorities in what Hollifield (2004) calls "the liberal paradox." Such scholarship gives us a sense that nations might strike this balance differently from one another, positing a theory of *domestic divergence* that stands in contrast to both varieties of convergence proponents.

When domestic divergence scholars account for cross-national differences, their explanations tend to be judicially focused, based on the notion that if states have become reluctant asylum seeker hosts, enacting policies that reflect this reluctance, cross-national differences must be explained by looking beyond legislative politics. Joppke (1998a:140–141), for example, suggests that the U.S. Constitution has made it more difficult for courts in the United States to ignore violations of noncitizen rights than their German and British counterparts. Soennecken (2008) suggests that nongovernmental organizations in Germany and Canada have had varying levels of success in assisting refugees in court because the two countries have very different traditional levels of access to the judiciary. It makes sense why domestic divergence scholars would choose to examine nonlegislative institutional players. However, by focusing on just one institutional player, comparative studies run the risk of assuming that courts play an equivalently important role in the overall RSD regime of each state.

The debates between international/exclusionary convergence and domestic divergence have dominated scholarly inquiry about migration in a globalizing world. They set up an image of two competing forces—the centrifugal force of exclusion and the centripetal force of inclusion—as a political battle. However, if we look closely at the dynamics of RSD regimes, we see there are many other forces in play besides the politics of migration. Domestic divergence theory is right to suggest that international human rights law cannot work the same way in every place it settles. But we need to know more about the mechanisms and causes of divergence. Rather than try to adjudicate between the international/exclusionary convergence and domestic divergence schools of thought, I identify who the key domestic decision makers are in each state, and examine how they might be influenced by international human rights norms, liberal constitutionalism, or an exclusionary political agenda, and under what circumstances. Instructive comparisons can be drawn only by comparing the overall political and institutional context of the three countries. A public law approach enables a focus on the dynamic interplay between the constitutional, administrative, and legislative actors that make up the institutional context of each place.

The Insights of Public Law

Although political science has long embraced comparison of every other aspect of political life, within public law, the subfield of comparative constitutionalism is only now beginning to flourish. Traditionally, public law scholars interested in constitutions have assumed that national legal institutions reflect the distinct culture and history of the place in which they developed (Alford 1986, Schauer 1993). This particularist approach downplays the existence of cultural commonalities across jurisdictions and ignores the fact that many legal institutions are transplanted into new countries through colonialism and globalization. By suggesting that there is nothing universal about the way law or courts work, this approach has had the unfortunate effect of discouraging scholars from engaging in comparison.

Recent scholarship in comparative constitutional law has focused on documenting a global trend toward an expansion of judicial power (see, for example, Holland 1991, Tate and Vallinder 1995, Epp 1998, Klug 2000, Ferejohn 2002, Ginsburg 2003, Hirschl 2004, Erdos 2010). All over the world, democracies new and old are shifting toward a judicialization of politics—a "reliance on adjudicative means for clarifying and settling fundamental moral controversies and highly contentious political questions" (Hirschl 2002:211). This line of scholarship has found that, in many migration destinations, the judicial branch is exhibiting an increasing willingness to limit legislatures and executives, make substantive policy, and assert individual rights.

In particular, both Hirschl (2004) and Epp (1998) have found that judicialization has brought courts into the center of national debates about equality, freedom, and justice. They also both suggest that courts tend to protect rights for which there is some degree of public support. Although these scholars have laid an excellent foundation for future research in comparative constitutional law, all their case studies focus on the way in which courts have treated citizens. Thus, we do not know as much as we could about how both the form and consequences of judicialization might operate in relation to noncitizens, despite the fact that many of the same countries currently experiencing a well-documented judicialization are also hosting large numbers of noncitizens.

There is almost no scholarship comparing the actions of courts on migration matters cross-nationally, and the few theories that do exist contradict each other. First, Joppke's (2001:359) comparative study of migration policy in the United States, the United Kingdom, and Germany suggests that there exists "a line, differently drawn in different polities and varying over time, that prudent and self-limiting courts will not transgress" when extending rights to noncitizens. He suggests that courts will not defend extremely unpopular subgroups and are not likely to push for changes to citizenship requirements. In contrast, Dauvergne (2008:68) argues that, in the "dark story" of state crackdown on asylum seeking, there is a "glimmer of a new way of thinking about refugee law" as evidenced by court decisions that push back on deterrent policies and assert the rights of asylum seekers. Finally, Price (2009) reverses the causality and suggests that, because courts have expanded their interpretation of the refugee definition far beyond what the drafters of the 1951 definition originally intended, and beyond what acceding states believed they were agreeing to, courts have created a backlash and contributed to the rise of restrictive policies in the West. None of these studies have developed specific hypotheses about factors that might limit or empower courts in a given moment. Clearly, there is more work to be done to conceptualize the place of courts in asylum policy regimes. In particular, we need to move beyond the assumption that courts always operate as a force to temper politics and expand rights. Rather, we need to conceptualize courts as political actors with distinct interests, priorities, and powers.

Scholars within law schools who focus specifically on refugee law tend to shy away from comparisons, preferring to be experts either in the laws and jurisprudence of the country in which they practice or in the international legal guidance emanating from the United Nations. When they do compare, these studies tend to leave the United States out. For example, consider a line in the introduction of an article comparing Australian and Canadian High Court decisions: "U.S. refugee law and policy has always tended to be influenced in a greater extent by foreign policy concerns, with the result that jurisprudence in this area is less comparable" (Dauvergne 1998:78). A deeper look at the refugee status determination programs of the United States, Canada, and Australia demonstrates that this idea of American exceptionalism is unproductive. Instructive comparisons can be drawn not just between the legal reasoning in the most high-profile cases, but also by comparing the overall political and institutional context of the three countries.

Although the field of comparative constitutional law is relatively new, there is a much more longstanding international orientation to the strain of public law scholarship concerned with administrative law. Despite the fact that RSD is one of the most frequent forms of administrative decision making that a liberal democracy must conduct, there has been limited academic study of how administrative RSD processes work, how they differ from one another, and how they interact with other players in the policy arena. Equally surprising, scholars of asylum have focused on either the legislative process or the judicial branch, although administrative agencies are an extremely significant (if not the central) component of the domestic implementation of international law protecting refugees. These agencies are the exclusive point of contact the vast majority of asylum seekers have with the government of the receiving country, and so they are an essential part of the admissions and border control apparatus in any country. They are also precedent setters, laying the groundwork for the interpretation of asylum law before the courts get to see it in particular appeals.

One of the key building blocks of comparative administrative law is a distinction between adversarial and inquisitorial styles of decision making, a conceptual dichotomy dating back to medieval times (Damaska 1986:3). The adversarial style takes the shape of a triad: two disputants arguing their respective cases before a passive judge, who must resolve the dispute by deciding which case is more persuasive (Shapiro 1981, Stone Sweet 1999). In an adversarial process, justice is based on the premise that an impartial judge decides between competing versions of the story after hearing both sides argued forcefully. Unlike this courtroom-like setting, inquisitorial hearings are designed to be nonadversarial and nonlegalistic, taking the form of a dyad between the person whose fate is to be decided and the person deciding it. The inquisitorial decision maker engages in a conversation with the parties, and the facts must be discovered through a collaborative process of research and questioning. Justice is demonstrated through the decision maker's commitment to an active investigatory process.

Although the adversarial and inquisitorial ideal types are still at the core of cross-national comparisons of decision-making styles, in more recent work, Kagan (2001:9–10) has expanded on Damaska's concepts by building a two-by-two matrix of four dispute resolution models, enabling a more detailed comparison of styles. On one axis is a distinction between whether the decision making is formal (based on legal rules and precedents) or informal (based on discretion and case-by-case considerations). The other axis divides decision making according to whether it is more hierarchical and centralized or whether it is characterized by the participation of multiple disputing parties. In one corner of the Kagan matrix stands *adversarial legalism,* in which decision making is formal but fragmented and participatory. Kagan (2001:1) argues that this category is an accurate description of "the American way of law." When decision making is formal, but decisions are made in a more hierarchical and centralized fashion, we see *bureaucratic legalism,* the second ideal style of dispute resolution. The third type occurs when decisions are made by a centralized decision maker, but they are made more informally. Kagan (2001) calls this model *professional judgment,* which is a highly inquisitorial style. Lastly, if the decision making is both informal and participatory, not controlled by a single decision maker, Kagan (2001) calls this fourth type of decision making *mediation.*

In this book, I use the Kagan/Damaska typologies as a way of understanding the administrative component of each nation's RSD regime. RSD is formal if it is based on legal precedent and subject to regular judicial review. It is informal if it does not follow a clear precedent and is conducted in a discretionary, case-by-case manner. RSD procedures follow adversarial legalism if a government prosecutor is used to challenge asylum claims, and a judge decides between the competing positions. In contrast, the inquisitorial form requires much more active decision makers. Instead of placing the responsibility for the collection of evidence and the presentation of arguments on the disputing parties themselves, the inquisitorial process combines the role of investigator and decision maker into one. RSD is inquisitorial if the asylum seeker goes before a decision maker who both researches and decides the claim.

In the three states examined in this book, we see multiple distinct types of decision making at work. In the United States, RSD involves an inquisitorial process at the initial stage, but not all applicants have access to it, and it is only one stage of many. Thus, the overwhelming tone of the American RSD regime is that of Kagan's (2001) adversarial legalism. In sharp contrast, the Canadian RSD regime follows a typical professional judgment model. The Australian RSD regime is the most complex of the three. It is highly fragmented, and the judiciary plays an active role, which suggests elements of adversarial legalism. However, most of the stages of decision making have adopted an inquisitorial style. Thus, Australia's regime is a hybrid that might perhaps be named *bureaucratic adversarialism.* Because the Australian system is ultimately a hybrid of the American and Canadian models, it serves as a fascinating point of comparison for understanding the structural position of administrative agencies within government, and the power of those agencies to make decisions affecting individuals.

A public law approach to comparing RSD illustrates how different decision-making styles are linked to different conceptions of administrative justice (Adler 2003). Administrative justice is about the procedures agencies must follow in order to be fair, and the scope of judicial review of their actions if they are accused of not being fair. Some approaches to administrative justice prioritize predictability and consistency, others prefer flexibility and the consideration of particular circumstances. Some forms of decision making value efficiency and expediency very highly; others sacrifice speed to allow multiple opportunities for each side to be heard. In every country that uses judicial review of administrative decision making, review is designed to prevent arbitrary use of power by government agents, but each country has a different standard that outlines when courts can step in, and when they should sit out and defer to agency expertise (Stewart 2003).

How administrative agencies define procedural fairness and address the challenges of RSD affects the degree to which the politics of deterrence and exclusion translates into individual RSD decisions and influences their outcomes. As I will demonstrate, some models allow for more insulation from migration politics and some models limit discretion in favor of predictable outcomes that are sometimes generous and sometimes highly restrictive. A public law approach illuminates the mechanisms behind these outcomes, breaking free of debates about international norms versus strategic interests.

The Challenges of RSD

In many ways, RSD is a uniquely challenging category of administrative decision because the stakes are so high. In addition, RSD is highly interpretive and speculative, especially because there is often very little factual information on which to base the decision. In determining whether an applicant's fear of persecution is indeed "well-founded," decision makers are often required to make inferences about the motivations of remote actors and the conditions in countries to which they have never been. Yet, the logic of RSD assumes that there is an essential "refugeeness" that can be discovered, or not, in each case.

Many cases hinge on the decision maker's assessment from afar of whether the government in the asylum seeker's home country could (if she were returned there) provide her with adequate protection from persecution by a third party, such as an abusive spouse or a guerrilla group. A large number of other cases center on the question of whether the past persecution experienced by the asylum seeker was really motivated by one of the reasons outlined in the Convention or was, instead, simply unlucky and random victimization from which no one is protected by international law.[2]

Just as frequently, the issue at hand is not whether the asylum seeker's experience fits with the refugee definition, but rather the veracity of the claimant's story. In these situations, the asylum seeker can fit easily within the definition if her story is true. These cases require what is known among asylum adjudicators as a *credibility determination*; put more basically, it is a decision about whether the asylum seeker is telling the truth and can back up her story with evidence. Some form of credibility determination precedes any decision about refugee status, and often obviates it. Although decision makers are usually required to legitimate their gut feelings with legally defensible arguments, there is a lot of leeway because, ultimately, their negative credibility finding is very difficult to reverse under judicial review.

Standards of proof are another very slippery area of RSD. Much of the time, evidence simply does not exist, and it is replaced by in-depth questioning around the details of the story, assessments from physicians and psychiatrists about the presence of physical or psychological scars from persecution, or the testimony of friends and family. As administrative agencies raise the requirements for more hard evidence, the prevalence of fraudulent documents also increases in a never-ending game of cat and mouse.[3] Accounts of the conditions in refugee-producing countries can be verified to a certain extent by reports from the U.S. Department of State and nongovernmental advocacy organizations such as Human Rights Watch and Amnesty International.[4] However, almost by definition, conditions can change very quickly in refugee-producing countries, and the more volatile the situation on the ground, the more likely country reports are to be out of date or inaccurate.

Decision makers are acutely aware that the incentives for asylum seekers to embellish or fabricate their stories are incredibly high. Suspicions abound among policymakers that many of the stories of persecution told in RSD hearings are fabricated, often purchased along with false identities from the smugglers and human traffickers who have turned asylum seeking into a lucrative black market. Thus, adjudicators are under pressure to enforce the border from within, and avoid granting asylum to a fraudulent applicant who is an economic migrant in an asylum seeker's clothing. Administrative agencies that conduct RSD are concerned about this type of error because it tends to bring about criticism from the political branches; politicians complain that accepting fraudulent claims wastes resources, undermines the legitimacy of the system, admits potential security risks, and creates warped incentives for similarly situated people to follow in their footsteps, sometimes risking their lives at sea or in the desert. Refugee status decision makers can also be pushed toward rejecting a claim not just by political pressure, but also by skepticism and experiences with fraud. Although the stories told in RSD hearings are often equal parts riveting and disturbing, decision makers can quickly become distrustful and burned out by the repeated experience of listening to them. Similar stories can become repetitive and begin to ring false, even when they are true.

On the other hand, RSD adjudicators are also under pressure to avoid refusing asylum to a legitimate asylum seeker (often described by administrators as "real refugees"). These "false negatives" are of concern not just for moral and humanitarian reasons; they also bring scrutiny from advocacy groups or from the judicial branch via appealed decisions because they raise questions about the procedural and substantive fairness of the process. During interviews, officials in charge of RSD agencies insisted they worry about these two types of errors—false positives and false negatives—equally. This insistence illustrates the highly political nature of their jobs.

There are many other barriers in the process of discovery. Cultural differences relating to how events are recounted and how time is conceptualized can often lead to misunderstandings and perceptions of obfuscation. As former Canadian Immigration and Refugee Board member Audrey Macklin puts it:

> Examining demeanor for clues to credibility presupposes that we know what truth telling looks like and that it looks the same on everybody. The stereotype goes something like this: truth tellers looks us in the eye, answer questions put to them in a straightforward manner, do not hesitate, show an "appropriate" amount of emotion, and are neither too laconic, nor too verbose. (Macklin 1998b:137)

The process of RSD can often be vulnerable to accusations of orientalism, because it assumes that behaviors such as making eye contact, and terms such as *family* are universally consistent when they are highly culturally contingent. Furthermore, true stories may seem improbable to decision makers simply because they are unimaginable within their own lived experience. Under these circumstances, even the most sympathetic decision makers may find it impossible to avoid letting personal bias, including class bias, affect their reasoning.[5] The fact that most stories are translated by an interpreter can further limit the potential for a personal connection between the adjudicator and the asylum seeker. Translation slip-ups can also make a clear assessment of credibility more difficult.

Perhaps most important, people who are forced to retell the stories of traumatic experiences can seem unemotional, or become confused about repressed details, which can make them seem like they are lying.[6] Consider the following example from a Toronto refugee lawyer:

> A case where I was sure I would win (and it nearly killed me when we didn't) was an Iraqi boy who fled the army, was caught and then

tortured. He was electrocuted till the muscles in his leg ripped, and you could tell by talking to him that if anyone had been tortured, it was him. The problem was, because of that he could not give coherent testimony. It was gibberish. It wasn't lies, it just didn't make sense.... I'm a big boy, I win and I lose. But this one brought me to tears. I will never forget that case. (author interview, 5/09/2007)

In determining the legitimacy of asylum seekers' stories, adjudicators must interpret the legal language of the 1951 Convention Relating to the Status of Refugees and the 1967 Protocol to the Convention, as well as extensive domestic legislation, case law, and regulations that are supposed to bring clarity and consistency to the process. Yet, the legal definition of a refugee raises as many questions as it answers, especially when viewed in light of the current realities of global migration. For example, do today's refugees fit the definition laid out in the 1951 Convention as neatly as those of the past? Does the priority that the Convention definition placed on political exile implicitly privilege the stories of those who are fleeing certain types of regimes? Can the definition be elastic enough to accommodate the claims of people who could never have been in the minds of the Convention's framers? These questions are not just esoteric thought experiments, they are central to cases that RSD adjudicators must decide every day.

The concept of RSD assumes there is a percentage of asylum seekers who have the qualities of a true refugee, which can be discovered through regularized inquiry, allowing states to separate and distinguish refugees from other migrants. The realities of asylum seeking and administrative decision making cast serious doubt on that assumption. Yet, the conceptualization of refugee and migrant as distinct categories has been remarkably enduring both among scholars of refugee law and refugee advocates. The UNHCR has promoted the distinction for decades, insisting that "refugees are not migrants" (Feller 2005). The UNHCR is concerned about "mixed migration," the phenomenon in which migrants with many different motivations for leaving their home country arrive in receiving states together, sometimes literally in the same boat (Loescher 2003). In the face of these situations, the UN agency prioritizes the task of "disentangling refugees from migrants to ensure their proper protection" (UNHCR 2011:5).

It is strategically necessary for the UNHCR to promote this distinction to maximize its political influence and to achieve refugee protection for many vulnerable migrants. However, by adopting this framework, the academic literature tends to echo the priorities and categories of policymakers. Thus, scholars have frequently neglected to analyze and illuminate the circumstances under which states might choose to categorize asylum seekers as either refugees or migrants in different political moments. Much of the debate in the academic literature has focused on the policy question of whether contemporary asylum seekers are true refugees deserving of the protection accorded to them by their special status under international law or whether they are disingenuous economic migrants trying to "skip the queue."

As early as the late 1980s, some scholars were already making the argument that shifts toward deterrence policies in Europe were due to a difference in the asylum seekers themselves. For example, according to Martin (1988), the "new asylum seekers" were less likely to fit the refugee definition than asylum seekers of the past. Rather than escaping persecution, they were seeking better economic fortunes. Because they used the asylum process as a back door to avoid the long lines for other forms of migration to industrialized states, they caused receiving nations to lose patience with laws that could have been used to protect genuine refugees.[7] Price (2009:202) has recently made a very similar argument, suggesting that "fraudulent or bad faith" asylum claims have increased since the asylum boom of the 1990s. Because global acceptance rates for refugee visa applications declined during the period in which application rates rose, he concludes that "the policy dilemma faced by Western states is how to remain open to genuine refugees while at the same time preventing asylum from being exploited by those who are not entitled to it" (Price 2009:203).[8] This association between unsuccessful asylum claims and actively fraudulent or undeserving claims requires much more elaboration. It assumes that RSD processes are accurately discovering true refugees and that all denied applications are disingenuous ones. It also assumes that genuine refugees will not be prevented by policies of deterrence from lodging a claim in the first place.

By arguing over whether contemporary asylum seekers are "real refugees," academics reinforce the constructed divide between the categories of migrant and refugee, ignoring the fact that when states assign whole groups of migrants to one category or the other, there are contextual political reasons for doing so. As Black (2001:63) argued, "the uncritical use of the term in scholarly literature can contribute to the perception of the naturalness of the category of refugees and of differential policies towards those who do and those who do not qualify for the label." The act of a state granting asylum has always been highly political (Kanstroom 2010). It is political in the sense that it rewards relief to those whose political activity has led to their persecution, and it is political in the sense that it inevitably weights some kinds of political activity—and some kinds of persecution—more heavily than others. Chimni (1998) observed that the 1951 definition of a refugee was based on a Cold War model that conceptualized refugees as political dissidents. He argues that this "exilic bias" disadvantages asylum seekers from the developing world, who often do not fit that model as neatly (Chimni 1998:351). Receiving states today must determine how to handle those migrants that fall in the vast gray middle between obvious refugees and obvious economic migrants, and there is a great deal of variation in how they draw that line.

Why Compare the United States, Canada, and Australia?

The United States, Canada, and Australia are fascinating cases for a comparative study of RSD processes because the three states share so many common features in terms of politics, history, and culture, and thus can be considered to be "most-similar systems" (Mill 1843, Przeworski and Teune 1970). By holding many common domestic factors reasonably constant, a cross-national comparison of RSD in the United States, Canada, and Australia enables us to isolate the factors that lead to divergent outcomes.

First, the three countries are naturally and frequently grouped together by immigration scholars as "classic countries of immigration" because they have a history of population growth via large-scale migration, and an integral part of their national identity stems from being a migrant destination (Brubaker 1995, Freeman 1995, Joppke 1998b, Cornelius et al 2004). Since 1965, the United States has tended to prioritize family reunification in its immigration policy, whereas Canada and Australia have been more concerned with attracting people with particular job skills; however, employment needs are an important part of the American immigration calculus as well (Reitz 1998, Borjas 2001, Wolgin 2011). Although the U.S. Department of Homeland Security has become more focused on internal enforcement, all three states have active immigration bureaucracies that place a high level of emphasis on selectivity and control (Freeman and Jupp 1992, Kelley and Trebilcock 1998, Ngai 2004, Tavan 2005).

The second major commonality is the way in which immigration has come to mean racial and ethnic diversification in all three places. Each country had longstanding racial restrictions on migration that were lifted in 1965 (United States), 1967 (Canada), and 1973 (Australia). Today, the vast majority of migrants to these countries are from Asia, Africa, and Latin America. Each state has taken a different approach to assimilation and incorporation in the face of this newfound diversity. The United States has a famously laissez-faire approach to immigrant incorporation, leaving much of the assimilation work to civil society organizations or to the immigrants' own initiative (Glazer 1998, Bloemraad 2006). Canada and Australia have tended to have more proactive, interventionist policies designed to encourage naturalization, but while Canada has embraced the concept of multiculturalism (Kelley and Trebilcock 1998, Bloemraad 2006), Australia has never fully committed to the concept of rights-based, multicultural citizenship. Rather, its policies are more focused on assimilation through English acquisition and the adoption of Australian culture and values (Markus

1994, Castles and Vasta 2004, Tavan 2005). Despite these policy variations, anxiety about the shrinking white majority and disputes about the proper way to accommodate cultural, religious, and linguistic differences have been dominant themes in the politics of all three states for several decades.

Third, beyond their common roots as nations of immigrants, the United States, Canada, and Australia have all used their immigration policies to extend protection to displaced people in need, and at various times have engaged in generous refugee resettlement programs.[9] Throughout the Cold War, none of the three states made much of a distinction between asylum policy and refugee resettlement more generally, because both issues were located within the foreign policy agendas of these nations. In the United States, refugee resettlement was dominated by the executive branch and was geared almost exclusively toward people fleeing communist enemies, such as Hungarian freedom fighters during the 1950s and, later, Vietnamese allied with the United States during the 1970s (Hohl 1978, Zolberg 2009). Beginning with the Cuban Revolution of 1959, the United States became a country of direct asylum for the first time, but because the new Cuban government was allied with the Soviet Union, accepting people who were leaving Cuba seemed perfectly compatible with the American mission of refugee resettlement during the Cold War, despite the unauthorized nature of their arrival (Loescher and Scanlan 1986, Zucker and Zucker 1992). During the 1980s, as asylum seekers from a wide variety of nations began to flock to America, those from communist countries were again given top priority.

The United States was not unique in its focus on people escaping communism. When Canada became involved in refugee resettlement during the 1970s, it created prioritized categories for Indochinese and Eastern Europeans (Kelley and Trebilcock 1998:406). Similarly, Australia's resettlement from camps of Vietnamese refugees during the 1970s and 1980s served the dual purposes of taking a stance in the Cold War, and establishing Australia as a member of the international humanitarian community (Gibney 2004). Australia's first foray into the granting of refugee status visas to asylum seekers within its domestic territory involved the large number of Chinese students who were studying there when the Tiananmen Square massacre happened in 1989. Thus, in all three nations, decisions about both refugee resettlement and domestic asylum claims were made with an outward focus during the Cold War.

More recently, a fourth commonality has emerged, one that is particularly germane to this study: the United States, Canada, and Australia have become popular asylum seeker destinations that conduct RSD on a relatively large scale. The United States consistently receives more asylum applications than any other country; in 2012, it received 17.4% of the total number of asylum applications lodged worldwide. Canada tends to hover in the top five most common receiving countries; in 2008 it was the second most popular and in 2012 it was sixth, with 4.3% of worldwide applications. That same year, Australia was 11th with 3.3% of the total, despite its relatively inaccessible location. Canada receives far more asylum seekers per capita than the other two countries because it has a population of only one-tenth of the United States. During the five-year period between 2006 and 2010, Canada received one asylum application for every 236 residents. Thus, asylum seekers are a much more visible presence in Canada, because the ratio for the United States was more than four times less, at one asylum application per every 1,200 residents, and the ratio for Australia was one asylum seeker for every 835 residents.[10]

A fifth important similarity among the three countries lies in their common legal traditions and strong judiciaries. All three nations drew heavily on British common law when designing their legal systems. Australia (in 1900), and to a lesser extent Canada (in 1867), drew on the U.S. Constitution of 1787 as a guide when drafting their own, and courts in all three nations use similar common law logic today. In addition, courts in all three countries share a uniquely high level of independence and power to weigh in on the actions of government. In fact, until after the Second World War, the United States, Canada, and Australia were the only three countries in the world to have well-established judicial review (Shapiro and Stone Sweet 2002). During the past few decades, all three countries have achieved "increasing constitutional independence," with more attention to the "progressive elaboration of rights" for citizens than in the past (Scheppele 2003:14).

An additional, related commonality is that, in recent years, the separation of powers has become an important issue in the immigration politics of all three states, and asylum claims have become a dominant part of the business of the federal courts. All three countries have federal systems in which immigration policy is dictated primarily at the level of the national government, although in all three countries constitutional questions have arisen about the extent of the federal government's immigration power. Although Australia and Canada are parliamentary systems and the United States has a president, all three countries have large immigration bureaucracies, and all three allow courts to review decisions made by those agencies. The extent of this power of judicial review has been another question with which all three states have wrestled.

The final common factor that makes this cross-national comparison compelling is that the contemporary asylum control policies of the United States, Canada, and Australia have become remarkably similar to one another. I discuss the details of this convergence in much more detail in Chapter 3, but at this point it is worth noting that, since the end of the Cold War, the asylum policies of the United States, Canada, and Australia have become more focused on keeping asylum seekers out. Because they require individualized assessment, asylum seekers make border enforcement more complicated, and if they make it across the border, they represent a costly administrative burden. Thus, in all three countries, asylum policymaking is dominated by an awareness of the cost of conducting RSD and concerns about border security. Because all three countries have become reluctant asylum seeker hosts, and have put policies in place that reflect this reluctance, the politics of deterrence can essentially be held constant across the three country cases.

In sum, the United States, Canada, and Australia have remarkably common histories of mass migration and refugee resettlement, and share current high levels of asylum seeking. They all have common law legal systems and strong courts, and wrestle with disputes regarding separation of powers. For these reasons, the variation in RSD outcomes cannot be attributed to different migration histories, asylum policies, or legal systems. Instead, the differences are a result of the administrative architecture that each country has set up for conducting RSD.

Data and Methods

To build a systemic comparison of three different RSD regimes, I used a combination of qualitative research methods. In particular, drawing on a year of fieldwork, I use in-depth elite interviews, courtroom observation, and case analysis to demonstrate why RSD regimes differ and how those cross-national differences matter both in terms of procedural justice and in terms of raw acceptance rates for asylum seekers.[11] I first built a historical narrative of the development of each RSD regime by creating a database of media coverage on issues related to asylum seekers in all three countries. I selected two major broadsheets from each country and searched their archives for the years 1980 to 2010. I excluded letters to the editor and book reviews, but included all news items, features, editorials, and op-eds with more than a brief passing reference to asylum policy. In the United States, I searched the *New York Times* and *Washington Post* for the terms *asylum* and *congress*, and ended up keeping 445 articles in the database, approximately one-fifth of the original number of articles collected. In Canada, I searched *The Globe and Mail* and *The Toronto Star*. Because the term *asylum* is never used in Canada, I searched for *refugee* and *parliament*, and ended up with 453 articles. Because the term *refugee* is much more general than *asylum*, including those resettled from overseas, I discarded far more articles in the Canadian search. In Australia, I searched *The Age* and *The Sydney Morning Herald* for the terms *asylum* and *parliament*, and ended up keeping 1,362 articles, also about one-fifth of the original hits. Ultimately, the database includes 2,260 articles across the six newspapers for the entire 32-year period. Not only was this collection of news accounts extremely helpful in piecing together the complex timelines of asylum policymaking in each country, it was also essential for identifying interview subjects and significant court cases.

I conducted 103 in-depth, in-person interviews (30 in the United States, 35 in Canada, and 38 in Australia). These interviews fell into three categories. First, in each capital city, I met with policy elites, including staff at the following relevant agencies: Department of Homeland Security, Department of Justice (both the Executive Office of Immigration Review and the Office of Immigration Litigation), and Department of State in the United States; Citizenship and Immigration Canada, the Immigration and Refugee Board, and the Department of Justice in Canada; and the Department of Migration and Citizenship, the Refugee Review Tribunal, and the Federal Court of Australia. The conversations focused on perceived challenges and successes in implementation, and relations with the advocacy community and with other actors responsible for asylum policy implementation. I also interviewed representatives of the UNHCR in each capital to discuss coordination with government, and how their offices handle instances of noncompliance with international law.

I also interviewed key refugee advocates from organizations the media had mentioned as having participated in lobbying efforts on asylum policy during the past 15 years, and that list asylum as an organizational focus. I interviewed a senior staff person at almost all of these organizations and then used these contacts to expand my list via snowball sampling—asking each contact if there were any significant organizations I had missed. My conversations with policy elites focused on their biggest priorities and challenges, relations with government, and strategies for achieving reform. Many policy elites had been working on this issue for decades, and provided me with a useful historical perspective and contemporary analysis of their policy environments. I collected literature from each advocate I interviewed and each government agency, many of which conduct their own research on asylum seeker policy. Although these documents have a distinct political slant, they are useful guides to the most pressing debates within the policy area.

In addition, I interviewed a sample of people who represent asylum seekers in RSD hearings and who were most often, but not exclusively, lawyers. Because there are hundreds of people who represent refugees in each country, I focused on one major refugee destination city per state: Toronto, San Francisco, and Sydney. I chose these cities because the majority of asylum hearings in Canada are conducted in Toronto and the vast majority of Australian hearings are conducted in Sydney. Hearings in the United States are distributed more evenly over a broader range of cities than in the other two countries, but San Francisco is one of the top four cities where asylum claims are heard in the United States. In each city, I took a random sample of representatives from a list I compiled using telephone books and Internet searches. I asked them about their experiences with the RSD regime, the advice they give their clients, the tactics they use to gain favorable decisions, and the concerns they have about the system as a whole. I conducted 50 interviews in this category (15–20 in each country).

Another key element of my fieldwork was observation of RSD hearings. In each country, I visited the administrative agencies responsible for RSD and I collected statistics, training materials, and operational regulations from the agencies. I observed multiple hearings at the San Francisco immigration court, and several appeals at the 9th Circuit Federal Court of Appeals. In Toronto, I observed hearings at the Immigration and Refugee Board, and appeals at the Federal Court of Canada. In Australia, all hearings at the Refugee Review Tribunal are closed, but I observed multiple first-level appeals of these hearings at the Federal Magistrates Court and further appeals at the Federal Court of Australia in Sydney.

To supplement my ethnographic data collection, I collected descriptive statistics from multiple sources in order to compare basic numbers across countries and over time. First, I used the UNHCR statistical yearbooks from 1980 to 2013 for information on the numbers of applications for asylum and acceptance rates reported by each nation. Second, I collected data from the federal courts of all three countries on applications for judicial review of asylum decision and success rates. Third, I collected data on acceptance rates, reversal rates, and rate of legal representation from the administrative agencies responsible for RSD in each country. Much of these data are not available publicly, but were provided to me after visiting the agencies personally and making a special request.

The final element of my research consisted of a detailed content analysis of 137 significant administrative, federal court, and high court decisions regarding asylum law. I selected these cases based on mentions in the database of news coverage, responses of interviewees to the question of which cases they viewed as important, and a survey of law review articles using the terms *refugee/asylum*, *administrative*, and *procedure*. This three-pronged approach was extremely helpful in identifying the most significant cases for defining the roles of each institutional player, and setting the parameters of procedural justice for asylum seekers. While analyzing the cases, I looked for patterns in case law development across the three states, and tracked the frequency and duration of unsettled legal questions in each place. I took particular note of instances of cross-fertilization (reference to an equivalent decision in another country), and the level of deference courts in each state afforded to the administrative agencies. The case analysis revealed a common theme across the three countries. Courts in all three jurisdictions have dealt, to some degree, with cases involving forced sterilization claims from the People's Republic of China, albeit in very different ways. Thus, the case analysis was particularly informative to my discussion about these types of claims in Chapter 8.

Through a combination of news coverage, interviews, observations, and case analysis, I developed a detailed picture of the institutional landscape for RSD in each of the three states. I also have a clear sense of how each RSD regime has developed over time, and the particular role of each institutional player. Rather than concluding that these three states are totally converging—either in favor of international legal norms or against them—a big-picture perspective informed by the subfield of public law allows for holistic comparisons that highlight the points of convergence among the states as well as the reasons for divergence.

CHAPTER 3

"Illegal Refugees" and the Rise of Restrictive Asylum Politics

Despite major differences in how refugee claims are processed *after* asylum seekers reach the United States, Canada, and Australia, policies governing asylum seekers' access to receiving states have converged with one another in multiple important ways during the past few decades. Contemporary policymakers in all three states have reconceptualized and recategorized asylum seekers as unauthorized migrants, introducing successively more elaborate and creative techniques for restricting access to their territories. In each country, a regime of deterrence has taken shape, the origins of which predate the renewed emphasis on border control and national security that was sparked by the terrorist attacks on the United States in September 2001. Those events only served to fuel the worldwide trend toward restriction that had already arisen. The result of this regime of deterrence is that asylum policy has been subsumed under national security concerns and the prevention of illegal migration. In all three countries, asylum seekers have been conceptually separated from refugees and thus have lost their insulation from the domestic politics of immigration control.

Many authors, particularly within the international relations subdiscipline of political science, have commented on the increasing resistance of western states to accept asylum seekers. However, the literature lacks a coherent theory about the specific mechanisms behind the rise of deterrence policies in individual states. Loescher (2003:11) observes that, since the end of the Cold War, "a growing state interest in keeping refugees out" has become a "worldwide trend." Gibney (2006:145–146) suggests that once asylum seeking became a "globalized" phenomenon, a backdoor way for the Third World to immigrate to the West, states "fell like dominos" and became reluctant asylum seeker destinations. Kneebone (2009:281) argues there are "broadly similar patterns in the response of...receiving countries to asylum seekers and refugees over the last decade...denying them access to their rights under international law," but she does not present an argument for why such a similar pattern has arisen in multiple countries at the same time. Gammeltoft-Hansen (2011) provides more specifics, describing a worldwide pattern in outsourcing and offshore processing of asylum policy. He wisely suggests that states are motivated to institute deterrence practices to "release themselves—de facto or de jure—from some of the constraints otherwise imposed by international law" (Gammeltoft-Hansen 2011:8). In contrast, Dauvergne (2008) presents the theory that policies focused on "making asylum illegal" are deeply linked to both economic globalization and changes in the way courts view human rights law. However, because asylum is just one example within a larger study of globalization and law, she does not examine any particular domestic context in detail.

Because the political mechanisms of the shift toward deterrence have been understudied, especially by scholars of domestic politics, there are many unanswered questions about whether the rise of such policies proceeded in the same way or for the same reasons in each country in which it has occurred. The balancing act between sovereign border control and liberal commitments to humanitarianism is a central challenge for migration states all over the world (Birrell 1992, Hollifield 2004, Hurrell 2010). In determining how to strike that balance, states share many common pressures and ideological commitments. However, these features also combine with factors that are particular to the domestic context. For example, the domestic politics around unauthorized migration and the impact of both the end of the Cold War and the post-September 11 "War on Terror" vary widely across receiving states. Thus, the rise of deterrence politics will have different internal mechanisms, even if the outcomes look similar from a distance, because policy regimes have developed over long stretches of time, incorporating global and local elements.

One very significant commonality among the three states in this study is that they all signed international treaties making commitments to refugee protection before they considered themselves to be countries of first asylum, and before asylum seekers had started coming to their shores in significant numbers. Thus, the rise of the regime of deterrence is, in part, a story of unintended consequences, because international commitments made by each country in a particular political moment came back to haunt future generations of policymakers. Had these countries' leaders anticipated the financial, security, and political challenges of the present-day situation, they might not have been as willing to make commitments that, at the time, were largely an abstraction.

Australia was the first of the three to ratify the Convention in 1954, but perhaps not for the most noble reasons. Fueled by fears of Japanese invasion during the Second World War, domestic politics during the postwar era led to a strong push by the Australian government to increase the white population via the importation of many thousands of European refugees (Tavan 2005). Even today, Australia's remarkably high percentage of foreign-born residents (almost one in four) can be partially attributed to the massive influx of Europeans during the postwar period (Reitz 1998). Even as late as 1981, 75% of Australia's foreign-born population was of European origin (Zappala and Castles 2000:35). Australia signed on to the Convention as a signal of its commitment to the resettlement of European refugees, paying very little (if any) attention to the components of the treaty that dealt with unauthorized arrivals. After the infamous White Australia policy was dismantled in 1973, Australia expanded its commitment to refugees by signing on to the 1967 Protocol, which amended the 1951 Convention to include non-European refugees. However, even at that time, the arrival of asylum seekers directly in Australia was not viewed as a concern, or even a possibility, by policymakers.

Although policymakers in the United States and Canada were less worried about an influx of Asians than their Australian counterparts during the 1950s and 1960s, they also did not view direct asylum as an immediate concern. Instead, policy decisions in these two countries were driven by strategic interests in the fight against communism. For this reason, American and Canadian policymakers essentially ignored the U.N. Convention and administered their own refugee policies by passing legislation that prioritized the admission of people whose exile was geopolitically strategic in the Cold War. Refugee admissions were dominated by the executive branch via executive order in the United States, and by the cabinet and the immigration bureaucracy via orders-in-council in Canada (Kelley and Trebilcock 1998, Bon Tempo 2008, Wolgin 2011). After years of nonattention to the international refugee protection regime, the United States ratified the Protocol (encompassing the Convention) in 1968, and Canada followed suit and ratified both in 1969. However, these gestures were mostly symbolic, as both countries continued to prioritize their refugee resettlement according to foreign-policy goals.[1] In addition, neither country established legislation codifying an official domestic refugee status determination policy until 1976 in Canada and 1980 in the United States.

Beyond a lack of historic concern about direct asylum arrivals, the second commonality among the United States, Canada, and Australia was the pressure each state felt as a result of the global asylum boom of the late 1980s and early 1990s. This precipitous rise in application numbers was related to the end of emigration restrictions in the former Soviet bloc, and the increase in the number of regional conflicts (such as wars in the former Yugoslavia and Rwanda) that arose once the stability of the Cold War period ended (Helton 2002:18). This boom reached Europe first and most dramatically, but soon began to extend to the United States, Canada, and Australia.

Figures 3.1 and 3.2 illustrate the rise and fall in the numbers of asylum seekers who filed an application for a refugee visa in the United States, Canada, and Australia between 1980 and 2012. All three countries have undoubtedly become

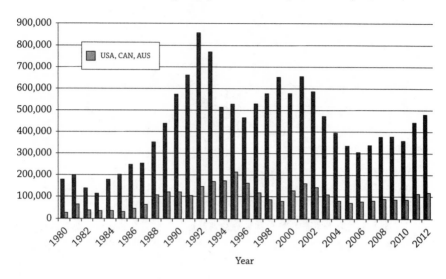

Figure 3.1 Asylum Applications Filed Worldwide and in the United States, Canada, Australia (1980–2012). Source: Compiled by author using UNHCR annual reports, 1980–2012. *Asylum levels and trends in industrialized countries.* Geneva Switzerland: UNHCR.

asylum seeker destinations, and reluctant ones. Although it is not possible to prove that deterrence policies are the only factor contributing to the decline in annual asylum applications lodged since the mid 1990s, the worldwide displacement caused by war, repression, and poverty has not markedly declined during the period. In addition, changes in the cost and availability of international air travel, and a growing black market for travel documents, have reduced other barriers to escape. Over time, deterrent measures have enabled all industrialized receiving states to cut back on the number of asylum seekers who access their RSD procedures, although they have not returned to the low Cold War levels.

One of the most challenging aspects of implementing asylum policy is the clandestine element that inevitably comes along with asylum seekers' movement. A person cannot go to the American, Canadian, or Australian embassy in their home country and apply for a refugee visa, or a visa to travel to one of those countries to seek asylum. For this reason, those who wish to flee often do so under false pretenses; they get temporary student, tourist, or business visas if they can; they often buy false documents, or they simply sneak over a border.

Public opinion in receiving states is very sensitive to incidences of asylum seekers attempting to enter surreptitiously. Explosions of media coverage on asylum seeker issues do not necessarily occur when asylum applications levels are at their highest. Instead, coverage tends to coincide with incidents such as the boat "invasions" of 1988 and 2010 in Canada, and 2001 in Australia. Figure 3.3

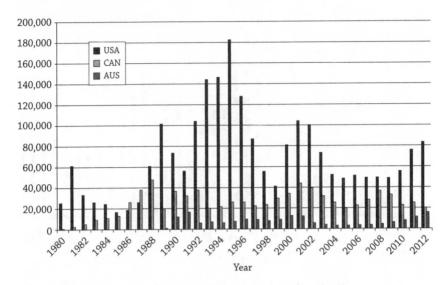

Figure 3.2 Asylum Applications Filed in the United States, Canada, and Australia (1980–2012). Source: Compiled by author using UNHCR annual reports, 1980–2012. *Asylum levels and trends in industrialized countries.* Geneva Switzerland: UNHCR.

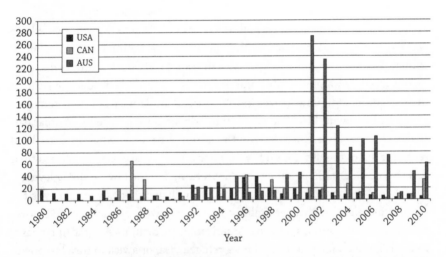

Figure 3.3 Media Coverage of Asylum Policy in the United States, Canada, and Australia in Articles per Year (1980–2010). Database compiled by author.

illustrates how the three states differ on the salience of asylum seekers in public debate by tracing the volume of media coverage of asylum seeker issues from 1980 to 2010. Measured by level of media coverage, public salience of this issue is greatest in Australia, where instances of boat arrivals have been disproportionately reported in the Australian press, especially during the 21st century. In addition, much of the legislation dictating admissions policies for asylum seekers, and even the structure of the RSD system, has been passed in response to these crises of unauthorized boat arrivals.

Part of the explanation for the variation in asylum seeker salience is the degree to which asylum seekers are associated with unauthorized migrants in the public eye. Because both Canada and Australia have historically had relative success in controlling unauthorized migration, asylum seekers in general—and boat arrivals in particular—are a direct threat to the continuation of that success. The sheer difficulty of clandestine arrival in Australia combined with the universal visa requirement means there are very, very few undocumented immigrants, most of whom are visa "overstayers." When asylum seekers arrive by boat, they are a striking visual representation of a loss of border control. In contrast, the United States is faced with geographic realities that make it far more accessible to people from developing countries than either Canada or Australia. Thus, the concept of undocumented immigration has been a feature of American immigration policy since at least the 1960s (Ngai 2004). In addition, because asylum seekers have been arriving by boat from Cuba and Haiti since the 1970s, the phenomena of boat arrivals is a longstanding one in the United States, and is less likely to inspire media-generated crises.

Although the timing, level, and public visibility of unauthorized arrivals has varied across the three countries, asylum seekers have eventually been reconceptualized as illegal immigrants in all three places. In the remainder of this chapter, I explain how, despite many differences, three separate states came to the common conclusion that asylum seekers should be actively deterred. I take up the story of each country in turn, describing the particular trajectory of each toward a regime of deterrence.

The United States

During the late 1960s and early 1970s, only a very small number of individual defectors and dissidents sought asylum each year in the United States (INS Statistical Yearbook 1996: Table 27). Further, asylum seeking remained conceptually linked to American refugee policy and thus was insulated from the domestic politics of immigration control. As the 1970s progressed, however, the United States began to experience the phenomenon of unwanted asylum seekers for the first time. Spurred by political instability and repression in Haiti, large numbers of people began to flee that country and seek refuge in the United States. Prior to this moment, the United States had admitted refugees and asylum seekers either by making proactive, strategic choices about which groups to admit from overseas or by allowing occasional individual dissidents to stay. Haitians did not fit into either category; they came in large numbers, their admission provided no geopolitical strategic value, and they were poor and black. Thus, the arrival of Haitians placed a strain on the neat conceptual separation between refugees and migrants that the system had allowed through much of the Cold War (Hamlin 2012a).

Meanwhile, the Nixon, Ford, and Carter administrations were using their executive parole power to admit large numbers of Vietnamese allied with the United States, as well as Cubans fleeing the Castro regime, all with little congressional input. Because the Constitution grants control over immigration matters to the legislative branch, by the late 1970s there was increasing congressional frustration over this presidential power grab, as well as a growing consensus that legislation was needed to remedy the confusing and inadequate patchwork of federal refugee policies and resettlement programs.[2] Ultimately, these forces combined to help spur legislative reform (Kennedy 1981, Anker and Posner 1981).

The 1980 Refugee Act was designed to limit executive control of the policy area and, for the first time in U.S. law, it officially codified a system of refugee status determination based on the UN Convention definition. Thus, on paper, the 1980 Act represented a major transition from the previous ad hoc, executive-driven, group-based system to an individualized, nonideological administrative process.[3] However, refugee admissions had been group based and dominated by the executive branch for so long that it was difficult to shake these entrenched practices, and presidents had no incentives to willingly relinquish power over this issue. Thus, presidents Carter and then Reagan both were able to appeal to Cold War necessities to reassert themselves into the policy arena almost immediately after the Act's passage.

First, in spring and summer 1980, President Carter used his parole power to admit 130,000 Cubans via the Mariel Boatlift. He submitted legislation that would classify them as "special entrants," sidestepping the newly created individualized RSD process (Zucker and Zucker 1987, Bon Tempo 2008). Second, after the election of 1980, the new Reagan administration developed a policy of Coast Guard interdiction at sea, in which officials from the Immigration and Naturalization Services (INS) identified boats with Haitians, boarded them, and conducted cursory assessments of eligibility for asylum. During the first five years of the program, the U.S. government interdicted 3,000 Haitians at sea. None were granted asylum—or were even brought to the U.S. mainland for a full hearing. Instead, the Coast Guard escorted the boats back to Haiti (Loescher and Scanlan 1986:194). Third, although the INS was technically responsible for conducting individual-level assessment of onshore asylum claims, during the 1980s the U.S. State Department submitted recommendations in each case, which the INS followed 95% of the time. These decisions followed striking group-based patterns, suggesting that the ideological commitments of the Cold War remained the single most reliable predictor for success of an asylum application. Approval rates varied from more than 70% for applicants from the USSR to around 2% for Haitians, Guatemalans, Hondurans, and Salvadorans (Feen 1985, Government Accounting Office 1987, Zucker and Zucker 1991).

The treatment of Haitian and Central American asylum seekers galvanized the burgeoning domestic advocacy community, and the categorization of asylum seekers became the focal point of an intense political struggle. Because the legal definition of a refugee had been officially expanded, advocates could argue that the actions of the Reagan administration were legally untenable, and use the new refugee definition as a powerful "source of legal authority" (author interview, 6/15/2010; Hamlin and Wolgin 2012). It took time, however, for this movement to gain momentum and to build up the infrastructure necessary for sustained legal advocacy (Yarnold 1990). The American Civil Liberties Union did not found its Immigrants Rights Project, which included a legal defense program for asylum seekers, until 1987, and much of the resistance to the asylum policies of the 1980s took place at the grassroots level. Legislation such as the 1986 Immigration Reform and Control Act reemphasized the importance of legality and enforcement. Yet, human rights groups, with the strong support of churches across the country, began a widespread civil disobedience campaign that became known as a sanctuary movement, to help refugees from El Salvador and Guatemala cross the border illegally and seek safe haven in the United States.[4] Thus, the border became a fraught symbol of an increasingly militarized struggle, and asylum seekers trying to enter the United States from the south became illegal border crossers.

By the 1990s, the range of interests engaged with refugee and asylum policy had grown, making it a more complicated and contentious policy area than ever before. The collapse of the Soviet Union and subsequent end of the Cold War had weakened the ideological framework that dominated American refugee and asylum policy since the 1950s, and advocates had mobilized to highlight the tensions and hypocrisy in the existing system. The INS found itself under intense pressure and criticism as several advocacy groups, including Amnesty International U.S.A and the Lawyers Committee for Human Rights, released reports on the implementation of the new asylum program's first decade, drawing universally negative conclusions. One study described the 1980s as "a period of failure and neglect."[5]

In response to sustained advocacy and freed from the counterveiling pressure of the fight against communism, the INS initiated a number of reforms during the early 1990s. In many ways, these reforms represented the delayed implementation of the asylum program created by the Refugee Act ten years earlier. First, the INS established a specialized Asylum Corps in 1990. This new group of mid-level bureaucrats trained in international refugee law assessed eligibility for refugee status based on the wording of the UN refugee definition. Second, to support the work of the Asylum Corps, the INS also set up a documentation center containing an extensive database of information about country conditions, including U.S. State Department country reports but also information provided by Human Rights Watch and Amnesty International about sending country conditions (Beyer 1992). These changes were designed to insulate the RSD process from direct U.S. State Department influence and were met with approval by refugee advocates (U.S. Commission on Immigration Reform 1997). This burst of humanitarianism did not last long, however. By 1994, the tone of the asylum policy debate was completely different than it had been three years earlier.

During the transition out of the Cold War framework, institutional *and* ideological strains combined to give leverage to those lawmakers who wanted to put an end to the asylum system altogether. Institutionally, the early 1990s saw an asylum boom that put the system under intense caseload stress just after the reforms had created a more costly and time-consuming RSD procedure. The collapse of the Soviet Union and the Chinese crackdown after the massacre at Tiananmen Square in 1989, followed by the coup that removed Haitian President Aristide from power in September 1991, left the new Asylum Corps swamped with an immense backlog of cases. Throughout a 10-year period, annual applications increased more than 10-fold, from 16,622 new applicants in 1985 to 182,769 applicants in 1995. By the end of the 1994 fiscal year, the backlog at the Asylum Office was 425,000 cases (INS Statistical Yearbook, 1994).

The rapid change in political commitment to the asylum system was not caused by the administrative costs of the asylum boom alone, however. The boom placed a huge institutional strain on the American RSD system that only exacerbated the already apparent ideological friction. Without a Cold War rationale for the program, the expansionist humanitarian side of the debate faltered, and political support for a thorough administrative procedure was short-lived. Thus, during a critical juncture in asylum policymaking, both the institutional and ideological capacity of the American asylum system was put to the test. By 1994, the modern era of asylum policymaking was born—one that is focused on reducing administrative burdens and is characterized by high levels of interbranch conflict, because both the courts and Congress became far more active players in asylum policy than ever before (Legomsky 1996).

Although the regime of deterrence did not fully take hold until after the 1994 congressional election, there were signs of crumbling support for the newly reformed system during the years leading up to that election. These symptoms of withdrawal from the humanitarian commitments of the early 1990s played out across three high-profile, dramatic controversies, culminating in what the

New York Times labeled the "Refugee Panic Attack of 1993."[6] First, there was a mass influx of Haitians, spurring the Bush administration to renew the policy of Coast Guard interdiction that had been so effective in preventing asylum seekers ten years earlier. The Coast Guard began a program of bringing Haitian asylum seekers to Guantanamo Bay, Cuba, rather than to the United States, where they could access the judicial appeals process.[7] The reintroduction of this divisive policy led to a back-and-forth between the courts and the executive branch that ended up being drawn out across two presidential administrations.

Controversy over interdiction was fueled by newly empowered legal advocacy organizations. These advocates appealed to international human rights norms such as *nonrefoulement* (the obligation not to return someone to a country where they will be persecuted). In November 1991, a federal district court judge issued an injunction preventing the forcible return of asylum seekers to Haiti (*Haitian Refugee Center, Inc. v. Baker*, No. 91-2653-CIV [S.D.Fla. Dec. 20, 1991]). This court order was quickly overturned by the 11th Circuit Court of Appeals, which decided the interdiction policy was a legitimate exercise of executive power (*Haitian Refugee Center, Inc. v. Baker*, 949 F.2d 1109 [11th Cir. 1991]). The Haitian Refugee Center appealed this decision to the Supreme Court, but, on January 31, 1992, the Court denied *certiorari*, refusing to hear the case, and thus allowing the logic of the 11th Circuit Court of Appeals to stand. The policy of forced return to Haiti was soon resumed. When the number of people leaving Haiti did not decline, and the Coast Guard interdiction program became overwhelmed, President Bush issued an Executive Order on May 24, 1992, calling on the Coast Guard to summarily return all vessels without any onboard asylum hearing.[8]

Presidential candidate Bill Clinton publicly criticized the Executive Order as both immoral and illegal, and after he took office in 1993, the United States returned to its previous policy of detaining Haitian boat people at the military base at Guantanamo Bay, Cuba. However, because this program was extremely costly and had no clear end point, after only six months, President Clinton resorted to the same program of repatriation for which he had strongly criticized his predecessor. Again, the issue went to the Supreme Court and, on June 22, 1993, the Court upheld the policy in an eight-to-one decision. The court announced that neither the Immigration and Nationality Act, or Article 33 of the 1951 Refugee Convention prevented the president from issuing an Executive Order of interdiction because these texts did not apply to aliens outside U.S. territory (*Sale v. Haitian Centers Council*, 113 S. Ct. 2549 [1993]). There was widespread outrage among advocates in the aftermath of the ruling. For example, Frank Sharry, executive director of the National Immigration Forum said: "now that no refugees are seen as strategic assets in geopolitical confrontation, they all have become solely a headache."[9]

Meanwhile, in June 1993, the tanker ship *Golden Venture* ran aground in New York harbor, and almost 300 Chinese people attempting to smuggle themselves into the United States jumped ship and tried to swim to shore. Six of them drowned. Most of the survivors sought asylum from China's forced sterilization policy, and top INS officials argued that the Bush administration's promise of protection from that policy had created warped incentives for people to risk their lives and hire smugglers to get to the United States. The INS detained and then denied asylum to almost all of the people onboard.[10]

The third contributor to the asylum crisis of 1993 was the discovery that Ramzi Ahmed Yousef, a planner of the World Trade Center bombing in February of that year, had filed an asylum application and had been allowed to live freely in the United States for years while his claim was pending.[11] This illustration of the perils of the administrative backlog received media attention, and even Senator Kennedy—a drafter of the 1980 Refugee Act and longtime champion of refugees—stated that the asylum seeker system had fallen apart and needed an overhaul. Thus, the American asylum program was in jeopardy only a few years after the creation of an unbiased, independent RSD process.[12]

After the 1994 election, the new Republican majority in Congress drafted the 1996 Illegal Immigration Reform and Immigrant Responsibility Act (IIRIRA). This act cemented the new era of asylum policy in the United States by subsuming the asylum program within a larger scale overhaul of illegal immigration control. In fact, the bill came very close to including a provision that would put an end to domestic asylum hearings altogether—a section that was removed during the eleventh hour as a result of extensive lobbying by refugee advocates and the support of several key members of Congress (author interview, 2/12/2007; see also Schrag 2000).

Although the IIRIRA did not end asylum for all, it shifted the focus of asylum policy to reducing incentives through stricter border control and crackdowns on exploitation of the process. The 1996 reforms placed a one-year time limit on applying for asylum, narrowed the grounds for which asylum could be granted, removed work rights for people whose asylum applications are pending, and instituted a policy of keeping as many people as possible in detention while their claims are investigated.[13] In addition, it created an Expedited Removal program, which prevents many would-be asylum applicants from accessing the RSD system at all, by processing claims at the border. Under this policy, a border control officer screens asylum seekers at the point of entry and makes an initial assessment of whether asylum seekers have a "credible fear" of persecution if returned to their home country. If so, the alien is referred for an asylum hearing. Part of what makes Expedited Removal so effective at reducing asylum applications is that it is up to the discretion of the individual immigration officer to decide how to pose questions about fear in the interview. If no fear is explicitly expressed and their documents are otherwise invalid for entry, the asylum seeker is summarily removed.

The magnitude of the Expedited Removal program is immense. A study commissioned by Congress found that of 177,040 people who were eligible for Expedited Removal in 2003, 171,664 either withdrew their application for entry voluntarily and left the United States or were deported after their initial interview. The remaining 3% were referred to an asylum hearing, in which most were not ultimately found to be refugees and were deported (U.S. Commission on International Religious Freedom 2005:32). More recent data from Immigration and Customs Enforcement (ICE) shows that the program has continued to grow each year since its inception and, in 2011 (the last year for which data are available), Expedited Removal accounted for 31.4% of the removals that ICE conducted (Immigration and Customs Enforcement, 2011). When the program was initially implemented, refugee advocates challenged it in court, but the D.C. Circuit Court decided the plaintiff organizations lacked standing to file suit on behalf of the asylum seekers who were being removed.[14] The asylum seekers themselves could not sue, because they were outside the border, and thus the jurisdiction of the United States. Expedited Removal has been regularly criticized by human rights groups and refugee advocates in the years since its inception for the lack of transparency or checks, but the Department of Homeland Security, which took over the program from the INS in 2003, has made few changes to the basic process (author interviews, 2/08/2007, 2/09/2007, 2/12/2007).

The other component of the 1996 legislation that has come under criticism by human rights organizations is the mandatory detention of asylum seekers who arrive without proper documentation.[15] Even those who can demonstrate they have a credible fear during their port-of-entry interview are detained until their hearing (although exceptions are made if bed space is not available) (Cole 2002, Congressional Research Service 2004). Including aliens who are awaiting deportation for criminal activity, the United States detains more than 375,000 noncitizens per year, with an average stay of 30 days in custody. The detention system has continued to grow; ICE, the branch of the Department of Homeland Security responsible for immigrant detention, doubled its custody operations budget between 2003 and 2009 to $1.7 billion per year.[16] The detention system has been roundly criticized for its poor conditions; its treatment of women, children, and the elderly; and for mingling asylum seekers with convicted criminals. Monitoring groups such as Human Rights First, which conducted in-depth studies of U.S. detention practices in 2004 and 2009, have raised concerns about the limited access to counsel for asylum seekers in detention and the potential of the detention environment to reactivate post-traumatic stress disorder stemming from past imprisonment and torture (Human Rights First 2004,

2009). Advocates also argue that, since the creation of the new Department of Homeland Security, the emphasis on security has led to more rights abuses of asylum seekers in detention. During the 2013 attempt at comprehensive immigration reform, the Democratic–controlled Senate passed a bill that would increase oversight of detention facilities to ensure detainees are "treated humanely" (S. 744, Border Security, Economic Opportunity, and Immigration Modernization Act, Section 3716[b]). However, detention is not an issue with much political traction, and the widespread use of detention for immigrants is a practice with support on both sides of the aisle.

Especially during the years after the terrorist attacks of September 11, 2001, support for increased border security was very strong among politicians in both political parties. However, a U.S. State Department official emphasized in an interview that "the idea that everything changed after 9/11 isn't really true. Changes were in the works before that. We had realized that we had gotten lazy, and needed to change the way we handled things" (author interview, 02/13/2007). During interviews, officials within the immigration bureaucracy also consistently expressed support for the commitments of the new era of asylum policy. A high-ranking Department of Justice lawyer lamented that there are still too many economically motivated migrants using the asylum system as a back door, causing a "flood" of applications. She concluded that "people file frivolous asylum claims in order to buy more time in the country, and since we've had serious talk about a guest worker program, those people think if they just hang on a little longer in the system, they will be able to stay" (author interview, 2/12/2007). Yet, a long-term Department of Homeland Security official suggested that policy developments have helped to close loopholes for economically motivated migrants to get in, saying: "things have improved a lot. It's not tied to getting a work permit anymore, so there is less incentive to seek asylum as a way to skip the queue" (author interview, 2/05/2007).

The current regime of deterrence has bipartisan support. In the United States, the 1996 IIRIRA was passed by a Republican Congress but signed into law by President Clinton. Congresses controlled by both political parties, as well as presidents George W. Bush and Barack Obama have continued to support the policies of deterrence that were outlined by the IIRIRA, and the Coast Guard interdiction-at-sea program continues to return people to Haiti, Cuba, Mexico, and the Dominican Republic (Frelick 2004, U.S. Coast Guard 2014). In 2005, Congress passed and President Bush signed the REAL ID Act, which was designed to crack down on illegal immigration, and included further restrictions on seeking asylum by increasing the requirements for verifying identity.

The extensive debates about comprehensive immigration reform in 2013 included little, if any, focus on asylum seekers. Instead, Congress concerned itself with the fate of millions of undocumented residents and whether they would be granted a path to U.S. citizenship. The reform proposal passed by the Senate in June 2013 included a provision eliminating the one-year bar on applying for asylum, but no other proposed changes to the current policies of deterrence.[17] The debates in the Republican–controlled House of Representatives focused heavily on enforcement and border control measures that, although not explicitly targeting asylum seekers, would have the side effect of enhanced deterrence for migrants seeking asylum.

Historians of migration to the United States tend to focus either on refugees or migrants, and the asylum seeker story frequently falls between the cracks. Bon Tempo's (2008:202) excellent history of American refugee policy touches only briefly on asylum seekers during the post Cold War period and does not discuss any deterrence policies. In the most comprehensive recent history of U.S. immigration policy, Tichenor (2002) describes the rise of restrictionist politics during the early 1990s, but does not link that debate to asylum policy trends. Schrag's (2000) fascinating discussion of the congressional battle over the American asylum program in 1996 provides a detailed insider perspective on deterrence politics, but the book is a close snapshot of a brief period, and does not connect that battle with the larger scale and longer term context of U.S. migration politics. He suggests the 1996 legislation may have been driven by a "temporary spike in public distress about immigration" and enabled by a Republican–controlled House of Representatives (Schrag 2000:225). But, as this section has illustrated, the contemporary American regime of deterrence has much earlier roots. It seems to have been sparked as soon as asylum seekers began to arrive in considerable numbers during the 1970s, and continues today as a durable policy regime.

Canada

Canada's transition to a regime of asylum seeker deterrence is a much more recent one than in the United States. For many decades prior to the shift, Canadian refugee policy was dominated by two themes that operated in tandem with one another. The first theme was Canada's role as a middle power, with a commitment to multilateralism that made it an influential player in global governance organizations (Vital 1967, Chapnik 2000). This critical aspect of Canada's identity led its government to prioritize compliance with international refugee protection standards and engage in close coordination with the UNHCR (Dirks 1985). The second theme was one of tight bureaucratic control of immigration admissions, through which Canada prioritized admission of those refugees from overseas who could fill particular needs in the labor force.

Policymakers during the postwar era believed that Canada's economic needs and international obligations could be met simultaneously through its immigration policy. For example, in 1966, the Canadian government restructured the bureaucracy to create the Department of Manpower and Immigration by combining the Department of Labor and the Department of Citizenship and Immigration into one agency (Dirks 1977:230). This new department was central in facilitating the admission of 11,000 Czechoslovakian refugees in 1968, most of whom were highly skilled and entered the workforce quickly (Adelman 1991:192).

When Liberal Party leader Pierre Trudeau became Prime Minister in 1968, refugee policy began to occupy a special place in Canadian immigration policy—one that was less concerned with the purely economic benefits of admission. This shift was partly due to increased economic prosperity that alleviated concerns about Canada's capacity to absorb low-income refugees into society. It also was a response to a growing humanitarian constituency both within the Canadian government and in civil society. First, in 1969, Canada became a signatory to the Refugee Convention. Then, during the early 1970s, Canada admitted thousands of Tibetans suffering from Chinese oppression, Ugandan Asians escaping Idi Amin, and Chilean leftists fleeing Pinochet (Adelman 1991:194). Canada also began to provide asylum to Americans avoiding the draft for the Vietnam War. None of these admissions were driven by economic interests. The Ugandan Asians were compelling because they were British citizens, and Chileans found support among the humanitarian community, who put a lot of pressure on the government to come to their aid (Dirks 1985:128). Together, these changes moved Canada into the position of a major refugee resettlement state by the mid 1970s.

The centerpiece of Canada's emergence as a leading place of refuge for the world's displaced people was the 1976 Immigration Act, which finally undertook a full-fledged legislative overhaul of refugee policy. The 1976 Act was a clear statement about Canada's place in the international community and its commitment to the international refugee regime. Much like the 1980 Refugee Act in the United States, the Act officially incorporated the UN Convention standards into law, making refugees a distinct category of entrants with a particular status (Adelman 1991:210). However, Canadian law went even further and broke refugees down into two main categories: Convention refugees and humanitarian refugees. Through this provision, Parliament preserved Canada's sovereign right to admit people from overseas who did not meet the Convention's specific definition (Adelman 1991:173). In other words, it preserved the ability to be more generous in admissions than the Convention required.

The 1976 Act also created a refugee status determination program for asylum seekers already within or arriving in Canada.[18] These claims were processed by the newly created Refugee Status Advisory Committee, which made its recommendations to the Minister of Immigration. The program was very small; it processed only a few hundred claims per year through the late 1970s, mostly in the form of paper applications. However, partially due to mounting tensions in the Indian state of Punjab and the high rejection rate of Central Americans in the United States during that period, Canada's application numbers began to increase at an unprecedented pace during the 1980s. Like the United States but on a smaller scale, Canada "moved from being a country of resettlement to a country of asylum for refugees" during the 1980s (Adelman 1991:217). By the middle of the decade, such large numbers of people were making in-country asylum claims that the system became completely overloaded, receiving almost 20,000 applications per year.

By 1985, Parliament was under the leadership of Mulroney's center-right Progressive Conservative Party. Alarmed by the size of the asylum backlog, the new Parliament commissioned a review of the system, which was conducted by Toronto Rabbi Gunther Plaut. His criticisms of the paper-based process received widespread attention in the media and from policymakers.[19] Among the 89 specific recommendations for improvement made in the report, the biggest concern he raised was the wait time of up to three years (Plaut 1985). In response to the report, Immigration Minister MacDonald said that she would make the creation of a new system a top priority.

In fact, an overhaul of the system became compulsory later that same year, when the Canadian Supreme Court handed down a ruling stating that the due process protections in the new Canadian Charter of Rights and Freedoms required in-person hearings for RSD applicants instead of paper applications (*Singh v. Minister of Employment and Immigration* [1985] 1 S.C.R. 177). In the aftermath of this decision, the Canadian government had to implement a new system with expanded due process protections, while at the same time manage the reality that lengthy administrative backlogs also would raise due process concerns.

Thus, in 1986, the Mulroney government instituted a one-time expedited review program that amounted to a general amnesty for people with pending asylum applications; approximately 85% of the 28,000 applicants processed that year were accepted (Dench 1999). The amnesty was designed to clear the decks and allow for a fresh start in asylum policymaking. It marked the high point of generosity for Canada's RSD regime, inspiring the UNHCR to award the Canadian people the Nansen Award. It was the only time UNHCR's highest honor has been awarded to a nation and not an individual. Particularly in contrast with the increasingly restrictive and ideological asylum policies of the United States during the 1980s, Canada gained a stellar reputation for humanitarian treatment of asylum seekers.

However, the Canadian system was not free from controversy, and the unbridled generosity of the 1986 program did not last as pressures on the system mounted. Accusations of bias were put forward by some in explanation of the low acceptance rate of Sikh applicants, and Haitians, many of whom sought asylum in French–speaking Montreal, also claimed they were disproportionately rejected.[20] By summer 1987, tensions ran high as the backlog of applications was again on the rise, and a ship smuggling 174 Sikhs was discovered off the coast of Nova Scotia.[21] The summer before, a ship filled with Sri Lankan Tamils had landed nearby, and concerns began to fester about whether this emerging pattern meant that Canada had become a destination for boat people. Meanwhile, a group of Turkish rejected asylum seekers mounted a dramatic protest of their impending deportation, marching from Montreal to Ottawa, camping out on Parliament Hill in a hunger strike, and demanding to be allowed to stay.[22] On April 2, 1988, the *Toronto Star* announced in a headline that the immigration system was "on [the] verge of collapse."[23]

Parliament called a special session to draw up legislation that would again overhaul the RSD program. However, because of its hasty construction and harsh new approach to asylum seeker policy, the 1988 reform bill was met with much criticism and subjected to many iterations and revisions.[24] Although a consensus had emerged that reform of some kind was needed, the 1988 reform efforts illustrated the tensions that were emerging between the longstanding Canadian commitment to internationalism and newer pressures on government to introduce deterrence policies. The result was a complicated hybrid mix of laws, not entirely compatible with one another. The first element of the legislation was the Refugee Reform Bill (also known as C-55), which included reforms to the inland RSD system. It expanded the number of people working for the Immigration Appeals Board to try and eliminate the backlog of asylum seekers awaiting hearings. Despite earlier attempts to fix this problem, including the amnesty just two years earlier, by the time C-55 was implemented, the number of asylum seekers awaiting hearings had again reached a huge backlog of 122,000 people (Dirks 1995:95). The bill also restructured the Immigration Appeals Board, renaming it the Immigration and Refugee Board (or IRB), and creating a new subdivision especially designed to handle refugee claims: the Convention Refugee Determination Division (Kelley and Trebilcock 1998:415).

Although C-55 tried to thicken the administrative system for RSD and bring the process more in line with the tenets of international law, ultimately the reforms of 1988 marked a turn toward deterrence in Canadian asylum policy and the beginning of convergence with the policies of the United States. C-55 also created a more aggressive and streamlined refugee status determination process, designed to cut back on the growing number of fraudulent claims by making the hearings faster. In addition, its companion bill, the Refugee Deterrents and Detention Bill of 1988 (known as C-84) allowed for the discretionary detention of asylum seekers whom immigration officials believed to be a security or flight risk (Helton 1991). When passed, the combined effect of the two 1988 acts was to make it "more difficult for a person to make a refugee claim in Canada, and indeed, to enter Canada in the first place" by shifting the burden of proof for making claims onto the asylum seeker (Kelley and Trebilcock 1998:418).

Because these acts were the first attempts the government had made in years to set limits on its general policy of open admission for asylum seekers, they were met with very high levels of opposition among refugee advocates and established immigrant communities. These groups expressed the sentiment that Canada was abandoning its historic role as a nation of immigrants (Hurwitz 1989, Young 1997:9). Nevertheless, the twin voices of restrictionism and fiscal conservatism had begun to take hold in the Canadian immigration debate, and gained momentum during the 1990s.[25] The 1988 legislation survived a Charter challenge in court only a few days after coming to force in January 1989 and was implemented.[26] In 1992, the Mulroney government passed bill C-86, unveiling a set of new deterrent provisions for asylum seekers, including a stricter standard at the port-of-entry interview, new limits on the right of rejected applicants to appeal, fingerprinting requirements for all claimants, and the imposition of heavy fines on airlines that bring people to Canada with false documents.[27]

By 1996, Chretien's Liberal Party government had come to power after almost a decade in opposition. The new Immigration Minister, Lucienne Robillard, announced that the entire immigration system, which was still based primarily on the 1976 Immigration Act, was in need of "an overhaul."[28] She appointed a panel to assess how the process could be streamlined to better prevent fraud, and throughout 1996 and 1997, the Ministry of Immigration and Citizenship considered a number of different changes to the RSD system, including a disbanding of the IRB.[29] Parliament could not come to a consensus about how to proceed with the reforms, and they were stalled. However, when a succession of boats filled with asylum seekers from China began to arrive in the summer of 1999, Minister Robillard renewed her calls for reforms to Canadian admissions policy and focused her remarks on the human smuggling angle of the issue.[30] After much debate and negotiation with immigrant advocates, the Immigration and Refugee Protection Act (IRPA) was passed in 2002.

The IRPA affected every aspect of the immigration and RSD systems, and embodied the new era of asylum policy in Canada—one that was focused on relieving administrative burdens. One of the main goals of the Act was to reduce the length of the asylum application process by placing heavy restrictions on judicial review of IRB decisions. To account for that cutback, the IRPA created a new division within the IRB, a Refugee Appeal Division (RAD), which would review negative decisions on their merits. Because the IRB backlog was a huge concern, the staff time required to support the RAD would be created through a shift from two-member panels to single-member hearings so that half the number of board members would be required for each case. Refugee advocates gave this new design grudging support, but felt betrayed when, in the immediate aftermath of IRPA's passage, the Immigration Minister announced that the RAD would not be implemented for budgetary reasons, whereas the cost-saving single-member hearings and judicial review restrictions would go ahead (Kitching 2007).[31] The RAD was not added until eight years later, when Parliament passed the Balanced Refugee Reform Act in 2010.

Another major component of the 2002 reforms was the signing, many years in the making, of an agreement between the United States and Canada regarding refugee claimants at the shared border between the two nations.[32] The most basic feature of the Safe Third Country agreement is that, with some notable exceptions, an asylum seeker must apply for refugee status in whichever of the two states they landed first. They cannot arrive in one country and travel to the other to make their application, and they cannot apply in one country after being rejected in the other—what some policymakers derisively call "shopping for asylum." Of course, because of the permeability of the border between the United States and Mexico, and the nature of international air travel, the vast majority of people affected by this agreement are those who attempt to enter Canada via the United States. An official at the Department of Citizenship and Immigration Canada (CIC) who had been an early drafter and promoter of the Safe Third Country agreement referred to the diversion of people away from the Canadian system as a "cost-sharing necessity" (author interview, 3/30/2007). During interviews, bureaucrats expressed a palpable sense of relief about the reduction of a secondary flow of asylum seekers from the United States, and the potential for a more manageable caseload in the aftermath of the Safe Third Country agreement (Arbel and Brenner 2013).

The effect of the Safe Third Country agreement is mitigated by the fact that asylum seekers who make it into the Canadian interior and file their application from within the country are not excluded from lodging their claim. However, uncertainty about the long-term impact of the agreement did not prevent a flurry of litigation regarding its legitimacy. In November 2007, a federal judge ruled that because the U.S. refugee system did not comply with the standards of the UNHCR, it could not be designated as a Safe Third Country, and ordered the agreement to come to an end.[33] The government got a stay from the Chief Justice of the Federal Court of Appeal, preventing the suspension of the agreement while both parties regrouped for a full hearing by the appeals court. In June 2008, that court overturned the federal judge's original ruling on the grounds that the case at hand could not be used to assess the overall safety of the U.S. system. Currently, the agreement continues to function, because in February 2009, the Supreme Court of Canada declined to hear an appeal of a decision that had been filed by a consortium of Canadian refugee advocates.[34]

During interviews, Canadian policymakers generally did not see a contradiction between Canada's commitment to humanitarian internationalism and the regime of deterrence, because they contrasted asylum seekers with refugees. They viewed asylum seekers as taking essential support away from genuine refugees, who are more deserving of assistance. For example, one top official in charge of both the overseas and domestic refugee programs within the CIC remarked:

> There are huge differences between the populations of domestic asylum seekers and people resettled from overseas. They come from completely different sets of nations. The overseas program focuses on the most needy, coming from camps. They need much more help in the resettlement program, they often need training on how to use electricity, they don't speak English, they often have incredible traumas. They are often women with children. The people who make it here [to seek asylum] in general have more money, more skills, speak English, are easier to integrate, often are single men. What is really frustrating is the domestic program costs so incredibly much more money, and so we can't spend those resources on helping the neediest people overseas. (author interview, 3/30/2007)

This official went on to argue that deportation should be invoked more frequently, because

> [t]he integrity of the program is threatened if you don't remove people, because then the public just sees it as "backdoor immigration." We can also do a better job of checking documents at foreign airports before people get on planes. We were the first to pioneer that strategy, but we could do more. (author interview, 3/30/2007)

As Zolberg (1992:105) observed, "the effectiveness of Canada's system is predicated on a level of border control that the United States cannot expect to achieve." For Canada to provide generous refugee resettlement programs and a rich administrative RSD, it needs to maintain high levels of control over the numbers of people who enter. During the 1980s, support for Canada's generous asylum program began to turn, as Canada found that it could not completely avoid the political pitfalls for which it had criticized the United States.[35] Critics

and proponents alike take pride in the leading role their country has historically taken in its humanitarian approach to RSD. Yet, Canada has led the way
in restrictive policymaking as well; it has introduced innovative border enforcement strategies, instituting port-of-entry interviews and carrier sanctions before
other nations, and it pushed aggressively for bilateral cooperation in asylum policy management with the United States. Despite Canada's reputation, it implemented harsher legislation limiting access to the asylum system six years before
the restrictive reforms passed in the United States in 1996.

In Canada today, the rhetoric of internationalism and humanitarianism
remains an important part of the policymaking process, but political support
for that process and the influence of the international refugee protection regime
both seem to be waning. In the current era of conservative government, aggressive deterrent efforts and the absence of certain procedural safeguards have led
to a disconnect between contemporary policies and the internationalist commitments and rights-expanding jurisprudence of the past. The 2012 Protecting
Canada's Immigration System Act ushered in yet more changes to the system,
which critics have suggested further cement Canada's retreat from humanitarianism. As a long-time Canadian lawyer and refugee advocate described the situation: "Imagine a beautiful church with a twelve-foot wall around it. You can't
pat yourself on the back and say you've taken care of it if no one makes it over
the wall, especially not the most vulnerable" (author interview, 5/11/2007).
Officials at UNHCR headquarters in Ottawa echoed that characterization when
describing their relationship with the Canadian government. A refugee protection officer told me: "[D]iplomacy is a key word. We have to be very judicious
about where we express disagreement and how" (author interview, 4/03/2007).
In response to such criticisms, Immigration Minister Jason Kenney insisted: "In
every respect, we are a model of generosity. Find me one other country that is
more generous with respect to immigration and refugees."[36] The commitment to
a hearing-based Canadian RSD process that was created by court order remains
in place today, but the current Canadian RSD regime is a long way from the one
that earned accolades from the UNHCR in 1986.

Australia

Australia differs from the United States and Canada in the sense that it has
always been an extremely reluctant asylum destination (Carens 1988). Although
Australia has been a nation of immigrants since its founding, it has had a history
of tight government control over migration, and a strong reluctance among policymakers to relinquish that control (Betts 2005, Tavan 2005). Further, asylum
seekers are the only substantial source of unauthorized migration into Australia

and are a highly visible aspect of the contemporary immigration policy debate. Because asylum has consistently been viewed as a domestic immigration control issue, Australia's approach to asylum seekers stands in contrast to its history of generosity in resettling refugees from overseas in carefully selected and controlled numbers (Gibney 2004). Australia's asylum politics is characterized by reactions to perceived threats, whether they come via uninvited boat arrivals, activist court decisions, or pressure to conform with international protection standards. Ever since asylum seekers began to arrive, policymakers have insisted on their sovereign right to control Australia's borders (Gelber and McDonald 2006).

Australia had a brief early encounter with asylum seeking during the late 1970s, when boat people from Vietnam arrived in Australia's northern waters in large numbers. Despite the fact that Australia was willingly resettling Vietnamese refugees from overseas camps at that time, the prospect of uncontrolled arrivals sparked a legislative flurry. In 1980, Parliament passed both the Migration Amendment Act and the Immigration (Unauthorized Arrivals) Act, designed to increase monitoring of the coast and to strengthen penalties for people smuggling (Schloenhardt 2003). This deterrent effort combined with Australia's distance from many of the refugee-producing conflicts of the 1980s seemed to have worked; for almost a decade, Australia received practically no more asylum seekers.

Then, in 1989, as a senior Department of Immigration and Citizenship (DIAC) official put it, the nation was "rudely drawn into the maelstrom of RSD overnight" (author interview, 10/05/2007). When the Chinese government cracked down on students during the repressive events of May and June 1989, Australian Prime Minister Hawke promised a safe haven for the Chinese students studying overseas in Australia.[37] Immediately, the immigration department received thousands of applications for asylum, which it was unprepared to manage. Later in 1989, boats began to arrive again off the northern coast of Australia, this time carrying Cambodians.[38] In response to this reemergence of boat arrivals, Prime Minister Hawke famously stated:

> Do not let any people, or any group of people in the world think that because Australia has that proud record, that all they need to do is break the rules, jump the queue, lob here and Bob's your uncle. Bob is not your uncle on this issue, other than in accordance with the appropriate rules. We will continue to be one of the most humanitarian countries in the world. But it is not an open door policy.[39]

By 1992, the backlog of applications had increased, and boats continued to arrive, leading the Australian Parliament to pass extensive amendments to the

1958 Migration Act. These reforms emphasized enhanced border control and established a universal visa requirement. After the regulations came into effect, those without a visa or those who overstayed their visa were subject to mandatory detention and removal (Crock 1998). In 1993, after discontent from religious and human rights leaders began to gain momentum, the government formed a committee to evaluate the practice of detaining unauthorized asylum seekers.[40] After several members of Parliament, as well as the media, were refused access to detention centers by the immigration department, Amnesty International and the UNHCR got involved.[41]

The advocates argued that conditions in the detention centers were unacceptable and, in particular, the detention of children received a great deal of negative media attention.[42] Although the number of detainees was small compared with the United States, the policy had become a political lightening rod, symbolic of a larger scale attitude toward asylum seekers. The asylum application rate was still quite low during the mid 1990s, but the Australian government was determined to reduce it even further, spurring several controversies. First, despite pressure both internally and internationally, the Australian government introduced yet another deterrent measure in late 1994 when it announced that people who sought asylum from China's One-Child policy would be found automatically ineligible for protection. Immigration Minister Bolkus said that this change was designed to "send a clear message" that Australia's "doors are closed."[43] In 1995, Minister Bolkus worked with the Chinese authorities to arrange the return of refused Chinese asylum seekers in custody in Australia.[44]

The second controversy occurred later in 1995, when a diplomatic crisis emerged regarding the fate of about 1,300 East Timorese asylum seekers. As Australian officials considered their cases, the Indonesian government indicated that it would be extremely unhappy if Australia were to find it to be a persecutor of its citizens.[45] The Australian government stalled and attempted unsuccessfully to get Portugal to grant the asylum seekers citizenship based on colonial ties.[46] The Indonesian government threatened that if Australia accepted the asylum claims of the East Timorese, it could expect thousands more arrivals to follow.[47] The fate of the asylum seekers, whose numbers had grown to 1,650 by that point, evolved into a protracted legal battle,[48] which eventually fizzled into an extended limbo as their applications were neither approved nor denied.[49] It was later discovered, through the leaking of a secret internal memo, that the Australian government had decided not to act one way or the other on their cases.[50] This issue was not settled until 2003, when after years of battles, threats of deportation, and a tense split within the coalition government, Immigration Minister Ruddock agreed to use his discretionary power to grant permanent residency (though not asylum) to the Timorese, who by then had been living in Australia for a decade.[51]

In the midst of the ongoing Timorese scandal, a new succession of boat arrivals commenced in the winter of 1999. What made this set of asylum seekers different from previous ones was that these people were not from the region. Rather, they were coming from Iraq, Iran, and Afghanistan, and could not have possibly come to Australia directly.[52] Despite the fact that almost all of them were eventually found to be genuine Convention refugees,[53] Parliament responded by passing the Border Protection Legislation Amendment Act of 1999, which made protection visas temporary and subject to reevaluation after three years, enhanced the penalties for people smuggling, and established a DNA and fingerprinting requirement for all asylum seekers.[54] Although intended as a strong deterrent for boat arrivals, asylum seekers continued to arrive through 2000 and 2001. After two years of buildup, the situation came to a head in August 2001, when a Norwegian tanker ship called the *MV Tampa* encountered a sinking vessel holding 438 asylum seekers from several Middle Eastern nations just outside of Australian territorial waters. By all accounts, the asylum seekers were in a desperate situation; their boat was sinking and they had run low on food and water. The captain of the *Tampa* brought all the asylum seekers onboard and attempted to bring them to Australia (Crock and Saul 2002).[55]

Prime Minister Howard chose this moment to take a high-profile stand on asylum seekers, and the Australian government refused to allow the refugees entry into the country.[56] His refusal resulted in a standoff that lasted for days and garnered worldwide media attention. Australian troops boarded the ship and provided emergency medical aid but were not allowed to speak to the asylum seekers lest they express a "well-founded fear of persecution."[57] Eventually, the *Tampa* was forced to be rerouted to makeshift camps in Papua New Guinea. At the time, Australian Prime Minister John Howard was in the midst of a reelection campaign, and in response to his government's actions surrounding what came to be known as the *Tampa* incident, he famously announced: "[W]e decide who comes into this country and the circumstances in which they come" (Howard 2001). Howard and his coalition government subsequently won that election comfortably, running in no small part on a restrictionist immigration ticket.

In the aftermath of the *Tampa* affair and Howard's reelection in 2001, Parliament revisited its policies regarding asylum seekers and passed a number of pieces of legislation related to restricting immigration to Australia, including the Border Protection Validation and Enforcement Powers Act 2001, and the Migration Legislation Amendment Act of 2001. This cluster of legislation came to be known as the *Pacific Solution*, which had four prongs.[58] First, it relied on an extensive interdiction-at-sea program, by which it turned away boats of people, usually arriving via Indonesia, who are assumed not to be eligible for refugee protection because of their circuitous route to Australia.[59] Second, the Australian government developed a Memorandum of Understanding with Indonesia aimed at cracking down on smuggling rings and preventing boats from leaving in the first place (Matthew 2003).[60] Third, Australia, via a series of acts of Parliament, some passed when boats were found approaching particular islands, excised more than 4,000 of Australia's islands from the Migration Zone.[61] The effect of excision is that Australia is not obligated to process the asylum claims of anyone who lands on them. Fourth, Australia moved its detention centers offshore, where they are also not subject to Australian law. A major center was located on the newly excised Christmas Island, and the other on the sovereign, but tiny, Pacific island nation of Nauru. In exchange for millions of dollars a year in development aid, the Nauru government allowed Australia to keep hundreds of detainees off Australian soil in detention centers run by the International Migration Organization, and out of its direct line of obligation under international law (Burnside 2007).

In addition to making it very difficult to reach Australia, the Howard government passed several measures designed to cut down on the incentives of the program for those who did make it. For example, people who were granted asylum after an unauthorized arrival were only granted a temporary, three-year "bridging visa," after which they had to be completely reassessed and considered for a permanent refugee visa. Asylum seekers on bridging visas did not receive access to the health and welfare benefits available to all other Australian residents, and were not able to sponsor their relatives for immigration to Australia. In contrast, asylum seekers who arrived on a valid tourist, student, or business visa and then applied for asylum were eligible to apply for a permanent visa directly. This double standard illustrated the degree to which asylum policy in Australia had become intertwined with immigration control. It was the uninvited arrival that raised the ire of politicians and policymakers alike. Phillip Ruddock, Immigration Minister from 2001 to 2007, made statements repeatedly and publicly asserting Australia's sovereign right to control its borders. For example, in June 2003, he complained:

> We must enforce our national right to determine who comes here to live, and when and how they do so. Let us hear no more of this nonsense that we live in a borderless world or that we owe a greater obligation than the people of other countries to those who would prefer to bend the rules and come to our shores illegally. (Ruddock 2003)

Although the Howard–Ruddock policies were extremely popular among the Australian public for a long time, a series of scandals eroded support for them in the years leading up to Howard's eventual defeat in the 2007 parliamentary election. First, in 2002, a boat in the Australian "search zone" sank, killing 353 asylum seekers and inspiring accusations that their distress calls had been ignored.[62] Later in 2002, a wave of unrest in the form of riots, hunger strikes, and symbolic sewing closed of prisoners' mouths made headlines as asylum seekers protested the conditions in detention centers (Ozdowski 2002, Brennan 2003, Mares 2003). Then, in 2005, a mentally ill Australian citizen of Philipina origin was discovered in an immigration detention center, having lived there, her schizophrenia untreated, for years. The public dismay this revelation caused was exacerbated by the Immigration Minister's refusal to apologize to her.[63] In addition, it was discovered that the Prime Minister had either lied or been misled by his advisors when he stated that asylum seekers throw their children overboard to provoke rescue, and commented that he did not want that type of person in Australia.[64]

In November 2007, Prime Minister Howard's party was defeated and he lost his own parliamentary seat, a fairly unusual fate for a Prime Minister. Although the election did not revolve solely around asylum issues, as the environment and Howard's ties to U.S. President George W. Bush were also hotly debated, the "Children Overboard" scandal discredited Howard among the public and contributed significantly to his personal unpopularity. The Howard government was replaced with a Labor Party government led by Kevin Rudd, who had promised to end many components of the Pacific Solution. In February 2008, the Rudd government announced the closure of the detention facility on the island nation of Nauru, leaving Australian territory Christmas Island as the only offshore detention center.

The Labor government soon found that it was difficult to sustain its opposition to the Pacific Solution. Despite the initial popularity of the Nauru closure, as asylum seekers continued to arrive in Australia in large numbers, political support for a regime of deterrence seemed to regain momentum quite quickly. Both the Rudd and Gillard governments continued to make extensive use of domestic detention facilities, and in March 2011, the severely overcrowded Christmas Island center was the site of an asylum seeker riot.[65] Opposition Leader Tony Abbott made it clear that if he were elected in the next election, he would reinstate the Pacific Solution, turning boats away before they became Australia's responsibility under international law.[66]

In the face of continued boat arrivals, in June 2012, Prime Minister Gillard appointed an expert panel to look into the issue of how "to prevent asylum seekers risking their lives on dangerous boat journeys to Australia" (Houston et al. 2012:9). The so-called Houston report was released in August 2012. It recommended an expansion of the overseas refugee resettlement program as an offset to an expanded effort to develop a regional solution to maritime asylum seeking, including enhanced cooperation with Indonesia, Malaysia, and Papua New Guinea. Citing the report's recommendations, the Labor government reopened the Nauru facility in August 2012. In a parallel with the experience of U.S. President Bill Clinton, who ran against President Bush's policy of interdicting Caribbean asylum seekers at sea but ended up replicating it, Prime Minister Gillard defended her government's approach by insisting (somewhat repetitively) that "in contrast [to the Pacific Solution] this solution has been born of a regional process motivated by the region's desire to tackle this regional challenge."[67]

The reopening of Nauru ended up costing the Labor government political capital on all sides of the ideological spectrum. First, the poor conditions were immediately slammed by the UNHCR as a violation of Australia's obligations under the Refugee Convention.[68] Second, in July 2013, major rioting by detainees led to a fire that caused serious damage to the facility.[69] Ultimately, despite what asylum seeker advocates viewed as backtracking and catering to the exclusionary right wing, the Labor Party lost the September 2013 federal election by a landslide—a defeat that many observers attributed in part to their perceived weakness on border control.[70] The current Abbott government has already engaged in negotiations with the Indonesian government, arguably a refugee-producing country itself, to return boats to Jakarta without processing.[71]

Even though the Liberal Party has consistently been more willing to run against boat people, and has been known for its harsh deterrence policies, since it became an asylum seeker destination, Australia has regularly increased border enforcement, regardless of the political party in power. The Migration Reform Act of 1992 and the Border Control Act of 1999 were passed by Labor–controlled Parliaments. The Pacific Solution was created with strong cross-party support under Prime Minister Howard's coalition government. Both parties now support interdiction at sea of maritime arrivals; they simply disagree about whether to turn them around or process them offshore.

Negative sentiment about asylum seekers, particularly offshore arrivals, is quite strong within the Australian immigration bureaucracy. In an interview, a senior Department of Immigration official responded to a question about whether Australia resists being a country of first asylum by saying:

> We have often been a first asylum country. We have had boat arrivals internal to the region for 30 years. It's just that there are an awful lot of countries between here and Afghanistan, so we are most definitely not the country of first asylum for them. Our stance is that the front door is open to refugees, so there is no need for them to use the backdoor. And the thing is, the ones who come, the majority of them are not refugees, so our decision makers can get cynical. There is so much chaff, but they have to presume it's all wheat. It's a tough job. (author interview, 10/05/2007)

In fact, the vast majority of asylum seekers who arrive by boat are eventually found by Australia's own decision makers to be genuine refugees. Another top Australian official commented on this paradox without indicating any sense of irony:

> The lawful group of applicants reflect the lawful migration flows into Australia. They are more cashed up, and they generally have an approval rate of 25% to 30% at the primary stage, and another 10% in review. Unauthorized arrivals are quite different. They are mostly Afghans, Iranians, Iraqis, with a smattering of others, and their acceptance rates are much higher. Iraqis have an acceptance rate of 89%; Afghanis, 85%; and Iranians, about 50% at the primary stage. They are a totally different cohort. They come from countries where there are serious human rights problems. (author interview, 10/05/2007)[72]

International organizations continue to have a weak presence in Australia. A recent report by the UN stated: "Australia should take urgent and adequate measures to ensure that nobody is returned to a country where there are substantial grounds to believe they are at risk of being deprived of their life or being tortured or subjected to other cruel, inhuman or degrading treatment or punishment" (United Nations Human Rights Committee 2009). An official at the small UNHCR office in Canberra said that, although it has been an uphill battle to establish a UN presence in Australia, "we have developed as an organization here. We started the office in 1996, and I'd say we have really come of age as an organization in this region to the point where now we are asked to make comment before changes are made" (author interview, 10/02/2007). But, he went on to say, "we have to keep our powder dry" in deciding when to take a stand, and "must have concern for the political environment at the time so that we keep our good working relationship with the government."

Despite the fact that it receives a comparatively small number of asylum seekers each year, many of whom are from the most war-torn regions of the world, Australia's asylum regime is still the most aggressively restrictive of the three countries, and has been consistently focused on deterrence since Australia first became an asylum seeker destination. The extensive media coverage of asylum policy in Australia illustrates the high political salience of the issue; in addition, the hostility that advocates and bureaucrats expressed toward each other in interviews confirms the contentious nature of the issue. The Australian case suggests an unfounded fear of invasion that shows no signs of fading from the political agenda.

Conclusions

RSD remains a key, but weakening, feature of global immigration policy. No host country has threatened to abandon the 1951 Convention altogether, and no country has managed to completely prevent asylum seekers from arriving. However, the power of the international refugee protection regime is wearing thin. Geopolitical interests perpetuated this regime for many decades, and because receiving states could select which refugees to resettle, how many, and when, they could comply with international treaties without making major compromises. Only now, when conforming to refugee protection commitments has become inconvenient and expensive, is the regime being truly put to the test. Indeed, Hammerstad's (2010:247) recent study of the UNHCR concluded even that agency has recently adopted a discourse of securitization, because it believes that it must "relate to these asylum fears and the language of security enveloping them" to remain relevant to donor states.

Asylum seekers highlight the modern dilemma states face in protecting borders *and* human rights. Policy developments since the 1970s suggest this dilemma has been resolved, at least for now, in favor of border control. Because the rise of deterrence regimes has become a universal reaction to unauthorized asylum seeker arrivals, it calls into question the degree to which the international protection regime ever carried weight. This long-term view reminds us that deterrence politics is not particularly new. Instead, it is simply applied more universally today, to all unauthorized migrants asking to be categorized as refugees, rather than selectively to the unauthorized migrants with no geopolitical strategic value.

The domestic political mechanisms behind the adoption of deterrence policies were different for each of the three receiving states, depending on the place of asylum seekers within the larger politics of immigration in each country. In the United States, asylum policy was initially dominated by a Cold War mind-set that allowed for selective generosity, and then became subsumed under a focus on terrorism and border control, which required more universal restriction. However, border control and territorial protection have been themes of American migration policy since the mid 20th century, and are as old as the international category of a refugee. Restrictionism was applied to Haitian asylum seekers from the time of the first arrivals during the mid 1970s. Similarly, Canada's focus on immigration control through an active bureaucracy was compatible with refugee admissions for many decades. When the two elements of Canadian immigration policy came to be in tension, deterrence won out via a public reaction against big government and a push for bureaucratic efficiency.

The Australian story is slightly different because it has always conceptually separated asylum seekers from overseas refugee resettlement due to a longstanding fear of invasion.

In a world where the gray zone between voluntary and forced migration is ever expanding, and the question of whether asylum seekers deserve refugee protection is left wide open by receiving states, the procedural rights of these unwelcome visitors become more important—and more contentious. Just as the politics behind the rise of deterrent policies was different in each country, the domestic RSD regime by which asylum claims are processed is unique to the receiving state. Next, in Part II, I turn to the RSD regimes of the United States, Canada, and Australia.

PART

II

THREE RSD REGIMES COMPARED

CHAPTER 4

Courting Asylum: The Judicialization of RSD in the United States

On December 26, 2005, the *New York Times* ran a story about the U.S. asylum system that included some notably fervent public bickering. The article focused on the tale of an applicant for refugee status from China called Qun Wang, but the larger dispute was about the relative ability of different agencies to make a high-quality RSD.[1] Wang had arrived in Newark, New Jersey, and applied for asylum for himself and his wife based on the claim that she had been sterilized against her will in China. They both feared retribution from the Chinese government for fleeing if they were forced to return to their home country. The controversy arose over the handling of his claim at the administrative level. Wang's application had been denied by an Immigration Judge (IJ) who stated in her decision that his sexist comments during the RSD hearing had led her to conclude (in something of a nonsequitur) "he's a horrible father as far as the court's concerned." On appeal to the 3rd Circuit Court of Appeals, the federal judge who reviewed the case was outraged by the personal bias displayed in the administrative decision and sent the case back for a rehearing, complaining in the opinion that "the tone, the tenor, the disparagement, and the sarcasm of the IJ seem more appropriate to a court television show than a federal court proceeding."

The president of the National Association of Immigration Judges was not impressed by this public critique of administrative agency decision making from the judicial branch. She defended her colleague to the *Times* by responding that "the vast majority of IJ's do an excellent job given such a large caseload.... To go name-calling and having an open season on [administrative] judges, it's crossing the line of civility." However, the article went on to quote the Chief Judge from the U.S. 2nd Circuit Court of Appeals, asserting that "we're the first meaningful review that the petitioner has." In other words, according to some powerful members of the U.S. judiciary, RSD at the immigration court level does not meet basic standards of administrative justice.

As this incident suggests, a person who applies for refugee status in the United States enters a terrain that is fraught with turf wars and interbranch conflict. The contemporary American RSD regime is permeated by a domestic institutional politics of wrangling for control of the process that brings the courts into the center of the issue, and is reliant on lawyers to make a good case. This structure makes the American RSD system the paradigm of an adversarial, legalistic decision-making style in four key ways emphasized by Kagan (2001). First, decision making about asylum claims is fragmented across multiple government agencies. Second, asylum policy in the United States is highly participatory, and allows for multiple perspectives to be presented and weighed, which can serve as a powerful check against bias or error. Third, decisions at all but one of the key stages in the process are made in a typical adversarial style involving a lot of rules and procedures that constrain decision makers. Fourth, advocates often criticize decisions for being unpredictable, inconsistent, and costly—the three pejorative hallmarks of adversarial legalism.

Although adversarial legalism has some well-documented pathologies, it springs from a deeply rooted conception in American politics of administrative justice as something that occurs through thorough vetting of an issue. In an ideal world, a fragmented adversarial system allows for a multiplicity of perspectives to be presented, so all players get their day in court. Furthermore, because one of the key players in the American RSD regime is the judicial branch, and specifically the U.S. Courts of Appeals, much of the controversy within the regime is about constitutional questions such as what qualifies as due process, and which actor is more qualified to make RSD decisions—generalist judges or specialized administrative decision makers. On one side, the decision makers in the administrative agencies believe the judicial branch is meddling too often and not allowing them to do their job. On the other side, the federal judges feel overloaded with picking up the pieces from asylum decisions that have not been made correctly.

Because there is intense disagreement among judges, lawyers, administrators, advocates, and politicians about whether due process rights are best protected at an administrative or judicial level, the system has not committed to investing heavily in any one stage. For its part, Congress seems willing to limit the role of the judiciary in RSD without investing in administrative improvements, raising concerns among advocates that the RSD system is not properly insulated from restrictive, anti-immigrant politics. The Courts of Appeals have pushed back, reasserting their role as the protector of due process rights for asylum seekers, and the superior interpreter of the law. Remarkably, in the face of so much controversy, the assumption undergirding this system is that if an applicant gets the opportunity to have multiple "kicks at the can" (as several interviewees described the process), then justice will prevail eventually.

In this chapter, I present a detailed picture of what RSD looks like when it occurs within a system of administrative justice based on the principles of adversarial legalism. The commitments that drive this particular RSD regime structure are a powerful mechanism of cross-national divergence. The structure has become particularly significant because the increase in asylum seeking during the 1980s contributed to a shift in American immigration law. As opposed to a focus on international human rights concepts, the U.S. Courts of Appeals are motivated to police the interbranch dynamics around deference to administrative agencies and to protect constitutional due process rights for noncitizens, even as national border control policy has become harsher and more suspicious of them. These constitutional questions have nothing to do with asylum policy; RSD is just one battlefield on which these questions are being played out. Thus, immigration law is more centrally connected to major questions of constitutional and administrative law than ever before. Asylum seekers are able to make claims for refugee status in the United States because of international legal standards of protection, but the rights that asylum seekers assert in court are distinctly domestic and serve as a fulcrum for courts to assert their institutional power.

The Process and the Players

The structure of the American RSD regime is fragmented from the moment asylum seekers begin the process because there are two distinct points of entry to the system (Figure 4.1). The first is known as an affirmative asylum application, which is begun when a person proactively files a 12-page I-589 form: Application for Asylum and For Withholding of Removal. Affirmative claims must be filed within one year of entering the country and may be filed regardless of whether the asylum seeker initially entered illegally or legally. After the form is filed, the applicant is asked to appear for an RSD hearing at the Asylum Office. Currently, the Asylum Office is a subsection of the Bureau of Citizenship and Immigration Services, which falls within the Department of Homeland Security.[2] The hearing is inquisitorial and takes place in a small room with a bureaucrat who is trained in international and domestic asylum law but is not necessarily a lawyer. Applicants may bring a friend or counsel for support, but the hearing is a conversation between the applicant and the Officer.[3]

The Asylum Office was established in 1990 as an ideologically neutral, nonadversarial decision-making body that would address concerns about administrative justice that arose as a result of Cold War–era biases in the previous system. The Asylum Office was designed to follow a professional judgment model of decision making because it used highly trained, specialist decision makers in an

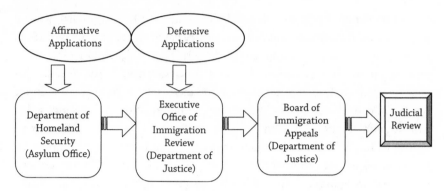

Figure 4.1 The RSD Process in the United States.

informal setting (Kagan 2001). However, almost immediately after the establishment of the Asylum Corps, this new approach to refugee status decision
making was put to the test by the asylum boom of the early 1990s. The Asylum
Office became swamped with an immense number of cases and, as mentioned in
the previous chapter, by the end of the 1994 fiscal year, the backlog was 425,000
cases (INS 1994). The high cost of processing asylum claims in this manner
tested politicians' commitment to the professional judgment model and gave
leverage to those lawmakers who wanted to put an end to the asylum system
altogether. In 1995 and 1996, these legislators came very close to succeeding; up
until days before passage of the 1996 IIRIRA, it included a provision that essentially removed the asylum program from U.S. law (Schrag 2000). The system
ultimately survived as a result of intense lobbying by refugee advocates, but the
IIRIRA still brought some significant reforms to the process.

One of the consequences of the 1996 IIRIRA is that, today, only about half
of asylum applicants have access to the Asylum Corps decision makers for their
initial decision. The other half of applicants is funneled directly into the highly
adversarial and legalistic administrative immigration court system, called the
Executive Office of Immigration Review (EOIR), which is housed within the
Department of Justice. These hearings are known as defensive asylum hearings,
because they are defending against deportation, and asylum seekers get tracked
into them in three ways. First, they may be found by ICE at a port of entry to
be without valid travel documents. Second, they may be found by immigration
officials to be in the United States illegally and placed in a removal proceeding.
If anyone in these two groups express a desire to seek asylum, they skip the affirmative hearing stage and are sent directly to a defensive hearing. The third path
to the EOIR is via the Asylum Office. All applications that are not accepted at
the affirmative stage are referred automatically to a defensive hearing before an
IJ, and thus join up with the defensive stream of cases.

Defensive hearings are adversarial; they are held in a courtroom setting before an administrative IJ.[4] IJs hear only immigration matters, but are not trained experts in asylum issues. The Department of Homeland Security is represented in the hearing by a lawyer whose job is to argue that the applicant does not qualify for asylum and should be deported. Applicants are encouraged to represent themselves with counsel, although the government does not provide one because deportation hearings are civil proceedings, not criminal trials.[5] The burden of proof in a defensive hearing is on the asylum seeker, and they may be cross-examined by the government attorney about the details of their claim. The IJ must decide between granting refugee status or ordering the applicant removed from the country.

The two-tiered system was created because Congress decided that some asylum seekers deserved more "kicks at the can" than others. Affirmative applicants were seen as more legitimate, and therefore more deserving, of a thorough system of administrative justice. Lawmakers created the distinction between affirmative and defensive claims because they did not want to encourage people to file frivolous asylum claims as a means of delaying their deportation. They also did not want to reward people for entering the country illegally by allowing them access to the Asylum Office, which has a reputation for generosity. Certainly, the two tracks of the American asylum system have very different trajectories in terms of their likelihood of acceptance. About one-third of affirmative applications are accepted at the initial stage,[6] and during the second stage, those who originally made affirmative claims have much better prospects of success than defensive applicants. In recent years the acceptance rate for these claims has consistently been more than 50%. Taking both stages together, about two-thirds of affirmative applicants are eventually granted asylum compared with the 35% grant rate for defensive applicants in 2012 (EOIR 2013).

Part of this difference may stem from the fact that people with strong claims are more likely to file affirmative applications after reaching the United States, and people with weaker claims may choose to wait until they are caught without papers to file for a withholding of removal from the country (Chen 2007). In fact, many lawyers told me that if clients come to them with a weak case, they advise them not to file an affirmative claim because it brings attention to themselves. One lawyer said, "If you are an honest lawyer, you won't do it, because if you aren't careful, they will get deported and it will break your heart." Instead, those with weak claims often choose to take their chances living illegally in the United States rather than apply for asylum and risk deportation.

Although their paths to asylum are different, the makeup of the affirmative and defensive populations of applicants is, in general, quite similar in terms of country of origin. During the past several years, the top three source countries in both categories have been the People's Republic of China, Ethiopia, and Egypt.

However, the defensive group has more Chinese applicants than any other country of origin, and the affirmative group is more evenly divided by country of origin. The affirmative group also tends to have more applicants from the region, including Colombians, Venezuelans, Salvadorans, and Guatemalans, whereas the defensive group has more applicants from farther afield, including large numbers of Indians, Nepalese, and Africans from a variety of countries (DHS 2013). This difference suggests that ease of travel to the United States, rather than legitimacy of the claim, may be another factor in determining whether asylum seekers get tracked as affirmative or defensive applicants.

If applicants are unsuccessful at the EOIR, they are deported unless they file an appeal with the central headquarters of the office, called the Board of Immigration Appeals (BIA). The BIA, located in Falls Church, Virginia (a suburb of Washington, DC), does not hold in-person hearings, but conducts on-paper reviews of the decisions of IJs. It consists of as many as 15 members, who are appointed as delegates of the Attorney General. Beyond the BIA, the last remaining recourse is to apply for judicial review in whichever region the initial asylum claim was filed. There are 12 regional circuit Courts of Appeals in the United States, which tend to be highly involved in reviewing RSD decisions (Carp and Stidham 2001). On rare occasions, the Supreme Court will step in to hear a case, especially if the issue at hand has been resolved differently across multiple circuit Courts of Appeals, a situation known as 'splits in the circuits'. In the vast majority of cases however, the U.S. Court of Appeals is the very last chance a failed asylum seeker has to prevent deportation. Thus, a case that travels from the Asylum Office to a federal court has been heard in four distinct institutional bodies, each with its own style and reputation. The assumption behind this design is that, after four considerations, any errors in the initial decision are discovered and resolved.

Administrative Insulation and Agency Interaction

Although the concept of administrative justice behind the American RSD regime is one of multiplicity and thorough vetting, because the American RSD regime is so fragmented and so dominated by adversarial decision-making bodies, a side effect is that there are multiple entry points for exclusionary politics to influence the process. However, although the American RSD regime as a whole is subject to a lot of criticism by refugee advocates, some stages of the process are far more respected and trusted than others. Generally speaking, asylum seeker advocates reserve their ire for the more adversarial stages of the administrative RSD process, with the strongest criticism aimed at the BIA, which is seen as transparently exclusionary.

According to asylum seeker advocates, the Asylum Office is the most politically insulated stage of the RSD regime. Although previous research has concluded that Asylum Officers are influenced not just by humanitarian concerns, but also by the strategic interests of the United States, this research looked at the Asylum Office in a vacuum, not relative to the other stages of the process (Salehyan and Rosenblum 2004). In contrast to IJs or federal judges, Asylum Officers receive extensive training in international refugee law. They are the furthest removed from judicial review, their decisions occur in private, and the decisions are not precedent setting. During interviews, staff members at the Asylum Office claimed they have a better reputation for refugee protection and are more removed from politics than the EOIR. This self-assessment was confirmed by advocates and lawyers who, without exception, reported more trust in and more satisfaction with the decision-making process at the Asylum Office. Still, lawyers suggested repeatedly that "the individual officers are a big variable." As one lawyer put it:

> Some will deny no matter what. I try to circumvent that by asking right off the bat at the Asylum Office what the concerns are that would prevent the officer from granting, and sometimes that works.... That's why a good attorney is critical. (author interview, 8/28/2007)

A recent large-scale quantitative study of grant rates across decision makers confirmed that, indeed, there is quite a bit of variation across individual Asylum Officers. However, the study found that the variation was far greater across the IJs at the EOIR (Ramji-Nogales et al. 2007, 2009). In fact, the IJs' grant rates varied dramatically, both across regions of the United States and among judges within the same region. Ramji-Nogales et al. (2009) found several instances of different judges in the same court with grant rates ranging from less than 5% to more than 80%, even when examining cases from the same sending country. They concluded that the random assignment of applicants to individual judges was tantamount to "refugee roulette." During interviews, lawyers confirmed these findings. One lawyer complained:

> It's a lottery draw of which judge you get at EOIR. Some are superstars, but one is the worst human being: he's idiosyncratic and unpredictable. He's a loose cannon, and gets really angry sometimes. (author interview, 8/24/2007)

Another lawyer suggested that there are some IJs with whom he doesn't even bother trying. He explained, "You can find out who the judge is ahead of time, and this absolutely influences our decision of whether even to take the case and how to prepare for it" (author interview, 9/14/2007). The fact that some applicants may have trouble finding legal counsel because of who they have been scheduled to appear before raises troubling questions about access to justice in the American asylum system.

Because IJ are political appointments, the type of person who becomes one varies across presidential administrations. Democrats have tended to appoint more women, people of color, and former advocates with experience representing asylum seekers. Republicans have tended to appoint IJs from out of the enforcement side.[7] Not surprisingly, the "refugee roulette" study found that personal background is a significant factor affecting the decision making of IJs. In particular, being female and having prior work experience as an immigration lawyer were the two best predictors of greater than average acceptance rates. A more recent political science study expanded on these findings, describing "a complex reality in which judicial policy proclivities do not have a constant influence in every context" (Camp Kieth et al. 2013:281). Instead, this study found that IJs with a background in enforcement were less likely to grant asylum to applicants from states to whom the United States gives military aid, and from states that are known to send large numbers of illegal immigrants to the United States. In other words, judges are influenced by both American strategic interests and exclusionary border control politics, but some judges are more likely to be swayed by those concerns than others. Presidents can appoint IJs with backgrounds that make them more likely to be sympathetic or tough on RSD applicants, but IJs from previous administrations remain, adding to the large variation across judges. In an interview, an immigration lawyer commented that after eight years of Bush administration appointments there were "less and less" of the "sympathetic" former lawyers on the bench (author interview, 8/23/2007). President Obama has been more likely to appoint judges who fit the profile of a sympathetic decision-maker, tipping the scales back the other way.

Beyond the variability and unpredictability of the EOIR, there is quite a bit of evidence to suggest that there are problems with the professionalism and legal quality of its decision making. These problems are most likely the result of the poor resources the agency receives, combined with the highly politicized climate in which IJs must operate. Well-known conservative Judge Richard Posner of the 7th Circuit Court of Appeals has been one of the most vocal critics of the Executive Office of Immigration Review, lambasting the quality of their decisions in his own written opinions, and in speeches to the Bar. In April 2008, he called the asylum system "inadequate" and went on to state that "there's simply a problem with the IJs having the knowledge that they need." He went on to add that the BIA "does not have the resources to give more than a perfunctory review."[8] Equally vehement critiques of administrative RSD have come from the opposite end of the ideological spectrum as well. For example, Judge Marsha Berzon of the 9th Circuit in San Francisco called a decision by an IJ "literally incomprehensible," "incoherent" and "indecipherable" and said that the decision "defies parsing under ordinary rules of English grammar."⁹

In response to these types of criticism from the judicial branch, in 2006, Attorney General Gonzales wrote a memorandum to the IJs, raising a concern that "there are some judges whose conduct can aptly be described as intemperate or even abusive and whose work must improve" (Gonzales 2006). The EOIR claims to be working on reducing tension with the judicial branch. For example, a high-level EOIR official acknowledged during an interview that "we've been chipping away at some of the animosity between some of the circuit judges and the EOIR." She went on to say that the EOIR has begun to do outreach among federal judges:

> I think these conversations have helped judges understand more the conditions under which we work. Like, we only have one-eighth of a law clerk per judge. When they understand our lack of resources, they are more understanding about the quality of the decisions that are being made. (author interview, 2/12/2007)

The BIA has an even worse reputation among both judges and advocates than the immigration courts. First, it has long suffered from limited political support, because opponents of the RSD process see it as an excessive waste of resources, and refugee protection advocates see it as a sham, lacking in the resources to conduct rigorous review. In addition, the BIA is not well regarded by many reviewing judges. As the senior counsel for the BIA told me, "Some Circuits, like the 9th and 2nd, don't actually see the BIA as experts." For example, in his 1996 study of the American courts, Judge Posner called the work of the BIA "dismal" and "perfunctory" (Posner 1996:265). He went on to suggest:

> It would be easier and cheaper for Congress to establish within the board...a tier of *credible* appellate judges who would write real opinions in all but the frivolous cases than to continue expanding the federal courts so that they can keep up with the flow of administrative review cases. (Posner 1996:266)

Critiques of the BIA increased when, in 2002, under pressure from the Bush administration, Attorney General John Ashcroft initiated procedures that were designed to reduce the immense backlog of cases the agency then faced. These "streamlining" reforms included more frequent reliance on decisions by one board member instead of three-member panels, a policy of "deference" to the conclusions drawn by IJs, an end to independent BIA fact-finding, and the use "Affirmances without Opinion" (AWO), which uphold the decision of the

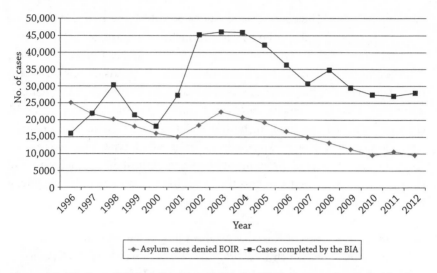

Figure 4.2 Number of Asylum Cases Denied by the EOIR Compared with the Number of Cases Completed by the BIA (1996–2012). Source: EOIR Statistical Yearbooks, 2000 to 2012.

IJ with no elaboration of the legal issues involved. The reforms also included a reduction over time of the BIA from 15 to 11 members—a change designed to increase the internal consistency and "collegiality" of BIA decision making by removing Clinton–appointed members (U.S. Department of Justice 2002, 2006). The BIA had already begun to increase the speed with which they finalized cases prior to the 2002 reforms (Figure 4.2), but these innovations quickly resulted in a dramatic increase in the number of cases the BIA was able to process in a year. Since then, the BIA has continued to move through its caseload very quickly, even as the number of cases processed at the EOIR has remained steady, and even declined slightly.[10]

The BIA has therefore succeeded in drastically reducing its backlog, but at the expense of further damaging its public image. During interviews, lawyers said they simply expect the decision to be upheld at that review stage, and view the BIA as "a pit stop on the way to the 9th Circuit" (author interview, 8/24/2007). One lawyer called the BIA "a rubber stamp" and said the AWOs are "a cop-out; we used to get real judicial review there, but now the appeals we send are just sent back within a matter of months" (author interview, 8/23/2007). Another said, "Every case gets appealed [to federal court], even if it's the weakest, because we know the BIA doesn't grant anything" (author interview, 8/27/2007).[11] According to the American Bar Association, these accusations have some truth to them. A study they conducted found that, before the 2002 reforms, the BIA would find in favor of the asylum applicant 25% of the time. Afterward, the rate was 10% (American Bar Association 2003). These statistics fuel suspicions among advocates that the streamlining reforms were a political move designed to reject more applicants.

Although increased judicial review was probably an unintended consequence of the BIA streamlining, a larger proportion of BIA decisions are now being reviewed than ever before, placing the agency under closer judicial scrutiny. Prior to 2002, only about 7% of BIA decisions were reviewed in federal court each year. Since the reforms, approximately a quarter of BIA decisions are being reviewed annually, more than three times as many as previously (Palmer et al. 2005). Ultimately then, because the Courts of Appeals have taken their role in the American RSD regime seriously, a lack of political investment in the administrative system has led to more judicial involvement and less agency independence.

Impact: The Judicialization of RSD

The judicialization of the American RSD regime is now a key mechanism of cross-national divergence. The U.S. Courts of Appeals have become central players in the regime, a shift that has highlighted the distinct institutional role these courts play within the judicial branch. The Supreme Court and Courts of Appeals are often at odds with one another, because, as Law (2010:15) argues, they operate in different institutional contexts and "play different roles...within the same policy area." Specifically, Law (2010) suggests the Courts of Appeals view themselves as error correctors for the administrative decisions of the BIA, and have been quite active in reviewing them. Because they hear far more cases than the Supreme Court ever can, they are largely "insulated from Supreme Court supervision" and function as "independent policy makers" (Law 2010:15). Furthermore, because the 9th Circuit hears approximately half of all immigration appeals, and is widely regarded as having a liberal ideological slant, its particular self-perception as an active error corrector results in high levels of conflict between that court and both the BIA and the Supreme Court. This tension within the judicial branch, which is usually considered to be a single institutional player in the American RSD regime, further illustrates the degree to which the system is fragmented, unpredictable, and contradictory.

In contrast to the current active involvement of the Courts of Appeals, the Supreme Court has, historically, played a much more limited role in American immigration law. Since the era of Chinese Exclusion, it has operated as a precedent setter with a focus on national sovereignty, asserting that Congress has a "plenary power" to regulate immigration without judicial intervention (Chin 2004, 2005).[12] The Supreme Court has maintained a focus on sovereignty and congressional plenary power over immigration even in light of America's adoption of various international treaties governing refugee protection. Because of its status as a global superpower, the United States has been notoriously disinclined to bend any of its policies—but in particular those related to border control—to international pressure. Neither judges nor policymakers take international soft law guidance into account when conducting legal interpretation, and rare instances of judicial reference to international developments are met with great skepticism by conservative judges.[13] The legacy of the plenary power doctrine is that immigrants who are attempting to enter to the United States have no access to constitutional rights or international protection treaties. Using the plenary power doctrine, the Supreme Court has upheld the deterrent policy of interdicting asylum seekers at sea, and allows the expedited removal of asylum seekers who attempt entry into the United States without valid travel documents (*Sale v. Haitian Centers. Council*, 509 U.S. 155 [1993]).

In contrast, those who have made it into the territory of the United States are entitled to a process governed by constitutional due process protections. The Supreme Court has repeatedly found that constitutional rights apply to all immigrants physically present in the United States, even if they entered the country illegally (see, for example, *Matthews v. Diaz*, 426 U.S. 67 [1976], *Plyler v. Doe*, 457 U.S. 202 [1982], and *INS v. St. Cyr*, 533 U.S. 289 [2001]). For example, the Supreme Court pushed back quite aggressively when Congress tried to strip courts of their jurisdiction to review the new detention standards in immigration reforms of 1996. IIRIRA states that if deportation cannot be secured within the customary 90-day window, deportees may be detained for an additional amount of time. It also asserts that "no court shall have jurisdiction to review [decisions] specified to be in the discretion of the Attorney General." However, in *Zadvydas v. Davis* (533 U.S. 678, 2001), Justice Breyer read a six-month detention limit into the statute to avoid the due process concerns that would have arisen from a different statutory interpretation. He stated that if the statute had intended to provide for indefinite detention, it would have posed a "serious constitutional threat." The Court went on to emphasize "the distinction between an alien who has effected entry into the United States and one who has never entered," saying that it "runs throughout immigration law," and further asserted that the plenary power of the political branches over immigration "is subject to important constitutional limitations."

Similarly, in *Demore v. Kim* (538 U.S. 510, 2003) the Supreme Court found that its jurisdiction had not been stripped from reviewing habeas corpus claims because Congress had not shown clearly enough that it intended to limit judicial review of constitutional claims (Motomura 2005). The Court rejected the idea that habeas claims in individual cases could not be subject to judicial review and claimed that "extent of [the Attorney General's] authority is not a matter of discretion" (Loughran 2004). Both of these decisions rest on the assumption that detention of someone being deported is subject to more due process considerations than detention of someone who has never been officially admitted.

Because the constitutional rights of noncitizens hinge on whether they have crossed the border, Bosniak (2008:4, 99) has called the immigration law of the United States "hard on the outside and soft on the inside" and "Janus–like," referring to the two-faced Roman god. The Supreme Court is deferential to Congress when it comes to setting admissions and border control policy, but the Court has clearly demonstrated that this deference does not extend to constitutional concerns about noncitizens inside the territory. Thus, when questions about administrative due process arise, it is left to the Courts of Appeals to assess whether the agency interpreted the statute correctly and provided due process in the removal hearing.

The constitutional right to due process was initially conceived as a protection for those facing criminal charges, but during the second half of the 20th century, the United States experienced a vast expansion of procedural rights in several areas beyond criminal procedure and a greater expectation among the American public that "total justice" could be achieved (Friedman 1985). As the administrative state expanded, the number of people affected by administrative action grew, as did the range of people eligible for judicial review (Stewart 2003). This expansion of due process rights to include many new groups has been called a due process revolution, because it swept through the courts and forced judges to decide how best to assess the actions of administrative agencies (Mashaw 1985). The popular expectation of total justice through administrative law is one of the changes in American law that has fueled the rise of adversarial legalism (Kagan 2001).

The resulting challenge of American administrative law is to strike a delicate balance between protecting individuals against rights violations or misinterpretation of statute by government agencies while maintaining a degree of deference to administrative decisions that are made by experts. The dominant legal rule governing this issue is that of *Chevron* deference—the concept, laid out first in *Chevron v. Natural Resources Defense Council* (467 U.S. 837, 1984)—that when a statute is ambiguous, the agency interpretation should be presumed to be correct because administrative decision makers are specialists. However, there is some room for ambiguity and judicial discretion because courts are allowed to strike down agency interpretations that they deem to be unreasonable. This provision is often used by the federal Courts of Appeals when reviewing immigration decisions, especially in light of the accusations of malpractice at the BIA. In a study conducted soon after the *Chevron* decision, Schuck and Elliott (1991:1027) found the likelihood of court intervention varies, depending on "the area of law and the policy domain in question." Cross and Tiller (1998) found the policy preferences of the judge (based on partisan identification) are a significant predictor of the decision to affirm or remand an agency decision. In addition, the Supreme Court decision in *United States v. Mead Corporation* (533 U.S. 218, 2001), a case unrelated to migration, weakens the force of *Chevron* slightly by introducing a more stringent standard of review. As this decision illustrates, in a legal system characterized by adversarial legalism, even the boundaries of each player's institutional role are contestable and in flux.

Currently, the circuit Courts of Appeals are reviewing administrative immigration decisions at startlingly high levels (Palmer 2006). On all topics combined, the Courts of Appeals received only 5,500 more cases in 2012 than they did in 1996. During the same period, cases originating from the BIA rose by almost 6,000 cases.[14] Thus, while other areas of litigation declined, including criminal cases and bankruptcies, immigration appeals accounted for most (if not all) of the increase in caseload throughout this 16-year period. To put it another way, in 1996, immigration appeals were 2% of the total caseload of the U.S. Courts of Appeals; by 2012, they had become just more than 12% of the cases on the docket.[15]

There has been much debate about whether the changes in BIA procedure are the cause of the extremely rapid increase in the number of immigration cases brought into the federal court system via an application for judicial review (Figure 4.3). A spike is certainly noticeable immediately after the 2002 reforms, but this phenomenon actually began during the 1980s and gained momentum during the 1990s (Posner 1996, Law 2010). As early as 1996, Judge Posner observed that the Courts of Appeals' caseload had grown much faster than that of the District Courts since the 1980s, and suggested that the difference was a result, in part, of the growth in appeals from administrative agencies, which go directly to the Courts of Appeals. In particular, he wrote, "were it not for the tremendous increase in appeals from the Immigration and Naturalization Service, the number of administrative appeals would actually have declined [between 1983 and 1995] because of the deregulation movement" (Posner 1996:110). Today, the percentage of immigration cases has increased to a startling 84% of all administrative appeals into federal court (Administrative Office of U.S. Courts 2012). As a result, many law schools are hiring immigration experts to teach their administrative law courses.

The immigration litigation explosion has not been distributed evenly across the federal Courts of Appeals. Together, the 9th Circuit, which includes California and Arizona, and the 2nd Circuit, which includes New York, process the vast majority of the total immigration caseload each year. In 2012, the 9th Circuit received 50% of the total immigration caseload at the federal court level; the 2nd Circuit received 20% (Administrative Office of U.S. Courts 2013). The Courts of Appeals do not keep statistics that track the specific issues raised

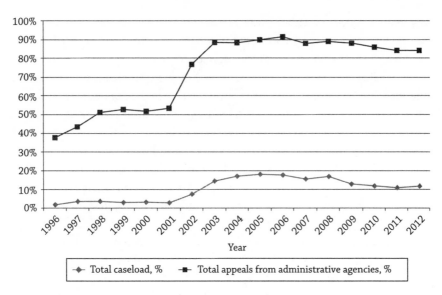

Figure 4.3 Immigration Cases as a Percentage of Administrative Appeals and as a Percentage of the Total Caseload of the Federal Courts of Appeals (1996–2012). Source: Judicial Business. Annual report of the Administrative Office of U.S. Courts, 2000–2012.

in cases before them and could not provide hard numbers on the proportion of the appeals from the BIA each year that are RSD matters.[16] However, it is likely that RSD cases are a very large contributor to the overall immigration caseload increase and may even make up a disproportionate set of the cases under federal court review. Applications for asylum are an exception to the jurisdiction-stripping measure passed by Congress in the immigration reforms of 1996 (IIRIRA, 1996, amending United States Code 1252a(2)(B)(ii)). In his 2006 testimony to Congress about the increase in immigration litigation, Chief Judge Walker of the 2nd Circuit claimed that more than 90% of the immigration cases they are asked to review "raise asylum issues" (Senate Hearing 109-537, "Immigration Litigation Reduction").

The Courts of Appeals, and in particular the overburdened 9th Circuit, seem to be taking their role as error correctors very seriously. Based on anonymous interviews with 9th Circuit judges, Law (2010:186) found they "simply did not trust the adjudications at the BIA and as a result felt obligated to give immigration cases much closer scrutiny than they would another type of administrative case." This scrutiny has led to frequent reversal of the BIA, which has regularly triggered Supreme Court chastisement of the 9th Circuit for taking their oversight too far. For example, in 2002, the Solicitor General petitioned the Supreme Court to hear the case *INS v. Ventura* (537 U.S. 12, 2002), in which the 9th Circuit had not returned an RSD case to the BIA for a rehearing after discovering problems with the way the case was handled. Instead, it granted asylum to an applicant for a reason the BIA had not considered. The 9th Circuit justified this decision in its majority opinion stating: "it is clear that we would be compelled to reverse the BIA's decision if the BIA decided the matter against the applicant." In his petition to the Supreme Court, the Solicitor General cited at least eight other similar cases, calling this kind of power grab by circuit courts "a recurring error." The Supreme Court issued a brief *per curiam* (summary) ruling in favor of the government in *INS v. Ventura*, but in 2006 the same issue again reached the Supreme Court, in the case of *Gonzales v. Thomas* (547 U.S. 183, 2006). Again, the Supreme Court issued another *per curiam* opinion without hearing oral arguments, and stated sternly in their opinion that "the 9th Circuit's failure to remand is legally erroneous, and that error is obvious in light of *Ventura*, itself a summary reversal." The 9th Circuit's deliberate contravening of Supreme Court decisions is evidence of the level of disdain with which some in the federal courts view the BIA, but also of the distinct institutional role the Courts of Appeals have come to play within the judicial branch, and the high level of insulation they ultimately feel from the Supreme Court.

The judicialization of immigration matters and the resulting tensions within the judicial branch have not gone unnoticed by Congress. However, a deep-seated commitment to the multiplicity of perspectives that comes with adversarial legalism has made it difficult, if not impossible, to reverse the trend. In March 2006, while the Senate was at work on a comprehensive immigration reform bill, a proposal was made to consolidate all appeals from the BIA into the single Court of Appeals for the Federal Circuit in Washington, DC. This proposal was designed to reduce the heavy burden on the caseload of the Courts of Appeals in other circuits, and to resolve the problem of inconsistent rulings across circuits (Section 501 of Senate Bill 2454, Securing America's Borders Act, introduced by Senate Majority Leader Frist on March 16, 2006). However, the proposal for centralization fell flat, especially among federal judges. The Judicial Conference, which is a policy body made up of the senior federal court judges, sent two letters to the Senate Judiciary Committee opposing this proposal, and five judges from the Conference testified before the Committee to voice their concerns in more detail (U.S. Federal Courts, 2006). Objections ranged from the impracticality of increasing the caseload at the Federal Circuit Court of Appeals by an estimated seven- to ninefold, the ineffectiveness of the proposal as a solution to the overload of the administrative agencies, and the commitment of the U.S. judicial branch to avoid specialization among its judges (Senate Hearing 109-537, "Immigration Litigation Reduction"; hearing before the Committee on the Judiciary, United States Senate, 109th Congress, April 3, 2006). Ultimately, Congress did not pass comprehensive immigration reform in 2006, so the proposal was not enacted, and during the 2013 reform debates, this idea did not resurface as an option.

Instead of finding a solution to the immigration litigation explosion, Congress has taken action to further judicialize the process, albeit inadvertently. In 2005, it passed the REAL ID Act, making the process even more reliant on lawyers. The REAL ID Act raises the burden of proof for asylum seekers in RSD hearings by requiring more documentary evidence of persecution (Neuman 2006, Bohmer and Shuman 2007:8). In interviews, lawyers reported on the challenges that this new standard has created in proving certain claims of persecution. One told me, "[T]here has been increased rigidification. In the past, we could win on testimony. Now we have to get documents that may not exist" (author interview, 8/23/2007). Another said that REAL ID had noticeably "tightened the screws" on the asylum process (author interview, 8/24/2007). A third said that "the expectation for supporting documentation has gone up, and there is less reliance on testimony" (author interview, 8/23/2007). Ironically, then, the response of Congress to judicial criticism of the administrative RSD process was to limit expert discretion within that process, making it much more difficult for asylum seekers to win their cases, and making the whole system much more reliant on lawyers. This setup is where the potential pathologies of adversarial legalism come to the fore. It is very costly, and if there is not a political commitment to investing in it, the benefits of fragmentation can be lost.

As my interviews revealed, many contemporary immigration lawyers view themselves as administrative practitioners and are ill equipped for work in the federal Courts of Appeals. The lawyers I interviewed pointed out that, although their practice had historically been based in the administrative settings of the Asylum Office and EOIR, they were finding themselves in federal court more and more. But they often confessed insecurity about their knowledge of the workings of the Courts of Appeals, and admitted that they referred their cases to colleagues with more experience if they reached the 9th Circuit. As one lawyer put it, "I refer my federal court work to other lawyers. The 9th Circuit is too much work, and I don't have backup, not many resources" (author interview, 9/12/2007). Another told me, "I do work for other attorneys when their cases get to the 9th Circuit because it can be intimidating if you don't do it regularly. It has a specific format" (author interview, 9/13/2007). Perhaps because of this increasing demand, more and more law schools are teaching immigration law as a regular course, and more lawyers are selecting immigration law as a field, despite low pay. In the five years between 2003 and 2008, the membership of the American Immigration Lawyers Association nearly doubled, growing to more than 11,000.[17] However, it may take a long time to fill the need for lawyers who are able to litigate complex matters at the Court of Appeals level.

Conclusions

Despite the fact that the initial stage of RSD in the United States is an example of the professional judgment model of decision making, because it is only one small part of a much larger system, this stage ultimately gets subsumed into the overall picture of a regime that is highly adversarial, legalistic, and contentious. Although some asylum seekers only experience the initial stage at the Asylum Office, the tenor of the regime as a whole is of adversarial legalism. There are different points of access to the process, different sites and forms of decision making, and low levels of insulation from political tinkering, as evidenced by the 2002 streamlining of the BIA and the REAL ID Act of 2005.

The American RSD regime has long embodied the tension between those in government who would like to see the program scrapped, those who see it as a screening process for potential threats, and those who value the ideal of offering protection in a neutral setting that is insulated from political influences. However, although the battles of the 1980s and 1990s tended to be about limiting political influence over the administrative process—and designing the process to reduce fraud—current battles are about the role of courts in adjudicating asylum, and the degree of deference that should be afforded to administrative agencies by courts. In other words, the immigration litigation explosion has judicialized the American RSD regime. Today, when federal courts review cases of administrative decision making, at least eight of ten times that case is an immigration case in which the judge must evaluate the interpretation of an important statute by the administrative agency.

The judicialization of asylum policy in the United States has been fueled in part by a lack of political will to invest in quality administrative decision making. The EOIR, and particularly the BIA, are subject to endless criticism from both politicians and judges, but they suffer from chronic underfunding. The American system does not provide expert fact-finding with any consistency. Thus, the federal Courts of Appeals have asserted themselves into this policy area and now show great reluctance to let it go. The Supreme Court has tried to limit this trend, and Congress has responded by creating legislation that strips court jurisdiction and limits administrative discretion, but these steps do not seem to have reduced the likelihood of Courts of Appeals to overturn asylum denials (Benson 2006). High levels of judicial oversight have led to turf battles, inconsistency, and unpredictability. There are 12 different circuits among the Courts of Appeals, each engaged in active review, with very little coordination from above, and regular splits in their jurisprudential paths. In particular, the liberal 9th Circuit has taken on the mantle of asylum seeker protection. As a lawyer for the Department of Justice who has to defend administrative decisions in federal court put it: "In those circuits with an activist bench, the law is totally debatable" (author interview, 2/12/2007). Certainly, other circuits have not always adopted the generous interpretation of the law that many 9th Circuit decisions promote. Thus, asylum seekers' fate may depend literally on where they crossed the border.

Despite all the inconsistencies and weaknesses of the American RSD regime, I found widespread support for fragmentation across my interviews of both policymakers and advocates. There was no shortage of concerns among advocates about the unfairness of the system in practice, especially a sense that the multiple layers to the process merely represented increasingly narrow hoops through which they have to jump to be heard. Nevertheless, advocates frequently pointed to the fact that the system allows for a lot of innovation in legal argument, and not once did an interviewee suggest that the system should be more centralized. Even among those whose jobs are oriented around enforcement of the law and reduction of false claims, policymakers expressed that they saw the value in strong judicial involvement, but lamented the time and cost it required. For example, a high-level Department of Justice lawyer from the Office of Immigration Litigation, which is responsible for defending RSD rejections in federal court, told me:

> The current system allows for diversity of opinion, which allows issues to be sufficiently vetted. The UNHCR doesn't want an adversarial system, but we have the best of both because we give people a chance with a nonadversarial system first.... People get their first bite of the apple with a very liberal rule, and if they still get denied, then they get three more bites at the apple, which is a lot, and it costs our taxpayers hundreds of thousands of dollars per alien per year, while they drag out their case. (author interview, 2/12/2007)

On both sides of the issues, interviewees expressed palpable frustration with the process, but saw the fragmentation and multiplicity as inevitable features of a thorough and just administrative process. The fragmentation and reliance on lawyers that characterize adversarial legalism, and American politics more generally, is not systematically good for asylum seekers, but its unpredictability and variability lead to more positive outcomes than a systematically restrictive regime.

The current state of the American RSD regime highlights important questions about the direction of American administrative law and the new, powerful role of the judicial branch in policymaking, particularly its mid-level Courts of Appeals. These questions have much larger ramifications beyond asylum policy. RSD has simply become a major battlefield for this dispute.

CHAPTER 5

The "Cadillac" Bureaucracy: RSD in Canada

In the spring of 2010, after many years of debate, the Canadian Parliament passed the Balanced Refugee Reform Act (BRRA), introducing some changes to the Canadian RSD regime. After the act was passed, the Canadian Bar Association, which had opposed previous versions of the bill, offered cautious praise for the final version. "Some of the concerns about the bill have been adequately addressed," it said in a statement. "This speaks well of the willingness of the minister and MPs from all parties to respond to legitimate criticism" (Canadian Bar Association 2010). In a similarly supportive vein, well-known refugee advocate and former IRB Chairman Peter Showler wrote an op-ed about the BRRA. Although he had some concerns and cautioned that "the devil is in the details," he stated that "the government has made a practical and legitimate attempt to balance fairness with prompt refugee claim processing."[1]

The Canadian RSD regime does not just differ from its neighbor to the south in terms of geniality. Its structural orientation is also completely different because the regime is based on a concept of administrative justice that prioritizes efficiency and expertise in decision making. Compared with the fragmentation and institutional conflict of the American RSD regime, the Canadian system is characterized by the vertical accountability and legal informality typical of the professional judgment model of decision making (Kagan 2001:10). The Canadian regime is highly centralized, and by enacting the BRRA, the Canadian Parliament consolidated even more authority and invested even more resources in the administrative tribunal, the IRB, reinvesting in the professional judgment approach after a period of political skepticism about it. Additional reforms that went into effect at the end of 2012 also emphasized expediency, efficiency, and bureaucratic expertise.[2]

While it is certainly not free from criticism, the IRB currently enjoys a relatively strong reputation among policymakers and refugee advocates alike. Many interviewees (although some with sarcasm in their voice), referred to the

Canadian RSD process as the "Cadillac system" of the world, because of how much time and resources are devoted to researching each case. The bureaucrats who conduct RSD in Canada have high levels of discretion to make decisions without legislative tinkering or judicial oversight, and the interactions between the courts and the administrative tribunal are less frequent and less fraught. In addition, the relatively low level of court involvement is uncontroversial, because most people seem to trust the system and think extensive judicial review is unnecessary. As a senior IRB official put it, "we are Canadian, so the relationship [between the courts and administrative agencies] is cordial. We don't have the same tensions and pressures that exist in the United States" (author interview, 3/29/2007).

An important attribute of the Canadian RSD regime is the commitment Canada has made more generally to diplomacy and multilateralism. As a classic example of a middle-power country, Canada has maintained a seat at the global decision-making table through its role in international institutions, and its close relationship with the UNHCR is no exception (Pratt 1990). Canada's RSD regime has earned it an international reputation for efficiency and generosity among refugee advocates, both foreign and domestic. Nevertheless, as refugee arrivals have become more of a domestic policy issue, Canada's outward-focused protection agenda has had to be reconciled with the exclusionary politics of deterrence.

So far, the Canadian RSD regime has proved to be stable, resilient, and responsive. However, because the regime places all its eggs in one institutional basket—the IRB—the ramifications of malpractice in that agency are extremely consequential. Further, because the system is expensive to maintain and relies so heavily on the frontline decision-making process, ongoing political support is very important. In particular, the recent shift in the IRB toward fast-tracking claims from countries that the Minister has designated as unlikely to produce refugees has led many advocates to question whether the conservative Harper government is committed to maintaining a thorough process for all applicants. A system of administrative justice based on professional judgment is insulated from politics (in this case, the politics of deterrence) only to the degree that there is a political commitment to preserving and investing in the system.

The Process and the Players

An early interpretation of the 1982 Canadian Charter of Rights and Freedoms shaped the basic RSD system that is still in place today by establishing the idea that refugee applicants are entitled to a rich administrative RSD process. Prior to the Charter's passage, Canada's in-country RSD system was conducted on a fairly small scale by trained bureaucrats within the CIC. These decision makers evaluated refugee claims on paper, without conducting in-person oral hearings. The 1982 Charter amended the Constitution to include a set of individual rights that were outlined over decades of negotiation (Morton 1987, Manfredi 1993, Mandel 1994, Morton and Knopff 2000). After the Charter's passage, it was not immediately clear whether the individual rights it codified applied to people who had not been admitted to Canada, although it was generally believed they did not. Before long, a denied asylum seeker from India brought a Charter–based challenge to the Supreme Court, asking it to resolve the issue of the Charter's application to noncitizens. He claimed that Canada's existing RSD process violated Section 7 of the new Charter that guaranteed "everyone...the right to life, liberty and security of the person and the right not to be deprived thereof except in accordance with the principles of fundamental justice."

In the landmark *Singh v. Minister of Employment and Immigration* (1 S.C.R. 177, 1985) decision, the Supreme Court of Canada concluded, much to the surprise of many policymakers at the time, that the Charter did apply to noncitizens, even those who had not been granted legal entry to the country. A senior official at CIC who was around at the time of the *Singh* case reminisced that "when the Charter was passed, no one expected the *Singh* decision. No one thought the Charter would be applied to people who had not even entered the country officially, and there was some resistance to that" (author interview, 3/30/2007). The case is particularly significant because the Court did not base this decision on any obligations under international law. The source of rights on which Singh (a man who had been denied entry to Canada) drew was the newly amended Canadian Constitution.[3] The Court unanimously found that, because deportation of refugee claimants could result in their loss of life in their home country, aliens who are present in Canada and apply for refugee status should receive an in-person hearing that meets with the substantive and procedural protections of the Charter.[4]

The *Singh* decision had major ramifications for Canada's approach to processing asylum seekers because it led to the creation of the Refugee Protection Division (RPD) of the IRB in 1989. Although some officials within the government were initially reluctant to create an elaborate administrative apparatus for noncitizens, the IRB has nevertheless invested resources in creating a tribunal that would meet the standards of accuracy, active investigation, effective management, and a systemic perspective that Mashaw (1985:171) argues makes for true bureaucratic justice. Today, all Canadian RSD takes place within this one agency, which Kernerman (2008:232) has called "one of the most sophisticated refugee determination systems in the world" (Figure 5.1).

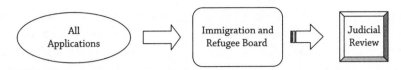

Figure 5.1 The RSD Process in Canada.

The Canadian RSD regime is clear about its aspiration to conduct decision making in the style of professional judgment. In its 2013/2014 annual report, in a subsection titled "Administrative Justice," the Chairperson of the IRB declared that the agency "strives to deliver a simpler, more accessible, and expeditious form of justice than that provided by the courts" (IRB 2014). Instead of the quasijudicial format used by the EOIR in the United States, the Canadian IRB conducts inquisitorial hearings and does not use lawyers to represent the government's position.[5] Rather, the tribunal engages in its own extensive research prior to the hearing. The IRB has several locations, but the large majority of claims are heard in the Toronto location.[6] This centralization makes a systemic perspective and active management more feasible because decision makers interact regularly and receive policy directives via a hierarchical leadership structure.

Unlike in the United States, the staff of the IRB is divided into regional teams that specialize in cases from one area of the world, including both Board Members and the Tribunal Officers who are assigned to them and assist them with research and preparation. The IRB houses a large documentation center with reports on conditions in refugee-producing countries all over the world. Information that the IRB collects on the case is shared with the claimant ahead of time. As a senior IRB official explained it, under an inquisitorial process, "we are not forcing the claimant to hire a lawyer because we are bearing the cost of the research" (author interview, 3/29/2007). This commitment to an active investigatory process stands in contrast with adversarial legalism, which is based on the premise that an impartial judge will decide whether the claimant is a refugee after hearing both sides argued forcefully.

When an asylum claim is filed, it is referred to the appropriate regional team within the RPD, where a staff member conducts basic triage on the case. Since the Protecting Canada's Immigration System Act went into effect at the end of 2012, claimants who come from a particular list of countries are sent to an expedited hearing. These designated countries of origin (DCOs) are those that the Minister of Citizenship and Immigration has determined to be democracies, and not generally refugee producing, such as the United States, Australia, Japan, and most countries in western Europe. In all RSD hearings, including the DCO cases, refugee claimants sit with an interpreter if they need one, and their counsel if they have one, and tell their story to a Board Member. The Member can choose to have a Tribunal Officer present to ask questions, or the member may ask questions directly. The counsel also asks questions, but it is up to the member to decide whether the counsel begins or ends the questioning period.[7]

Although refugee applicants are told by the IRB they do not need counsel, a culture has developed in which going alone to an RSD hearing has become the exception to the rule. This trend has arisen in part because most of the provincial governments spend taxpayer money on providing refugee claimants with an advocate through extensive legal aid programs. In addition, asylum seekers are also welcome to bring an immigration consultant with them instead of a lawyer. Consultants, who tend to come out of the refugee communities and serve as interpreters and guides to the system, cost significantly less than a lawyer but cannot be compensated through the legal aid system. Currently, about 90% of claimants attend their hearing with one of these two forms of representation.[8] Overall, about half the applicants who apply for refugee status in Canada are granted that status at the IRB, as opposed to the one in three who are successful in a similar style of decision making at the American Asylum Office.[9]

Having representation is correlated with success, although unrepresented asylum seekers may ultimately have lower grant rates at the IRB not because of the quality of their representation, but because of the strength of their case. According to internal statistics provided by the IRB, acceptance rates vary greatly based on whether claimants represent themselves or whether they have either a counsel or a consultant representing them. For example, in 2004, 2005, and 2006, represented claimants successfully gained a refugee visa at a rate of 43%, 48%, and 50%, respectively. In contrast, unrepresented claimants were successful between 10% and 11% of the time.[10] This discrepancy may be because refugee claimants who go to the IRB unrepresented made unsuccessful attempts to apply for a Legal Aid certificate. Further, the difficulty in securing a lawyer may explain why half of all unrepresented claimants end up abandoning their claim before it can be finalized, compared with only 8% of represented claimants.[11]

Since the rise of deterrence politics in Canada, debates over how best to reform the system have tested, but not ultimately severed, the Canadian government's commitment to a rich administrative RSD regime. The first big controversy arose over the question of adding an appeal stage to the process within the IRB. In 2002, Parliament revamped the IRB with the aim of reducing costs by shifting from two-member to single-member hearings for the initial assessment, but creating the RAD, which would conduct an on-paper review of negative decisions on their merits. This change was achieved through a delicate compromise guaranteed not to water down the quality of administrative assessment. However, after the act was passed, the CIC announced that as a result of "pressures on the system" implementation of the RAD would be delayed (CIC 2002).

Despite several attempts by some members of Parliament to pass another act forcing the implementation of the RAD, including a very near success in summer 2008, Parliament did not force the IRB to add the RAD for almost a decade after it was created on paper.[12] The CIC also did not push for its implementation; the head of asylum policy told me, "what we have is a very good front-end system that is very strong and thorough, which makes the appeal a bit redundant" (author interview, 3/30/2007).

The lack of a RAD remained an extremely sore point for refugee advocates throughout the decade. They felt betrayed by the CIC for compromising Canada's reputation for a thorough and rich process, and for focusing too much on cutting costs. When Parliament passed the Balanced Refugee Reform Act in 2010, it finally added the RAD as a second layer of RSD within the administrative tribunal. However, the Minister continued to stall by delaying the launch of the new division while additional reforms were debated. The RAD was finally opened on December 15, 2012, when the Protecting Canada's Immigration System Act went into force, but claimants from DCOs cannot access it and can only apply for judicial review in federal court if their claim is unsuccessful at the IRB.

Recent debates over the BRRA and Protecting Canada's Immigration System Act further illustrate the ways in which the professional judgment model has been vulnerable to exclusionary political pressure, but has ultimately prevailed. Both sets of reforms were designed to make the RSD process more expedient and to reduce the number of applications for judicial review, keeping claims within the administrative agency. As a result, the IRB has invested resources into processing claims more quickly than ever before, especially DOC applications from countries with low RSD acceptance rates.[13] During the debates over both acts, many members of Parliament expressed concern about the fairness and the constitutional ramifications of barring DOC applicants from the RAD.[14] It remains to be seen whether the fast-tracking of DOC claimants will be subject to a constitutional challenge, but it is certainly an unpopular development among refugee advocates—one that some point to as a sign of the demise of Canada's rich bureaucratic process (Canadian Association of Refugee Lawyers 2012).

Administrative Insulation and Agency Interaction

Despite recent controversies, the administrative insulation of the Canadian RSD regime is very high relative to other RSD regimes because it was designed to be insulated in two ways. First, the regime relies on active bureaucratic management and independence of the IRB from the immigration policymaking

aims of the CIC. Second, the regime requires low levels of judicial intervention beyond ensuring that fundamental constitutional protections are met.
This insulation and prioritization of a single, resource-rich frontline process
typifies the professional judgment model of administrative decision making. Unlike the United States, which houses the Asylum Corps within the
Department of Homeland Security, and places the EOIR under the ultimate
authority of the Attorney General, Canada's IRB is completely separate from
the CIC. The IRB is not totally immune to political tinkering, as the delay of
the implementation of the RAD, the creation of the DOC list, and ongoing
controversies about appointment of Board Members illustrate. Nevertheless,
a recent examination of Canada's RSD system in relation to the international
legal standards for RSD laid out by the UNHCR concluded the IRB meets
the UNHCR's desired standard of administrative independence (Heckman
2008).

Because of its insulation, the IRB enjoys a lot of flexibility and freedom to
develop its own procedures and create its own jurisprudence. It has issued
guidelines on particular procedural and jurisprudential issues, as well as highlighted certain cases as lead cases, or "Persuasive Decisions" as a means of
achieving consistency across cases. For example, Canada was the first country in
the world to create a specialized policy on handling gender-based RSD claims,
which it drafted with guidance from the UNHCR (IRB 1993, updated in 1996
and 2003). Supreme Court jurisprudence also supports the IRB's ability to give
its decision makers very specific directions about how to handle certain types
of cases. In the landmark administrative law case *I.W.A. v. Consolidated-Bathurst
Packaging Ltd.* (1 S.C.R. 282, 1990), the Supreme Court of Canada stated that
"the criteria for independence are not absence of influence but rather the freedom to decide according to one's own conscience and opinions." Subsequently,
the Federal Court has specifically upheld the legitimacy of the IRB's policy of
having Board Members consult with one another and with the Legal Services
Department in the writing of their written decisions (*Canada (Minister of
Employment and Immigration) v. Bovbel* [2 F.C. 563, 1994]). According to a
senior official at the IRB,

> [a] case cannot be overturned in court because it contradicts a simi-
> lar case...so we must find ways to build mechanisms for consistency
> for ourselves internally. That's why we make the guidelines—to give a
> sense of where we think we should be going with this. (author inter-
> view, 3/29/2007)

This active management is a prime example of a technique for ensuring bureaucratic justice within a professional judgement system.

IRB coordination is not always used to ensure a more generous approach to cases as it has been in the area of gender-based claims. The IRB first used this tactic in a restrictive vein during the late 1990s, when the number of Czech Roma refugee claimants began to increase suddenly and rapidly. In response, IRB management designated a January 1999 case as a "lead" case. In that case, the Board Member rejected the claim, the decision was distributed to all Board Members, and the rate of acceptance for Roma claimants decreased from 71% in December 1998 to 27% by March 1999 and then to 9% by June 1999.[15] The actions of the IRB were upheld in the Federal Court, but were struck down by the Federal Court of Appeal in 2006. The Federal Court of Appeal declined to address the question of whether the IRB is given statutory authority to generate lead cases in general. However, it concluded:

> Because Charter rights are at stake in refugee proceedings before the Board, the reasonable apprehension of bias standard is particularly demanding. The appellants could establish a reasonable apprehension of bias without proving the motivation of the Board in orchestrating the lead cases. (*Kozak v. Canada* (*Minister of Citizenship and Immigration*) [FCA 124, 2006])

The court went on to argue that because there was evidence that CIC officials had leaked news about the case to the Hungarian media in an attempt to dissuade potential applicants from leaving Hungary, "a person could reasonably conclude that the Lead Case strategy was not only designed to bring consistency to future decisions and to increase accuracy, but also to reduce the number of positive decisions that otherwise might be rendered" (*Kozak*, 2006). By this time, seven years had passed, and the tide of Roma claimants had long since turned. The lesson learned by the IRB from this incident was that, as long as it does not officially collaborate with the political branches in setting policy, active management in the form of specific guidance is an effective tool for ensuring consistency across decision makers.

Beyond the requirement that RSD be hearing centered, Canadian courts have given the tribunal a lot of flexibility and freedom to develop their own procedures and create their own jurisprudence. One of the reasons that courts play a relatively small role in the Canadian RSD regime is that Canada's era of judicial power with regard to individual rights is quite recent. Prior to the adoption of the Canadian Charter of Rights and Freedoms in 1982, courts were much more focused on policing the separation of powers between the federal and provincial governments, and on adjudicating economic matters than on protecting individual rights (Epp 1998).[16] Scholarship on the effect of the Charter has, in general, not paid much attention to the relationship between the constitutional amendment and Canadian administrative law (Sossin 2004). How Canadian courts have reconciled the new procedural fairness requirements with a long tradition of administrative deference is an area that has been surprisingly unexplored within political science.

After a period of uncertain jurisprudence around reconciling traditionally deferential administrative case law with the strictures of the newly codified procedural rights in the post-Charter era,[17] today the federal courts are working hard to maintain a hands-off approach. Unlike in the United States, where the standard of *Chevron* deference has reigned (at least formally) for decades, the Canadian Supreme Court has heard a long series of cases—mostly migration cases—designed to settle the issue of what the standard of judicial review of administrative decision making should be. In *Pushpanathan v. Canada, Minister of Citizenship and Immigration* (1 S.C.R 982, 1998), the Court essentially built a decision tree that assigned various questions and issues to one of the three levels of scrutiny that had emerged from the case law up to that point: correctness, simple reasonableness, and patent unreasonableness.[18] However, only one year later, in the case of *Baker v. Canada, Minister of Citizenship and Immigration* (2 S.C.R. 817, 1999), the Court lamented the difficulty in distinguishing between the two more deferential standards, questioning what the difference between reasonableness and patent unreasonableness was in practice (Dyzenhaus 2004). In 2002, *Suresh v. Canada, Minister of Citizenship and Immigration* (1 S.C.R. 3, 2002) further confused the landscape by introducing the question of national security to the already complex calculus. Thus, it was not surprising that the Canadian Supreme Court again revisited the issue in 2008, this time in a nonimmigration-related case: *Dunsmuir v. New Brunswick* (1 S.C.R. 190, 2008).

The Supreme Court used this opportunity to lay out a more unified vision of the relationship between fundamental values and administrative law than had ever before been articulated by the Court. In the beginning of the majority opinion, Justices Bastarache and Lebel summarized the post-Charter jurisprudence as follows:

> The recent history of judicial review in Canada has been marked by ebbs and flows of deference, confounding tests and new words for old problems, but no solutions that provide real guidance for litigants, counsel, administrative decision makers or judicial review judges. The time has arrived for a reassessment of the question. (*Dunsmuir*, 2008)

The Court first concluded that reasonableness and patent unreasonableness were too similar and should be collapsed into one standard. They then laid out a test for determining how to assign cases either to the correctness or the new reasonableness standard. The test essentially gives deference to agency decisions in policy areas in which (1) Parliament has expressed a desire to limit judicial review and (2) there is a regime of expertise in place within the administrative realm. However, it leaves room for "serious questions of general importance" to be examined more closely. The *Dunsmuir* decision suggests that courts should continue to give the IRB a high level of deference except on important constitutional questions.

This history of incremental jurisprudence around creating a standard of deference reveals an ironic comparison with the United States. Canadian administrative law is much more in flux than in America, where *Chevron* deference has been in place for many years. However, judicial involvement in administrative decision making is high in the United States and has been very low in Canada, despite some jurisprudential uncertainty about the correct standard of review. Further, the infrequency of judicial review in Canada combined with a unitary Federal Court, as opposed to the 11 separate American federal circuit courts, leads to a jurisprudential consistency that is unthinkable in the United States.

A rough comparison of the caseload trends in the United States and Canada suggests an ostensible parallel between the two states. Between 1995 and 2000, the Federal Court of Canada's immigration workload approximately doubled, and after the passage of the Immigration and Refugee Protection Act of 2002, there was an additional temporary surge in immigration cases as courts clarified new provisions in the law (Canadian Courts Administration Service Report 2003/4, Federal Court of Canada statistical reports for 2000 to 2012). By the end of 2006, it had become clear that "the workload of the Federal Court is intrinsically related to the volume of refugee claimants that the IRB is handling," and as a result, the CIC and the IRB pledged a "permanent transfer" of funds from their budgets to help offset the cost of processing the additional caseload (Canadian Courts Administration Service Report 2005/6). In 2012, more than 80% of proceedings commenced in the Federal Court were immigration matters. Two-thirds of those cases, or 56% of the total caseload, were RSD appeals. Each year since 2000, RSD cases have made up at least 45% of the total caseload of the Federal Court Trial Division, and in 10 of those years that percentage increased to more than 50% (Figure 5.2) (Federal Court of Canada statistical reports for 2000 to 2012).

Despite this heavy immigration and refugee caseload, a closer look makes clear that courts actually play a relatively minor role in the Canadian RSD regime. Unlike in the heavily judicialized American RSD regime, when Canadian courts receive an application for judicial review in an immigration case, they use a paper screening process that weeds out the vast majority of cases and lets the IRB decision stand without a court hearing (Federal Court of Canada statistical reports for 2005 to 2012). This requirement that immigrants and refugee claimants must apply for special permission (or "leave") to have their case heard does not apply

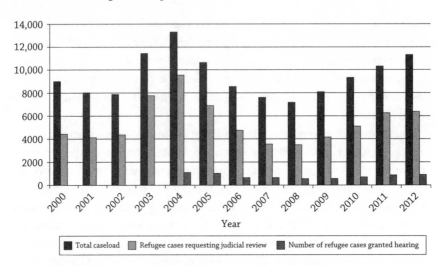

Figure 5.2 Federal Court Trial Division Caseload (2000–2012). Source: Federal Court of Canada statistical reports for the years 2000 to 2012. Data for the number of refugee cases granted judicial review begins in 2004.

to any other area of Canadian law, and the Federal Court is not required to give reasons for why a case is granted judicial review or not. This lack of transparency makes it impossible to assess whether applications are rejected because they are not seen as having merit or whether, as the statistics would imply, the Federal Court has adopted an unofficial policy of hearing only a specific ratio of the cases available, which has hovered steadily around 15% for a decade.[19] A recent study found that applicants who are represented by big law firms are more likely to be granted leave (Gould et al. 2010), although these firms are also less likely to take on weak claims. The claimants who are granted leave go on to a full court hearing, but even then, the prospect of reversal is extremely slim. The standard of review of an administrative decision is theoretically no more deferential than in the United States, and as in the United States, between 10% and 15% of cases that are granted a full hearing are successful in Federal Court. However, because so many cases are screened out, only about 1% of claims rejected by the IRB end up being over-turned by a court. Essentially, administrative decision makers operate without fear of reversal in Canada, because courts weigh in on the actions of the IRB very rarely.

If the Federal Court decides against a refugee claimant, the recourse for con-tinued legal action is, again, extremely limited. The Federal Court of Appeal can only hear a case if the Federal Court judge decides that "a serious question of general importance is involved" and agrees to certify that question (Immigration and Refugee Protection Act, 2002, Section 74). The question must be proposed by either the applicant or the respondent prior to knowledge of the judgment in the case. Because this process requires judges to choose to open themselves up to reversal, it is not surprising that only about 300 questions have been certified on any immigration matters since the Immigration and Refugee Protection Act went into force in 2002, even though the Federal Court has heard thousands of immigration cases during that period ("Immigration—Certified Questions," Federal Court of Canada, October 2013). Given the cost of taking a case to the Federal Court of Appeal, it is also not surprising that only about one-third of these 300 questions have been answered. In the rest of the cases, the appeal was never filed or the case was dismissed. Thus, of the tens of thousands of RSD cases the IRB has decided since 2002, only a handful have become a precedent-setting case at the Federal Court of Appeal.

Because the Canadian RSD regime is centered around such a resource-rich administrative process, both Canadian judges and refugee advocates are less critical about the quality of administrative RSD than they are in the United States. My courtroom observations of federal judicial review suggest that Canadian judges do feel frustration with the lack of legal rigor in many IRB decisions. However, the Canadian judiciary has not been publicly critical of the quality of RSD decision making as members of the American bench have been. Advocates are certainly focused on preventing the erosion of the professional judgment model, but their concerns are less despairing than their American counterparts.

Impact: Pressure on the IRB

Historically, administrative insulation has allowed for informality and a tendency toward generosity in the Canadian RSD regime, in part because the professional judgment model of decision making does not require the involvement of lawyers. According to a senior official at the IRB, "we have taken steps to dejudicialize the way we function.... The idea is that we can function without legal expertise. Our idea is that board members can acquire the substantive knowledge."[20] During interviews, some Canadian refugee advocates saw a benefit to the informality of the IRB because it often led members to accept applications that were not a solid fit with the legal definition of a refugee. As one lawyer put it, "If the member believes the person, they will find a way. You may get a 'sorry, you are just not a refugee' from a Federal Court judge, but not from the board members who are laypeople. They don't get training in being bound by law" (author interview, 5/7/2007). In my hearing room observations, I witnessed an exchange that corroborates this assessment:

BOARD MEMBER: Why do you fear returning to your country?
ASYLUM SEEKER: Because I want a better life for my children. I do not want them to grow up with drugs.

BOARD MEMBER: No one wants that for their children. I find the desire to avoid the drug cartels to be a political opinion, which is one of the five grounds in the Refugee Convention. I find you to be a Convention Refugee. (RSD hearing observation, IRB, Toronto, 5/17/2007)

Although the interpretive reasoning of this exchange may not have passed muster in a more adversarial legalistic setting, in professional judgment mode, decision makers are more able to read into the statements of asylum seekers and use their discretion in generous ways. This type of flexibility is less possible in an adversarial setting where the government is represented by legal counsel who will likely intervene if an asylum seeker is granted refugee status without a clear fit with the official definition.

This tendency toward generosity is not absolute, however. Generous acceptance rates are not an inevitable product of an institutional design based on professional judgment. There are several ways in which the informal, centralized professional judgment model can come under pressure and be used to advance restrictionist policy goals. First, the ideal of bureaucratic expertise can be undermined by the highly political nature of IRB member appointment and other political developments that underfund the process, which is designed to be resource rich. Second, board members frequently feel pressure to familiarize themselves with a growing body of case law to work with the lawyers who represent asylum seekers in the hearings. Last, the IRB has been faced with a burgeoning crisis in which Mexican asylum claims have come to dominate the caseload and strain the tradition of generosity that Canada has long embraced.

The first significant pressure comes from a reduced level of political support for an expensive and generous RSD regime. The most frequent complaint I heard from advocates was about a waning political commitment to the resource-heavy professional judgment model. In particular, a consistent and strenuous complaint I heard was about the current shortage of members on the IRB, which was conceived of by advocates as a political sabotage of the system. The IRB has suffered from political controversy regarding the appointment of members, and fewer new members have been appointed in recent years. As board member terms come to an end, they are not renewed. This situation has led to a board member shortage, which created a substantial backlog of cases after the board struggled to keep processing times down for many years.[21] Some advocates speculate that the reluctance to appoint new members is an attempt by the conservative Harper government to undermine the operation of the IRB and perhaps move back to a less independent administrative process. Others believe the IRB is simply falling victim to party politics in Parliament that have nothing to do with refugee policy. Either way, the increasing delay of hearing dates, and time pressure put on existing members, raises questions about achieving administrative justice under extreme caseload stress. The delayed implementation of the RAD also demonstrates that deterrence politics can bleed over into the administrative arena, and that political commitment to a thorough professional judgment model is vulnerable. Although there is no clear mechanism for how politicians or policymakers can force the IRB to crack down and be less generous, the political realities of the era of deterrence and austerity give the IRB incentive to actively and expediently manage its caseload.

The second pressure on the Canadian RSD regime is a move toward formalization of an inherently informal system. The jurisprudence around RSD has expanded, and despite the professed lack of need for prior legal experience among IRB members, once hired they are required to undergo training in the nuances of an increasingly complex body of law. The Senior Advisor of the Legal Services Branch of the IRB reported that the role of his office has increased over time, and that one of the main things they do is follow up with members whose decisions have been overturned in Federal Court to "raise flags about clear misunderstandings about the law." Referring to the board members, he said, "These guys aren't exactly Bora Laskin."[22] For practicality reasons, the legal training has to be perfunctory, and this can lead to additional confusion regarding interpretation of the law. One former member who is a lawyer said that he "disagreed and was upset" by the manner in which several legal issues were presented in the legal training he went through at the IRB, because he felt it was inaccurate and incomplete (author interview, 5/22/2007).

Many practitioners reported that this lack of legal training for IRB members can lead to confusion in the Canadian system, because it is common for a member without legal training to be confronted by an applicant's representative who is a lawyer. According to a lawyer who has been representing refugee claimants in Canada since the inception of the system, "the major thing that board members get wrong is the basic law. They don't understand what a balance of probabilities is" (author interview, 5/18/2007). Another experienced refugee lawyer stated, "Board members can't really handle innovative legal arguments. They are not interested in, and cannot cope with, jurisprudence. They actually don't like being presented with case law during hearings" (author interview, 5/24/2007). Another experienced lawyer suggested that members often seem afraid of what the counsel might throw at them: "Those members who are not lawyers are reluctant, intimidated about stepping outside the box because they believe that the law is the law. In legal practice, you realize it's for you to convince the court, but I think a nonlawyer will lack confidence to accept innovative arguments" (author interview, 5/30/2007).

Some lawyers reported that the mismatch between asylum advocates and adjudicators can lead to serious tensions in the hearing room:

> The problem with so many of them not being lawyers comes up in procedural issues and technical arguments, and if you point that out,

or object, they can get really uptight. For example, I had a case with a Portuguese interpreter who was terrible and the member wanted to continue because she knew Portuguese, and I tried to explain to her that we couldn't do that because there is a transcript.... But you have to be careful how technical you get with them, because you don't want to piss them off. (author interview, 5/14/2007)

Another source of tension and ambiguity is over the role of the Tribunal Officer in the hearing room. The position of these staff members is quite controversial, because they are ostensibly neutral, but if there are holes to be poked in a case, it is their job to do it. Thus, they can often end up acting like prosecutors in the hearing room, cross-examining the refugee claimant. Hearing room dynamics can sometimes slip into something that feels a lot like adversarial legalism. I witnessed this tendency toward adversarialism multiple times during the hearings I observed, and many lawyers I interviewed commented on it as well. I also frequently observed lawyers making submissions on behalf of their clients, claiming that the fact-finding of the tribunal was inadequate.

The third pressure on the Canadian RSD regime is the pressure to engage in bureaucratic triage stemming from the spike in asylum claims from Mexico. Although the global number of asylum seekers was in decline during the 2000s, the number of refugee applications in Canada increased during those years, primarily because of applications from Mexico. In 1994, Mexico was ranked 14th as a country of origin for refugee claimants in Canada. By 2004, it had jumped to become the number one source country; by 2007, the number of claims from Mexico had reached 23% of the total claims for that year—more than the number from the next three source countries of China, Haiti, and Colombia combined (IRB Annual Report 2006/2007). Before 2009, seeking asylum in Canada from Mexico was as straightforward as purchasing an airplane ticket. But, as the border between the United States and Mexico became more and more inaccessible during the crackdowns of the 1990s, policymakers believe that Canada became an entry point into the United States from the North. This theory is supported by the fact that Mexican asylum claims in Canada have a very high rate of abandonment—in other words, failure to appear at the RSD hearing. The generosity of Canada's RSD regime turned it into a magnet, both for those who used it as a gateway to the United States and those who actually appeared for their asylum hearing and sought to live in Canada with refugee status.

The IRB responded to the increase in Mexican asylum claims by using a similar tactic of coordination that it used to reduce Roma claims during the 1990s. In December 2006, IRB management labeled three decisions Persuasive Decisions, all of which were rejections. Persuasive Decisions differ from "lead" cases because they are selected as examples after the fact. It is clear from the text of the decisions the IRB Members did not intend to set a broad precedent when they wrote their reasons, because there is very little generally applicable language. Nevertheless, taken together, these cases promote the idea that the Mexican state does provide protection to its citizens, suggesting that Mexican claimants are not true refugees. In one case, a Member explicitly states the claimant "seems to be attempting to use the refugee system in order to gain entry into Canada" (IRB Decision TA4-18833, February 27, 2006). In another case involving a homosexual claimant who had escaped violent persecution in rural Mexico, an IRB Member concluded that the applicant could probably "relocate to Mexico City and access state protection if needed" (IRB Decisions TA4-10802 and TA4-10803, February 24, 2005).[23] After these decisions were issued, the acceptance rate for Mexican claims at the IRB went from 35% in 2006 to 15% in 2007, and by 2009 it was less than 10% (UNHCR Statistical Online Population Database). The post hoc designation of very particularized cases as Persuasive Decisions may be a questionable management strategy, but it clearly illustrates the willingness of the IRB to set its own jurisprudence and produce results without asking for guidance from the federal courts or intervention from the CIC.

Although the acceptance rate for Mexican claims dropped after the Persuasive Decisions were issued, the number of applicants continued to increase. In 2008, Canada received just over 8,000 Mexican applicants, up from around 1,000 per year during the late 1990s. Thus, in July 2009, the CIC added a visa requirement for visitors from Mexico, which cut down on the numbers drastically. In 2010, there were 1,300 applications, by 2011 the numbers had decreased further to 653, and in 2012 there were only 324 (UNHCR Statistical Online Population Database). Immigration Minister Jason Kenney defended the new visa require-ment to the media in 2009, saying:

> We're not talking about the kinds of people that are living in UN refu-
> gee camps by the millions who are victims of war and state-sponsored
> persecution…. It's an insult to the important concept of refugee pro-
> tection to allow it be systematically violated by people who are over-
> whelmingly economic immigrants.[24]

The determination of the CIC to eliminate Mexican asylum seeking became even more apparent in February 2013, when Minister Kenney listed Mexico as a DCO. This move prompted criticism from advocates, who questioned whether, given human rights abuses and the dominance of drug cartels, a blanket assess-ment could label Mexico as a country that does not produce refugees.[25] The han-dling of Mexican claims suggests that the IRB is not as insulated from the politics of deterrence as its reputation might suggest. Nevertheless, the acceptance rate of around 15% per year for Mexican asylum seekers in Canada is still far greater than in the United States, where it has hovered around 4% in recent years (UNHCR Statistical Online Population Database).

Conclusions

Both critics and proponents of the Canadian RSD regime take pride in the leading role their country has taken in its humanitarian approach to refugee policy over the past several decades. Yet, recent trends have led to a disconnect between the generosity of the past and the contemporary process. The combination of administrative insulation, a lack of political support for the expense and generosity of the system, and expanding jurisprudence has led to newfound pressures on the frontline agency making RSD decisions in Canada. Recent events suggest that the inner workings of the IRB are strained because the agency has to contend with heavy caseload stress. As a result of these changes, it has become more and more of a challenge to achieve a decision-making process that has political support, and that can function smoothly and without legal expertise. Some of these same trends are observable in the United States; a lack of political commitment, reduced investment of resources, and an increased reliance on lawyers are observable in both RSD regimes. However, because the American RSD regime is more fragmented and adversarial, these trends are amplified there, whereas in Canada there is a much greater barrier of resistance to and insulation from them.

Despite some real pressures on the system, a commitment to a system of administrative justice based on a centralized, resource-rich professional judgment model is still a powerful and enduring force in the Canadian RSD regime. It has been given a Constitutional basis via the *Singh* decision, and is a concrete example of Canada's humanitarian reputation. In interviews, advocates seemed to value this administrative insulation even while leveling harsh criticisms at other aspects of the Canadian RSD regime. The head of the biggest and most powerful refugee advocacy group in Canada told me: "The basic core of the system is good though. If I were to change it, it would be to increase the independence of the IRB. I have low faith in the federal courts. They don't have refugee experience" (author interview, 4/7/2007). Another advocate said: "I think the Canadian system is fantastic. We have a right to counsel, the hearing is in a good setting, not in a dusty refugee camp. Thanks to the rule of law, asylum seekers have some power, some recourse" (author interview, 5/29/2007). It remains to be seen whether the IRB has the institutional strength to withstand the internal challenges it faces, but past experience suggests that it is a resilient and innovative organization.

CHAPTER 6

The Battle of the "Bouncing Ball":
RSD in Australia

Australia is a relative newcomer to RSD, but it has generated more than enough legislation, jurisprudence, and controversy during the past few decades to make up for lost time. Especially since 2000, RSD has been brought to the center of a tense battle over judicial power, and a heated debate about the broader nature and source of rights in Australia. The issue of who has the ultimate authority over RSD has traveled back and forth between Parliament and the courts much like a "bouncing ball" crossing over the net in the Australian Open (Kneebone 2003:2). However, little progress has been made toward resolving many unanswered legal and political questions that will play out over the coming decades. For now, Australia has a reputation for restrictionism and harsh treatment of asylum seekers, but it is a contested reputation, and the terms of the contest are more judicialized than ever before.

A typical volley occurred on November 11, 2010, when the High Court handed down the twin decisions of *Plaintiff M61 and Plaintiff M69 v. Commonwealth of Australia* (HCA 41, 2010). The two asylum seekers in these cases were Sri Lankans who attempted to arrive by boat in October 2009 and were interdicted at sea. In keeping with Australia's policy toward so-called "offshore" asylum seekers, the two men were sent to a detention and processing center on Christmas Island, an Australian territory south of Indonesia. While the asylum seekers were in detention, the DIAC, in conjunction with a private contractor, determined them to be ineligible for refugee protection. However, the process they used was far less transparent than the RSD process available to typical "onshore" asylum seekers, who file for refugee protection when they arrive in Australia. In the unanimous *M61 and M69* opinion, the High Court ruled that the RSD process DIAC had offered to these men was inadequate, "denied [them] procedural fairness," and "had the consequence of depriving them of their liberty." The Court also found that the guiding legislation, the Migration Act, requires future

RSD processes to comply with principles of procedural fairness, regardless of whether the asylum seekers make their claims on- or offshore.

This decision called the longstanding Australian two-tiered RSD system into question; but, because it was based on a statutory interpretation and not the Australian Constitution, the decision pushed the issue back into Parliament's hands for clarification. Writing in the *Sydney Morning Herald*, law professor George Williams assessed the government's dilemma following the decision:

> It is now open for Parliament to, in turn, amend the [Migration] Act to prevent this. The problem with this path is that it would not preclude future High Court interpretation of the Act. History suggests that courts may find a way around even express words.... When Parliament closes off one avenue of appeal to the courts, judges may readily find another.[1]

The Australian Parliament has frequently amended the Migration Act to prevent asylum seekers from accessing thorough RSD hearings, to limit the power of courts to review RSD decisions, and to narrow the ways in which decision makers interpret the refugee definition (Vrachnas et al. 2005, Bagaric et al. 2006). The High Court has walked a fine line in response; it has deferred to Parliament by upholding many of its border control policies and limitations on asylum seeker rights within the Australian territory. However, the Court has been extremely successful in policing the separation of powers, and maintaining and reasserting its right to review administrative decisions. Parliament has only redoubled its attempts to keep the courts out of this policy area altogether.[2] However, struggles with the High Court continue because the Court holds a trump card—a constitutionally entrenched right to review all decisions made by "Officers of the Commonwealth" (Crock 2000).[3] Because this power is vested in the High Court alone, and not the other lower level federal courts, Australia's RSD regime is characterized by a politically charged, high-profile interbranch dispute.

The absent player in the Australian RSD regime is the administrative refugee status decision-making body, the Refugee Review Tribunal (RRT). Unlike the clear commitment to thorough vetting that characterizes administrative justice in the United States, or the focus on expertise and efficiency that constitutes Canadian administrative justice, the core value of the administrative process is less obvious in the Australian context. To carry the tennis metaphor further, the Australian administrative tribunal is like the net in the middle of a tennis match; it gets ignored in the excitement of watching the ball bounce back and forth. Because the battles over Australian RSD have centered on the ability of courts to review administrative decisions, and the reluctance of Parliament to allow such review, little progress has been made in terms of improving the quality or independence of the administrative process itself, and the administrative agencies do not have a strong identity that can be distinguished from the enforcement orientation of the Department of Immigration and Citizenship.

To confuse matters further, the Australian judicial branch is more involved in RSD than in Canada, but in less predictable ways than in the United States. Ironically, the Australian High Court is far more involved in RSD than the Supreme Court in either of the two other countries, but in a broader sense, the Australian High Court is the least powerful of the three judiciaries. For all of these reasons, the Australian RSD regime is a fascinating example of both the judicialization of politics and its limitations.

The Process and the Players

The lack of a single core value driving the concept of administrative justice in Australia is exemplified by the institutional design of the RSD regime. First, the regime does not rely on one ideal-type style of administrative decision making, such as adversarial legalism in the United States or professional judgment in Canada. Rather, it is a complex hybrid of the American and Canadian systems that could be labeled *bureaucratic adversarialism*. As in the United States, the administrative phase is fragmented, involving multiple distinct agencies. However, as with Canada, every stage of Australian RSD prior to federal court review is nonadversarial and nonlegalistic, without the active participation of lawyers or reliance on formal legal rules. On paper, the Australian regime has high levels of bureaucratic discretion, but it differs from the Canadian system because it lacks the centralization designed to ensure consistency, insulation from political pressure, and resource investment aimed at ensuring accuracy that characterizes a true model of bureaucratic justice (Mashaw 1985:172). It also lacks the teeth of the American system to vet cases thoroughly and to set legal precedents at the administrative level.

At the outset, Australia's restrictionist politics have ensured that many asylum seekers do not have access to the standard RSD process. As mentioned earlier, since 2001 Australia has distinguished between typical asylum seekers and "offshore" applicants, also known as irregular maritime arrivals who have entered Australian territorial waters but have not made it into Australia's "Migration Zone" (Bowen 2011).[4] Because offshore applicants have entered Australia via an excised portion of the Australian territory, they can only make an application for RSD if the Minister decides that it is "in the public interest" to allow the application.[5] The United States does have a policy of Expedited Removal for those who do not express a well-founded fear of persecution at a port of entry, and the U.S. also tracks its asylum applicants into two streams. However, neither Canada nor the United States has anything equivalent to this Australian policy of preventing people from applying for asylum who have arrived in the territory and have expressly asked to do so.

Unlike the Canadian IRB and the American Asylum Office, the frontline decisions conducted by the DIAC lack a history of commitment to neutrality and independence. The DIAC began to conduct RSD in earnest in 1989, when a large number of Chinese students who were living in Australia applied for asylum in the aftermath of the Tiananmen Square massacre. At that time, the DIAC also created an internal review body called the Refugee Status Review Committee, which examined negative decisions made by frontline decision makers and gave nonbinding recommendations about whether they should be sustained. This committee had no statutory basis and came under intense criticism from asylum seeker advocates because it included representatives from the Department of Foreign Affairs. This situation parallels the tension in the United States during the 1980s, when the State Department exercised great influence over RSD outcomes. Much like in the American case, Australian advocates expressed concerned that this process lacked transparency and that it may have enabled factors other than fit with the refugee definition to influence the process, such as foreign policy concerns.

Today, the DIAC is still the primary decision maker for both types of asylum seeker. For offshore applicants who are held on island detention centers, the DIAC is the only entity to which they have access. For onshore asylum seekers, the process is as shown in Figure 6.1. First, bureaucrats at the DIAC, which is based in the capital city, Canberra, conduct an on-paper assessment of the claim. DIAC decision makers have access to a large clearinghouse of country-of-origin information, but unlike in the United States and Canada, the vast majority of these cases are processed without a hearing. Department decision makers may interview applicants on a discretionary basis, but only do so less than 20% of

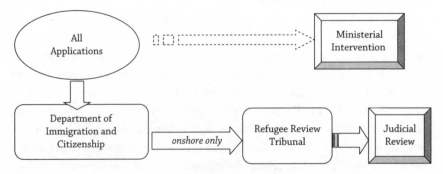

Figure 6.1 The RSD Process in Australia.

the time.[6] As in the United States, unauthorized arrivals are detained while their case is pending, whereas those who enter on a valid visa and then apply are not detained. Ironically, those who apply from detention tend to have an acceptance rate of more than 50%, and in the case of Afghanistan, which is the second largest sending country, recent acceptance rates have been more than 90% (author interview, 10/05/2007).[7] Those who arrive lawfully on a business, student, or tourist visa before applying for asylum tend to have much lower acceptance rates, approximately 25% to 30%, according to the head of the DIAC asylum program. This discrepancy is probably due in part to the fact that detained asylum seekers receive full legal representation and also because those entering with valid visas tend to come from countries such as China and India, which are less obviously refugee producing and have more economic migrants in the mix. China has been, by far, the biggest sending country of asylum seekers to Australia since 2002, but it has had grant rates well under 20% in recent years (UNHCR Statistical Online Population Database).

In another parallel with the United States, the Australian RSD process underwent a major reform in 1992, when Parliament amended the Migration Act and added the specialized RRT to the process. The Australian Parliament created the RRT because of concerns about the increasing number of applicants who were appealing negative DIAC decisions to the federal courts, and their increasing rate of success (McMillan 2011:22). At that point, the Refugee Status Review Committee was disbanded. Instead, the RRT is an administrative body that reviews DIAC decisions and, as in Canada, the tribunal is supposed to be independent from the department, which is focused on enforcement. Members of the tribunal are appointed based on recommendations of the Immigration Minister for terms of three years. About half the members are lawyers, but they come from a "broad range of professions" (RRT 2007).

The RRT conducts nonadversarial hearings primarily at the main office in Sydney, but also at a smaller one in Melbourne.[8] Similar to the Canadian model, RRT hearings are conducted in a private hearing room and tend to be in the form of "inquisitorial" conversations. Asylum applicants may bring a friend, relative, or counsel, and the counsel may be allowed to speak at the end of the hearing, but the process is designed not to require legal representation. There is no fee if the review results in a reversal of the DIAC decision, but if the original decision is upheld, a fee of $1,540 is billed to the applicant (RRT 2014). Australia is the only one of the three countries to impose this kind of financial burden on refugee applicants.

A recent comparison of migration policy in Canada and Australia stated that the Canadian IRB and Australian RRT are "highly comparable and similarly situated" (Dauvergne 2005:96). Although it is true that the two administrative tribunals are similar in many ways, there are several significant distinctions. First, the RRT was designed with the intention of keeping RSD cases out of the federal courts, not with the purpose of creating a process rich with both resources and procedural rights. Second, because the scope of RRT operations is much smaller than the IRB, and because the RRT is only one part of a multifaceted RSD regime, the RRT is far less involved than its Canadian counterpart in designing proactive policy. Thus, the RRT does not fulfill the parameters of professional judgment because it lacks the investment in active investigation and management to ensure consistency that characterizes that model.

These differences between the Australian and Canadian regimes illustrate the degree to which administrative law in Australia has yet to establish a core concept of administrative justice. In the United States, administrative courts are located solidly within the executive branch; in Canada, they are distinct and powerful bodies, and their independence is fiercely protected by law. In Australia, however, tribunals have an ambiguous place in constitutional law and there is much debate about where they fall between the executive and the judicial branches (Creyke 2007). The Refugee Review Tribunal is a subunit of the Migration Review Tribunal, which is Australia's largest administrative tribunal, but it is nowhere near as independent, or as respected, as its Canadian counterpart.

As in the United States and Canada, representation by counsel matters, although far fewer applicants in Australia are represented by some kind of advocate at their RRT hearing than in the other two states; in 2007 it was 44% and in 2011 it was 53%, most of whom were represented by migration agents, not lawyers.[9] Official statistics show that those who are represented at the RRT are three times more likely to be successful, although the head of the Australian RRT stated emphatically that these statistics are misleading, because people with weak cases are often unable to find someone to represent them (MRT/RRT 2011:40).[10] In contrast to the practitioners I interviewed in Canada and the United States, people who represent clients at the RRT are frequently not lawyers. Some of them work with church organizations and some are paid through the government funding program called the Immigration Advice and Application Assistance Scheme (IAAAS). When asylum seekers take their case to federal court, they are no longer eligible for legal aid except in a very limited number of cases the government has determined are jurisprudentially significant (author interview, Legal Aid Commission of New South Wales, 10/29/2007). Thus, many asylum seekers go to federal court without any kind of legal representation.

Besides judicial review, there is also another appeal that applicants may use if all other administrative avenues fail: ministerial intervention. The Immigration Minister has the power under Section 417 of the Migration Act to grant protected status to any immigrant. The decision need not be based on fit with the refugee definition; it is purely discretionary. Although there is no official procedure for how ministerial discretion works, and no way of predicting who will be successful, almost all rejected asylum seekers make an appeal to the Minister, even if they are also appealing their case to federal court (Taylor 2003). I discuss the ministerial intervention program in much more detail in Chapter 9.

Administrative Insulation and Agency Interactions

Australia's RSD regime is far less insulated from politics than its Canadian and American counterparts. In addition, Australian asylum seeker advocates tend to have a very tense relationship with policymakers rather than a seat at the table. This tension is apparent at every stage of the decision-making process. First and foremost, advocates are critical of the fact that ministerial intervention allows elected officials a direct hand in RSD, something that does not happen in either the United States or Canada. Because a very large proportion of rejected applicants view the intervention request as an essential step in the appeals process, this highly discretionary component exacerbates the impression among advocates and asylum seekers that the overall process does not have a clear commitment to administrative justice.

Beyond the Immigration Minister's direct role in the ministerial intervention process, the frontline decision makers who conduct RSD at the DIAC are designated representatives of the Minister of Immigration. Perhaps because they are geographically removed from the vast majority of asylum seekers and advocates who are in Sydney or Melbourne, and because the process occurs only on paper, advocates criticize the initial decision-making stage of RSD for being shrouded in secrecy, and view the bureaucrats making the decisions as lacking independence from the other more political functions of the department. During interviews, many advocates expressed a fervent belief that restrictionist political motives still influence RSD outcomes, and described to me conspiracy theories about ways in which the DIAC controls aspects of the process over which they do not hold any official jurisdiction. As one advocate put it, "I have been pleading with Immigration. I say to them, this is not about winning and losing. Of course you win. You have all the power. Just please stop doing this last minute, middle-of-the-night deportation stuff." Another advocate told me, "The culture in the Department is one of deterrence. The bias is consistently in favor of denying people protection." A third said, "[T]he distinction between policy and law is a fundamental principle of public administration, but today I feel like public servants are serving the Minister, not the public. And that's dangerous" (author interviews, 10/15/2007 and 10/16/2007).[11]

In contrast to this view, a very high-level DIAC official insisted that the Minister does not have any direct influence over individual decisions, and is kept

at "arms length" from the RSD that is conducted within the DIAC (author interview, 10/05/2007). However, the same official acknowledged that the DIAC is
in a delicate political situation because, unlike the IRB in Canada, it is responsible for conducting both RSD and migration enforcement:

> We have a very focused system in Australia, designed to put scrutiny
> on the Minister and the Department.... It produces removals quickly,
> but at a cost, which is a focus on us. And it's hard for the Department,
> because the issues are very complex, and we already feel pressure to get
> them right, and then being put in the spotlight just adds to the chal-
> lenge. Especially if we are being asked to implement unpopular policies.

The details that were revealed about the recent *M61* and *M69* cases suggest
it has been difficult for the DIAC to navigate the dual roles of enforcement and
adjudication, at least when dealing with offshore applicants.

The reputation of the RRT is only marginally better than that of the DIAC
decisions it must review; advocates often characterize it as toothless and easily
influenced by the Minister and the DIAC. As in the United States, the judicial
branch has also been critical of the quality of review at the RRT, accusing the
RRT of "bias" that has prevented "honest fact-finding."[12] Distrust of the RRT is
fueled by the fact that in the not-so-distant past, the Australian government has
come under fire by media and legal scholars for attempting to influence the decisions of RRT members, including not renewing the appointment of members
who have ruled against the government (Legomsky 1998). On average, the RRT
upholds the negative DIAC decision about 70% of the time, but according to one
study, RRT members' reversal rates decrease precipitously in the months leading
up to their reappointment (Legomsky 1998:250).[13] In 1998, the Immigration
Minister openly displayed a desire to influence the RRT by publicly warning
RRT members not to interpret the refugee definition in a way that was counter
to "the sovereignty of Parliament and the will of the Australian people."[14]

Perhaps because the RRT is under political pressure to enforce restrictive
migration policy, it does not display much of the proactive internal policymaking that a professional judgment-style agency such as the Canadian IRB produces. Like the Canadian tribunal, the RRT maintains the position that legal
training is not a necessary qualification for decision makers. But, unlike the IRB,
the RRT does not invest in thorough legal training and guidance. The head of the
RRT told me that "it's not a complex visa category.... So much of it is about the
facts, more than the interpretation of the law per se, so there is less need for legal
capacity" (author interview, 11/02/2007). Contradicting that view, a former
RRT member revealed that his "criticism of the tribunal is that they gave us too
little guidance. We had informal sounding boards in each other, but no seminars,

and little coordination" (author interview, 10/16/2007). Practitioners I spoke with indicated that RRT members tended to misunderstand their role and err on the side of skepticism, although the legal test is that an applicant must have a "real chance" of persecution.[15] As one lawyer put it, "the decision makers think it is their job to be suspicious and catch someone out, to focus on fine distinctions in what people say rather than applying legal tests" (author interview, 10/24/2007).

As in the United States and Canada, credibility determination has become a contentious issue in the Australian system because advocates see it as a tactic decision makers use to deny a case while insulating themselves from judicial review. In 2005, asylum lawyers and advocates made it a priority issue and lobbied the RRT at one of its biannual stakeholder meetings to reign in members who were hiding behind credibility as a basis for negative decisions, rather than making legal arguments. In response, the RRT released guidelines in October 2006 for its members on how to assess credibility properly. The guidelines state:

> Findings made by the Tribunal on credibility should be based on relevant and material facts. What is capable of being believed is not to be determined according to the member's subjective belief or gut feeling about whether an applicant is telling the truth or not. A member should focus on what is objectively or reasonably believable in the circumstances. (RRT 2006)

The RRT's creation of these guidelines is a move typical of an organization following the ideal type of decision making known as *bureaucratic legalism* (Kagan 2001). It introduces legal formalism as a strategy for reducing the discretion of individual decision makers and creates a more uniform standard. However, this incident is too isolated to support the conclusion that the RRT is consistently following a commitment to bureaucratic legalism, especially because there is not much evidence that the tribunal's sudden attempt to provide clear guidance to its members was successful. More than a year after the guidelines took effect, many advocates complained about the unpredictability of RRT member decision making. A lawyer who attends several hearings per week at the Sydney office said, "I never feel totally confident, even if it is a really strong case, because you never know who you will get" (author interview, 11/09/2007). As the head of the RRT acknowledged, achieving uniformity on this subject is next to impossible: "We have 70 to 80 members and of course there is a range of ways of dealing with credibility, which is a central aspect." He went on to say: "We are very cognizant of the fact that we have to meet a number of different objectives. We pull together many strands to achieve balance, but it is a constant challenge" (author interview, 11/02/2007).

Although the RRT must obviously handle pressure from Parliament, the DIAC, and the Immigration Minister, it is less clear what level of judicial scrutiny exists in the Australian RSD regime. From the perspective of the head of the RRT, it is high: "[W]e have a jurisprudence in Australia that is second to none. There is a lot of judicial scrutiny of the process . . . and courts will find it if there is any failure to deliver procedural fairness" (author interview, 11/02/2007). However, the actual role the judiciary plays has been much more variable, nuanced, and measured than this statement suggests. Parliament created the RRT to avoid high levels of judicial involvement in RSD, and has recently passed a variety of legislation designed to further limit judicial review of migration matters, including adding a privative clause to the Migration Act: a statutory removal of a court's ability to review decisions made under that piece of legislation. Nevertheless, the picture is complicated by the fact that the Australian courts, and in particular the High Court, have only increased their involvement in RSD over time.

To understand the place of the judiciary in the Australian RSD regime, then, we must take a slight detour to examine the development of Australian judicial power more generally. Australia was not designed to have a powerful judiciary, and has weak courts relative to the U.S. and Canada (Crock and McCallum 1994). Unlike Britain, Australia does have a written Constitution, but that document focuses on laying out the structure of government rather than codifying individual rights, and it does not contain a constitutionally framed right to procedural fairness. The question of whether Australia needs a Bill of Rights–style amendment to its Constitution is the subject of heated and ongoing debate in Australian political life, and has been the focus of several appointed commissions over the years (Galligan 1995, Williams 1999 and 2004). Opinions on the matter tend to be split along party lines, with the Labor (left of center) Party in favor of adding a Bill of Rights, and the Liberal (right of center) Party asserting that the current Constitution provides adequate individual rights protection. According to the common law tradition that Australia inherited from the British, there are certain basic principles thought to be so fundamental to a fair proceeding they need not be codified, such as having an unbiased decision maker and being informed of the charges one faces. Thus, opponents of a Bill of Rights–type amendment claim that it would make no difference to rights outcomes.

For now, the status of due process (and other individual rights) in Australia relies on a unique and complex blend of the common law conceptions of natural justice and more recently enacted statutory protections. One key early statute was the Administrative Decisions (Judicial Review) (ADJR) Act of 1977, which was the result of a period of reform and upheaval during the late 1960s and 1970s. This modest statute-based rights revolution was certainly limited compared with the rights movements in other countries, but the ADJR Act provided for judicial review of administrative decisions in federal courts beyond just the original jurisdiction of the High Court. It also specified a long list of conditions (in Sections 5(1)(a) and 6(1)(a)) to be considered a breach of the rules of natural justice and grounds for invalidating an administrative decision (Groves and Lee 2007). As a result of these developments in Australian administrative law, the power of the judicial branch, especially in the area of protecting individual rights, has been gradually expanding in the decades since.

Although the fairness of immigration decisions was not the intended focus of the ADJR Act, migration law has become one of the battlefields on which the extent of this relatively new judicial power is being contested. For example, in a series of cases in the years following the passage of the ADJR Act, the High Court applied the legislation to the migration context and thus asserted its authority to review deportation decisions. Most notably, in the 1985 case *Kioa v. West* (HCA 81) the High Court found that the standards of natural justice outlined in the act applied to decisions made by the DIAC.

The *Kioa* case represented a significant expansion of judicial power into a new policy area. However, as Australian courts have entered this area, they have, in general, adopted a pragmatic stance, balancing cost against their commitment to ensuring procedural fairness when reviewing migration decisions. For example, in 1993, the Federal Court concluded that "courts should be reluctant to impose in the name of procedural fairness detailed rules of practice, particularly in the area of high-volume decision making involving significant use of public resources" (*Zhang v. Minister for Immigration, Local Government and Ethnic Affairs* [45 FCR 384, 1993]). This position was reaffirmed by the High Court in 1994 in *Chen v. Minister for Immigration and Ethnic Affairs* (123 ALR 126, 1994), and again in the oft-cited High Court case of *Minister for Immigration and Ethnic Affairs v. Wu Shan Liang* (185 CLR 259, 1996). In that case, the majority stated:

> The reasons of an administrative decision maker are meant to inform and not to be scrutinized upon overzealous judicial review by seeking to discern whether some inadequacy may be gleaned from the way in which the reasons are expressed.

More recently, the High Court has recognized that courts should be careful not to impose time-consuming and expensive demands on administrative agencies (*Re Minister for Immigration and Multicultural Affairs; Ex parte PT* [178 ALR 497, 2001]). Thus, unlike in Canada, Australian courts have not forced the RRT to require an in-person hearing for RSD decisions.

Although the doctrine is certainly one of judicial deference, Australian judges also seem to share a commitment to counterbalance any legislative tinkering in the RSD process. This value is present in Australian courtrooms, and is even noticeable in many of the written opinions from the courts. As the Registrar of the Federal Court put it:

> The judiciary is not accepting that Parliament can limit their power "Argie Bargie." The Court says that Parliament is limited by the Constitution. Judges are very interested in procedural fairness. The idea of the day in court is very important to them, and they react emotionally to it. (author interview, 11/05/2007)

Similarly, a lawyer who represented asylum seekers in many of the major High Court cases of the past decade told me, "the High Court is fairly involved, and overturns decisions reasonably often, which means that tribunals are shown to be wrong, and this creates an 'in' for litigation" (author interview, 10/26/2007).

The most interesting aspect of the Australian judiciary's insistence on its right to review RSD is the fact that, in the vast majority of the instances when courts order a rehearing, the remands are based on very narrow procedural grounds. Thus, when the case is reheard by the RRT, the outcome is ultimately the same (Creyke and McMillan 2004). At first glance, the Australian RSD regime has high levels of judicial involvement that are very similar to those in the United States. However, unlike the American battle between the administrative agencies and the courts in which federal judges use their power of review to send a message about the low quality of administrative decision making, the Australian federal courts seem much more intent on sending a message to Parliament via the RRT. One lawyer told me, "we often end up seeking review based on minute technical grounds that don't have much to do with the claim" (author interview, 10/16/2007). The Registrar of the Federal Court echoed this statement, saying, "Usually, the jurisdictional error has nothing to do with the substance of the case, so a lot of them, even if they win in Federal Court, do not get a visa at the end of the day. Their long-term prospects do not change here" (author interview, 11/05/2007). Judicial review constitutes a burden on the federal courts, but the outcomes are more symbolic than substantive.

Judicial review rates have ebbed and flowed according to changes in legislation as well as new decisions outlining the grounds for review. The number of cases the RRT decides each year has been declining steadily since 2000, from more than 6,000 cases finalized each year to between 2,000 and 3,000 in the past several years (MRT/RRT 2001–2013). This decline is likely a result of the success of the deterrent policies that prevent asylum seekers from applying for refugee status in the first place. However, during this same period, the proportion of rejected applicants who seek a judicial remedy has demonstrated no clear pattern, fluctuating dramatically from a low of 12% in 2002 to a peak of 79% in 2006. In recent years, the proportion has remained more steady, around 20%

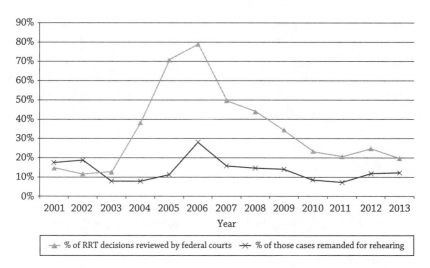

Figure 6.2 Refugee Review Tribunal Decisions and Judicial Review (2001–2013).
Source: MRT/RRT Annual Reports, 2001–2013.

(Figure 6.2). Interestingly, the years in which the courts were most involved in reviewing RRT decisions, they were also more likely to find in favor of the asylum seekers and remand the case to the RRT for a rehearing. As a result, the remand rates have also fluctuated, ranging from 7% to 28% of total cases reviewed.

In 2007, in its peak year of judicial involvement, migration matters made up 35% of the Federal Court workload, or 72% of the appellate work the Federal Court conducted (Federal Court of Australia, Annual Report 2010–11). A full 90% of these cases were refugee matters (author interview, 11/05/2007). These percentages have declined substantially since that time, and the Federal Court has adopted some strategies for efficient case management, such as combining cases that raise similar issues. However, migration cases still constitute a significant proportion of the total caseload. In addition, the migration caseload is disproportionately burdensome because a large number of applicants arrive at the Federal Court unrepresented. As the Registrar of the Court explained to me: "If the person is unrepresented, our case managers look for errors in the decision so that the case is not lopsided, because that is unpleasant for the judges." She went on to say that "refugee matters are not a jurisdiction of choice for most of the judges. Judges are frustrated because the feel they have no time to hear other matters" (author interview, 11/05/2007).

Thus, Australia's RSD regime is a fascinating paradox; traditionally weak courts are reluctantly becoming more involved in setting the parameters of procedural justice for asylum seekers. But, because judicial power is contested, courts self-limit the ways in which they assert themselves. This dynamic stands in sharp contrast to the Canadian system, which has powerful courts, but has restricted judicial review over RSD without ever banning it. It also differs from the American system, in which the courts' ability to conduct judicial review is both less controversial and more substantively meaningful. As with the administrative agencies, the role of courts in Australian politics is far less settled than in the United States or Canada, and asylum seekers frequently bring the cases that are being used to sort out these larger constitutional questions.

Impact: High-Profile Turf Battles

Despite the relative moderation of the Australian judiciary's rise to power, by the early 1990s the issue had inspired a political backlash, and the extent to which courts should be involved in reviewing migration decisions became a point of heated debate. This tension has only escalated in the decades since, and has become a focal point of interbranch conflict on multiple occasions, as Parliament has passed a long series of acts designed to limit the involvement of courts in migration decisions. Although the High Court has been quite active in pushing back against Parliament, it is ultimately limited in what it can do. Frequently, the stumbling block for the High Court is the lack of textualized, or enumerated, rights in the Australian Constitution that it can use to assert itself. Furthermore, the Court is ultimately quite calculating in the degree to which it is willing to limit itself in the name of parliamentary sovereignty.

The Australian High Court's strategic deference to Parliament may stem from the fact that Parliament has shown itself to be very willing to act on the migration issue, regardless of which party is in control. The Migration Act of 1958, which is the central piece of immigration legislation in Australia, has been amended many times to temper the degree to which the courts can specify procedural fairness requirements for migrants. The first legislative move was the Migration Reform Act of 1992, which replaced the ADJR Act for migration decisions. Instead, it outlined a specific codification of what the (more limited) natural justice requirements would be for administrative decisions about migration matters. In this way, Parliament attempted to remove the courts' ability to review several grounds that it asserted were being used by courts to look at the merits of cases.[16] The Migration Reform Act also established the RRT in an attempt to divert merits review away from the courts.

Since the RRT's creation in 1992, the backlash against expanded procedural rights for migrants has continued. In particular, Parliament has tried on several occasions to strip courts of their jurisdiction to hear appeals of RRT decisions, and the High Court has responded by routinely reasserting its constitutionally entrenched right to review decisions by commonwealth officers, even on the narrowest grounds. For example, in 2001, the Australian Parliament passed the

Migration Legislation Amendment (Judicial Review) Act, which added a privative clause to the Migration Act. Specifically, Parliament amended the Migration Act to say that decisions under that act are "final and conclusive" and "must not be challenged, appealed against, reviewed, quashed, or called in question in any court" (Migration Act 1958, Section 474, Part 1, (a) and (b)). This was a clear signal to the courts that their involvement in migration decision making was against the will of Parliament.

The High Court responded with a nuanced and calculated decision in *Plaintiff S157/2002 v. Commonwealth of Australia* (211 CLR 476, 2003). In a nod to Parliament, the Court found the addition of a privative clause to the Migration Act was constitutional. However, it went on to explain that any decision that was made in "jurisdictional error" would be "regarded, in law, as no decision at all" and so could not be considered a decision made under the Migration Act. In this way, the Court did not directly overturn an act of Parliament, but it eviscerated the intent of the Act by reasserting the right of courts to review all decisions that have been made in error.

Since the *S157* decision, Australian courts have defined jurisdictional error very broadly. For example, in the case of *SAAP & Anor v. Minister for Immigration and Multicultural and Indigenous Affairs* (215 ALR 162, 2005), the High Court found that the RRT had committed a jurisdictional error when it failed to give a written notice of reasons for denying an application, because written reasons were a component of the procedural fairness requirements laid out in Section 424A of the Migration Act. Because the High Court found that a common RRT practice was a jurisdictional error, 500 cases were remanded to the RRT for reconsideration. Also as a result of this decision, Parliament was forced to amend Section 424A to specify a new process for reporting adverse findings to a refugee applicant.[17]

Other examples of the back-and-forth between Parliament and the courts have included, first, the Federal Court's use of class actions to reverse large numbers of cases at once, and the subsequent banning of class actions via the Migration Legislation Amendment Act (No. 2) (2001); second, Parliament's establishment of time limits for bringing review requests in the Migration Litigation Reform Act (2005), and the subsequent invalidation of those time limits in the case of *Bodruddaza v. MIMA* (228 CLR 651, 2007); and third, and in many ways the most substantively significant skirmish, the amendment by Parliament of the Migration Act to narrow and specify the meaning of persecution to cases where there is a risk of "serious harm" and the persecution is "systematic."[18] This move was a direct response to High Court decisions that had interpreted the refugee definition more broadly.

Although there is no doubt that the Australian High Court has grown in power over time, and has triggered many parliamentary responses as a result, the Court still sets some clear limits on its own power. As a leading Australian refugee law scholar has said, refugee jurisprudence in Australia "is recent; it is generally fairly conservative; and it is domestic and textual in its focus, with relatively little attention paid to norms of international human rights law" (Crock 2004:53). The impact of these limitations is illustrated in stark terms by the case of *Al-Kateb v. Godwin and Minister for Immigration and Multicultural Affairs* (HCA 37, 2004). Al-Kateb was a stateless Palestinian whose asylum claim was rejected, but rather than being deported, he had been in immigration detention since 2000 because no country would accept him and he had nowhere to go. The High Court concluded that stateless asylum seekers whose petitions had been refused could be kept indefinitely in detention, despite the fact that they posed no threat to society. The Court ruled based on a strict constitutional interpretation, and claimed that Parliament had an unlimited power to detain. The Court acknowledged that the outcome was "tragic," but argued that in the absence of a Bill of Rights or constitutional amendment, there was little that it could do. The Al-Kateb majority also refused to use international law to circumvent textual limitations. Instead, it reaffirmed the sovereignty prerogative of Parliament, pronouncing that "the claim that the Constitution should be read consistently with the rules of international law has been decisively rejected by members of this Court on several occasions." This case illustrates the limits of Australia's rights revolution. Because it was procedural and statutory, rather than substantive and based on constitutional or international law, it can only go so far. Australia's politics have become more legalistic overall, and migration policymaking has become particularly judicialized, but the specific role that courts play is of a very different character than in the highly judicialized American context.

Conclusions

Australia's RSD regime has the low trust in administrative decision making, institutional fragmentation, and high levels of court review that can be found in the United States. However, it would be a mistake to characterize the Australian RSD regime as one of adversarial legalism. As in Canada, the focus of the Australian system is on bureaucratic and inquisitorial decision making. Australian courts are intent on protecting their power to review, and there has been a lot of back-and-forth and symbolic disputes. However, the lack of constitutional protections and historically limited power of courts, combined with a visceral commitment to restrictionism within the political branches, dilute the value of court review. More than in the United States or Canada, Australia's bureaucratic adversarialism produces results that are highly influenced by contentious restrictionist politics.

It should be noted, however, that this label of bureaucratic adversarialism is more tenuous than the adversarial legalism of the United States or the professional judgment of Canada. The character of Australia's RSD regime is less set than the other two systems in this study, perhaps because the regime is younger and administrative law is less developed. As a result, Australia has yet to establish a core value that drives its conceptualization of administrative justice. Rather, Australia's commitment to deterrent border control policies seems to be long-lasting, even as the 2001 drama of the *MV Tampa* tanker ship incident recedes into the background. As control of Parliament has changed hands over the years and the Pacific Solution era has faded, the general restrictionism of Australia's RSD regime has remained fairly stable.

Meanwhile, the power of the Australian courts has slowly grown. Since the *S157* decision of 2003, in which the High Court asserted its ability to review RRT decisions flawed by jurisdictional error, courts have become far more involved in the RSD regime. However, the courts do not seem to be driven by a policy preference for expansionist migration outcomes. Rather, the activist stance of the courts in protecting their jurisdiction is really about a bigger struggle over interbranch power dynamics that has yet to be resolved. So, the battle of the bouncing ball continues.

PART

III

THE DIFFERENCE AN RSD REGIME MAKES

CHAPTER 7

Asylum for Women: Reading Gender into the Refugee Definition

Imagine for a moment the story of a hypothetical, but prototypical, modern asylum seeker.[1] She was born into a tight-knit community in a small country, and at a young age was married off to a prominent member of the state police. From the earliest days of the marriage, it was an abusive one. Her husband was often drunk and would beat her regularly, sometimes until she lost consciousness. In one incident, he kicked her so hard that she miscarried a pregnancy. Over time, his abuse became increasingly sadistic; he whipped her with his pistol, broke a mirror over her head, and once tried to set her on fire. Her parents were no longer living so she could not return to their home, and when she tried to hide with her sister's family, he found her and was enraged, threatening to cut off her arms and legs if she ever tried to leave again. Her brother in-law took her to the local police, but they insisted that they were unable to intervene in such a private, personal matter, especially given the high-profile status of her husband. Eventually, knowing that her life was in danger, she decided to flee her country. Is she a refugee?

We know from Part II of this book that RSD regimes can have very different characters depending on the conceptions of administrative justice upon which they are based. In Part III, we turn our attentions to the question of how these differences affect the way in which particular asylum claims are handled. Specifically, I examine how different RSD regimes resolve areas of legal uncertainty, and how they generate policy when new issues arise. The UNHCR estimates that the majority of the refugees worldwide are women and children;[2] but, traditionally, the interpretation of the refugee definition and core legal precedents have been developed through the claims of men, who have long made up the majority of asylum seekers.[3] During the late 1980s and the early 1990s, the UNHCR pointed repeatedly to the plight of female asylum seekers as a burgeoning issue, and called on receiving nations to adapt their interpretation of the refugee definition to accept these claims as legitimate. Thus, in this chapter

I compare the responses of the United States, Canada, and Australia to the recent and rapid growth of gender-based asylum claims, and the powerful international pressure to recognize these claims as deserving refugee protection.

On the surface, the responses of these three countries to gender-based claims look remarkably similar. Canada issued guidelines on the handling of gender-based asylum claims in 1993, and the United States and Australia quickly followed suit, issuing their own guidelines in 1995 and 1996, respectively. The existence of these national-level guidelines suggests that all three regimes are respectful of international guidance and are open to recognizing gender-based claims. However, looking more closely at how this issue actually plays out across the three RSD regimes, we see three divergent trajectories that are predictable consequences of the character of each RSD regime more generally. Of particular importance in this case is the level of credence an RSD regime gives to international soft law. Furthermore, as this case study illustrates, the level of insulation and independence enjoyed by the administrative agencies making frontline RSD decisions has a significant impact on the outcomes of gender-based claims. Insulation enables a centralization of policymaking, which allows for stability and predictability of jurisprudence over time, and responsiveness to change. It does not lead automatically to more generous outcomes, but if there is a deliberate policy decision to be more generous, the impact of that decision is felt at all levels of a centralized RSD regime. In contrast, lower levels of insulation lead to interbranch conflict, unpredictability, and politicized decision making.

An examination of how gender-based claims are handled across three different jurisdictions also calls into question our notions of the globalization of law. Slaughter (2000:1104) argues that national-level courts can be vehicles of globalization through judges' exposure to international norms and their interactions (both formal and informal) with colleagues in other nations, leading to a vision of "a global community of law." An important feature of this process is what she calls judicial "cross-fertilization," the referencing of the decisions of other nations in written opinions (Slaughter 2004). Jacobsohn (2004) is more skeptical of this phenomenon. Instead of cross-fertilization, he calls this process "borrowing" and argues that the practice brings with it a potential for the "judicial misuse of foreign precedent" through the application of concepts that are inappropriate for the particularities of a given society (Jacobsohn 2004:1785). However, scholars are generally optimistic about the potential of cross-fertilization and judicial globalization. For example, Flaherty (2006:503) concludes that judicial globalization will "produce better considered and usually more just decisions" and "help fortify the international rule of law, and so foster greater global order and stability."

The three pathways taken by the United States, Canada, and Australia on gender-based asylum claims suggest a much more mixed picture of judicial globalization than is usually found in the scholarly literature. In all three countries, policymakers and interpreters of law have exhibited an awareness of international guidance on gender-based claims, and often made reference to developments in other countries. But, this acknowledgement of international legal developments has meant something very different in each country, depending on the individual character of the RSD regime. The case of gender-based asylum claims illustrates the fact that reference to international law and the borrowing of judicial opinions from other countries can be used as a decision-making tool in ways that are both expansive and restrictive. For this reason, I, like Jacobsohn (2004), prefer the term *borrowing*, because it indicates a strategic decision about when and what to borrow, as opposed to *cross-fertilization*, which suggests a natural process.

The stories of the United States, Canada, and Australia also suggest that the globalization of law operates at all levels of an RSD regime. The current literature on judicial globalization focuses exclusively on decisions made by courts at the highest level, often in the interpretation of constitutions. As the case of RSD vividly illustrates, by focusing only on constitutional courts, we miss the bottom-up element of judicial globalization by which low-level administrative tribunals are globalizing their approaches to judicial interpretation. This administrative globalization can take a more subtle form, avoiding the high-profile controversies often associated with the expanded power of constitutional courts.

Gender-Based Asylum Claims

A gender-based claim is a more particular concept than simply an asylum claim made by a woman; it is a request for protection from persecution that is leveled at the asylum seeker precisely because she is a woman. Gender-based claims pose a myriad of interpretive and administrative challenges for refugee status decision makers. First and foremost, the definition from the 1951 Convention Relating to the Status of Refugees makes no mention of gender, so women asylum seekers must fit their claims within one of the existing five categories. Some forms of gender-based claims can be subsumed under the grounds of political opinion, or perhaps religion, such as an opposition to Muslim laws about the subjugation of women. In general, however, most gender-based claims end up being considered under the rubric of membership in a particular social group—the part of the refugee definition that is the most fraught with interpretive challenges.[4]

The particular social group ground was not initially included in the refugee definition as it was being drafted, but as the end of the 1951 Convention drew near, the delegate from Sweden, Sture Petren, suggested that it should be added as an amendment, saying: "experience has shown that certain refugees are persecuted because they belonged to particular social groups. The draft provision made no provision for those cases, and one designed to cover them should accordingly be included." Without debate or dissenting votes, the phrase was then added to the definition (UN docs A/CONF.2/ SR.3 [Petren]). Courts often turn to the legislative history of a document as a means of illuminating the intent of the drafters, but there was almost no discussion of the phrase "membership in a particular social group" at the 1951 Convention, giving modern-day decision makers little to work with. Judging by the frequency with which court opinions interpreting the phrase mention and decry the lack of clear drafter intent, it has been a source of great frustration for decision makers that there is not more information about the motivation behind its addition.

Reliance on membership in a particular social group as a means of bringing women into the refugee definition presents some difficult legal questions. First, decision makers may not be willing to conclude that all the women in a country constitute a particular social group. Further, even if they go along with the idea of women as a group, decision makers must then also find that the persecution occurred *because* the individual is a woman, and not for some other reason. For example, a decision maker could conclude that a woman was beaten and abused by her husband's prominent family members not because of her gender, but because of an interfamily dispute that arose over her insufficient dowry. If, on the other hand, the particular social group is defined more specifically for each individual asylum claim, the logic can often become circular. For example: "women who are victims of domestic violence" defines the group by the persecution, whereas the refugee definition states that it protects people who are persecuted on account of their membership in a group. It is difficult to argue that women are targeted for domestic violence *because* of their association with domestic violence.

A related interpretive challenge posed by gender-based claims is the question of whether the forms of oppression experienced by women qualify as persecution. Part of the confusion stems from the fact that, often, the persecution of women either comes in the form of a generalized law that affects every female member of society and has the sanction and support of a majority of the population, or it comes in the form of private abuse, such as domestic violence, conducted by a nonstate actor. In this way, gender-based claims can be construed as alternatively too personal and too pervasive to fit the refugee definition.[5]

Traditionally, refugee status has been granted to those fleeing the oppression of their own government. When the persecution comes from a nonstate actor, as it often does with gender-based claims, the case is more difficult to prove. The asylum seeker has to show that the government cannot or will not provide protection. In the case of the hypothetical asylum seeker in the opening vignette, her husband's high-profile status as a member of the state police, combined with societal norms about respecting the internal dynamics of marriage, prevented the local police from intervening to protect her from spousal abuse. In cases like this one, the burden is on the asylum seeker to prove that her state lacked the capacity to protect her from harm.

Additional challenges of managing gender-based claims are less problems of legal interpretation and more practical matters. One frequent barrier to defining the oppression of women as rising to the level of persecution can come from the personal biases of RSD adjudicators. Decision makers in western countries are not immune from holding the sexist belief that women who object to oppressive traditions or cultural practices are merely rabble-rousers, rather than people with legitimate political opinions that deserve protection. Beyond that challenge, women who have been subjugated or abused are often not accustomed to speaking up about their experiences, especially in a formal hearing setting. The presence of a male RSD decision maker or a male interpreter from the home country can often be prohibitively intimidating for women who must give painful and intimate testimony. For all these reasons, gender-based claims require sensitive handling.

Even though there was no discussion of the intent behind including the particular social group clause when it was written in 1951, by the time the United States, Canada, and Australia had adopted the Convention and Protocol, and by the time they were interpreting it in their courts and applying the phrase to gender-based claims, a good deal of international soft law had developed around this issue (Fullerton 1993, Grahl-Madsen 2001). In 1985, the UNHCR Executive Committee suggested that women "who face harsh or inhumane treatment due to their having transgressed the social mores of the society in which they live" should be considered a particular social group. Then, in 1991, the UN issued an official guideline on the protection of refugee women that reiterated the position that women are a particular social group, and outlined a number of forms that gender-based persecution can take (UNHCR 1991). Again in 1993, the Executive Committee released a report suggesting that RSD decision makers be given special training in gender sensitivity (UNHCR 1993). The UNHCR has continued to update their guidelines every few years since, and takes an active role in encouraging receiving nations to be innovative and generous in applying the Refugee Convention to gender-based claims.[6]

The guidelines issued by the governments of the United States, Canada, and Australia all have the dual purpose of clarifying the confusion around how the refugee definition should be interpreted in relation to gender-based claims, and also outlining procedures for the sensitive handling of the RSD hearing itself. However, as the following accounts illustrate, each country has responded to the UN soft law guidelines quite differently.

Canada

The story of Canada's response to gender-based RSD claims should be discussed first, because Canada was the first country in the world to create a specialized policy designed to clarify the question of how to handle such claims. In keeping with the centralized, depoliticized bent of the Canadian RSD regime, these guidelines were developed autonomously within the administrative agency, the IRB. This agency is an independent tribunal designed to be isolated from the Department of Citizenship and Immigration and political pressure from Parliament. Removed from such pressures, the IRB based its guidelines very closely on the text of the soft law produced by the UNHCR, often quoting large sections of UN guidance verbatim.

Today, gender-based asylum claims are a fairly settled area of Canadian refugee law, because although the Canadian guidelines are not binding on courts, the courts have granted the IRB a huge amount of leeway to innovate in a proactive manner. The courts have upheld the gender guidelines repeatedly, making them the controlling policy on the issue at all levels of the RSD process. As one lawyer who regularly takes cases to the IRB put it: "The Board has been pretty good about the gender issue because it has been absorbed over there" (author interview, 5/29/2007). In other words, the professional judgment model of decision making prioritizes bureaucratic centralization and vertical accountability, which leads to consistency in outcomes. The IRB did not always have a clear approach to gender-based asylum claims, but once its leadership decided to embrace the guidance of the UNHCR, the agency adapted to change quickly and definitively, and has maintained a stable position on the issue ever since.

Canada's involvement in gender-based asylum claims was spurred by a high-profile controversy that hit the IRB soon after the creation of its specialized subunit, the Refugee Protection Division. The new decision-making body quickly became subject to intense criticism over the handling of a case, which came to be known as the *Nada* case. Nada was a Saudi Arabian woman whose refugee claim, filed in 1991, was based on the persecution she had suffered stemming from her refusal to wear a veil because she considered herself a feminist. The RSD decision maker denied her application, and wrote an opinion that would eventually become notorious:

> The claimant would do well, like all her compatriots, to abide by the laws of general application she opposes, and... to show consideration for the feelings of her father, who, like everyone else in her large family, was opposed to the liberalism of his daughter. (IRB Decision, file no. M91-04822, September 24, 1991)

The case received a lot of critical media attention and, under pressure from women's rights and human rights organizations, the Minister of Employment and Immigration eventually used his discretionary power to grant Nada refugee status.[7]

Although the IRB tries to maintain some distance from Parliament and the Minister, the Refugee Protection Division was still in its early stages of development at that point, and thus more susceptible to political pressure. In addition, by the early 1990s, the makeup of the IRB had been changing to include more female and minority members who themselves had been disturbed by the tone of the *Nada* decision. While this controversy was brewing, IRB Chairperson Nurjehan Mawani announced that she would be issuing groundbreaking guidelines for board members tasked with deciding claims based on gender persecution.[8] The final draft of the guidelines, titled *Women Refugee Claimants Fearing Gender-Related Persecution*, was issued on International Women's Day, March 9, 1993, and was the first statement by a government outlining procedures for handling gender-based refugee claims. The guidelines are designed to make RSD hearings more sensitive to those women who may find it difficult to speak about traumatic experiences, especially through a male interpreter or to a male board member.

However, beyond the goal of improving hearing room dynamics, much of the 20-page document is devoted to the legal question of how women can fit within the refugee definition, which does not explicitly include them. To that end, the guidelines state:

> The existing bank of jurisprudence on the meaning of persecution is based on, for the most part, the experience of male claimants. Aside from a few case of rape, the definition has not been applied to female-specific experiences, such as infanticide, genital mutilation, bride-burning, forced marriage, domestic violence, forced abortion, or compulsory sterilization. (IRB 1993:7)

The guidelines make frequent reference to the 1991 gender guidelines issued by the UNHCR, which argue that women who are persecuted because of their gender should be considered members of a particular social group under the refugee definition (UNHCR 1991).

Soon after the Canadian guidelines were released, the Canadian Supreme Court heard its first major case dealing with asylum, *Canada (Attorney General) v. Ward* (2 S.C.R 689, 1993). Although the case had nothing to do with gender, it had wide-reaching ramifications because the Court used the asylum claim of a former member of the Irish National Liberation Army (INLA) to outline its position on the concept of membership in a particular social group and its limits.

Ward claimed to fear for his life at the hands of his fellow members of the INLA because he believed they would act out of revenge for his defection from the group. He argued that this former association should be considered grounds for asylum based on membership in a social group.

In considering this argument, the Supreme Court of Canada engaged in some surprising judicial borrowing from its neighbor to the south. It looked very closely at the American BIA decision in the *Matter of Acosta* (Interim Decision #2986, 1985). The Court announced the administrative decision provided "a good working rule" for its own approach to the interpretation of the particular social group clause, and laid out a three-pronged test that is very similar to the BIA's logic in *Acosta*. The Court concluded that particular social groups are "(1) groups defined by an innate or unchangeable characteristic; (2) groups whose members voluntarily associate for reasons so fundamental to their human dignity that they should not be forced to forsake the association; and (3) groups associated by a former voluntary status, unalterable due to its historical permanence." Thus, because Ward could not undo his former status as a member of the INLA, he qualified as a Convention refugee under the third category. The Court also made a key finding for future gender-based claims, concluding that persecution need not be carried out by a member of the state, as long as the state is unable to provide adequate protection from it.

The *Ward* decision is a prime example of the globalization of law via judicial borrowing, but the ultimate lesson to be taken from it is ambiguous. The Canadian Supreme Court used the logic of a foreign decision-making body as a way of bolstering and justifying its conclusions in an area that neither Canadian courts nor the IRB had yet explored. However, it selected one case out of a diverse body of law in the United States without engaging in a thorough assessment of American jurisprudence on the particular social group question, which at the time was varied and occasionally contradicted the *Acosta* test. By following the expertise of an administrative agency, albeit from another country, the Court seems to have been attempting to give the *Ward* decision added legitimacy.

Although it was an unintended consequence, the selective borrowing from the *Acosta* decision by the Canadian Supreme Court trickled down to affect gender-based claims very directly. In 1996, the IRB updated its gender guidelines and added language referencing the conclusion in *Ward* (and, by extension, the BIA's logic in *Acosta*), that gender is an immutable characteristic fundamental to human dignity. The updated guidelines went on to clarify that women who are victims of persecution may be considered a particular social group, and that concerns about opening the floodgates to massive numbers of claims should not be a factor in decision making:

> The fact that the particular social group consists of large numbers of the female population in the country concerned is irrelevant—race,

religion, nationality and political opinion are also characteristics that
are shared by large numbers of people. (IRB 1996)

Because the IRB had committed itself to being a pioneer on gender issues, it
borrowed the logic of the *Acosta* decision and, ironically, took it much further
than any decision in the United States on women as a particular social group.

The IRB has continued to take pride in its reputation for leading the way on
gender-based asylum claims. In 2003, for the 10th anniversary of the original
guidelines, the IRB released a compendium of guiding cases on a wide variety
of gender-related refugee issues (IRB 2003). In addition, the UNHCR issued a
press release in which Commissioner Ruud Lubbers commended the Canadian
RSD system. Lubbers stated that "Canada was the trail-blazer in developing
an asylum process that takes proper account of gender-related persecution"
and hailed the news that the IRB accepts around 70% of gender-based asylum
claims, a rate well above the average acceptance rate for all claims (UNHCR
2003). A high level official at the CIC told me with pride:

> We look around a lot to see if what we are doing is consistent with other
> countries, and we found that on gender (domestic violence) we are
> a leader.... The international jurisprudence on gender is very mixed.
> (author interview, 4/03/2007)[9]

In fact, the variance between the gender-based asylum policy in the United
States and Canada has led to some major questions regarding whether the two
countries can collaborate on asylum policy via the Safe Third Country agreement. Under that agreement, asylum seekers cannot chose whether to file a refugee claim in one country over the other; instead, they must apply for refugee
status in the country where they first arrive. The assumption behind this agreement is that the RSD systems of the United States and Canada are equivalent.
However, the refugee advocacy community in Canada challenged the agreement
in court, arguing that among other shortcomings, the U.S. standard on gender
protection is insufficient, and if Canada is complicit in sending gender claimants
to the United States, where they are likely to be denied, Canada will be in violation of international law (Arnett 2005).[10]

The position of the Canadian advocates was upheld in the initial Federal
Court decision, but was overturned on appeal (*Canadian Council for Refugees,
Canadian Council of Churches, Amnesty International and John Doe vs. Her
Majesty the Queen,* (FCC 1262 [2007]). In February 2009, the Supreme Court
of Canada declined to hear the case, avoiding the awkwardness of potentially
declaring Canada's neighbor to the south to be in violation of international law.[11]
Nevertheless, the arguments put forward by both sides are illuminating. The

Canadian and American governments have asserted that both countries are in compliance with international law, and thus the difference in standards on gender stems from the fact that Canadian jurisprudence has gone above and beyond the norm in compliance levels. In other words, the Canadian government has invoked a generosity prerogative in this area, bringing in expert witnesses to testify to the more narrow gender jurisprudence of other nations, to show how Canada is an anomaly.[12]

For 20 years, Canada's gender story has been a clear example of the way in which a centralized bureaucratic approach to RSD can lead to rapid, responsive policy developments. It is also an example of the nonconfrontational relationship between the administrative agency and the courts. The gender guidelines were reaffirmed by the Supreme Court in *Ward*, but otherwise have seen very little court involvement, and no contention by courts that women cannot be considered a particular social group or that gender-based oppression should not be considered persecution. Courts have respected these basic premises laid out by the IRB. In addition, as we see in the next chapter, the gender guidelines have had wide-reaching impact on other precedent at the IRB, even in cases dealing with men. Thus, the example of Canada's gender interpretation demonstrates that liberalization and internationalization of legal interpretation can be spearheaded at the level of administrative tribunals. By examining only constitutional courts, we miss more low-profile developments in legal globalization in which jurisprudence percolates up to higher courts from below.

Although Canada's RSD regime has demonstrated a powerful commitment to its reputation as a pioneer on gender-based claims, it is not clear whether this commitment will endure as the 2010 BRRA is fully implemented. None of the procedural changes outlined in the BRRA are specific to gender-based claims, but because they are generally designed to make the process more expedient, some asylum seeker advocates have expressed concerns about how these changes will affect those making gender-based claims (Canadian Council for Refugees 2010, Sadrehashemi 2011). The core values of consistency and efficiency that undergird Canada's RSD regime have functioned in tandem with the IRB's commitment to generosity on the gender issue. However, this compatibility is not fixed in stone.

United States

The story of gender-based claims in the United States stands in sharp contrast to the Canadian trajectory because the United States has not prioritized the guidance of international soft law *or* the legal developments occurring in other nations. When the United States published its gender guidelines in 1995, they made only very brief mention of the 1993 Canadian guidelines and the UNHCR soft law upon which that document was based. The rest of the American guidelines are completely focused on the domestic context. They attempt to make sense of the mass of case law that, by 1995, had already developed around gender issues in the United States to "ensure uniformity and consistency in procedures and decisions" (Coven 1995). Since the guidelines were released, and despite some efforts on the part of policymakers within the immigration bureaucracy to ensure compliance with international law and uniformity of decision making, the reality of the situation continues to be a very mixed bag.

The American response to gender-based claims fits very neatly with the adversarial and legalist character of its RSD regime and with the fragmented American system of politics, law, and dispute resolution more generally. It has been a contentious, highly politicized, and litigious battle, involving many different institutional actors within both government and the advocacy community. Many central questions remain surprisingly unsettled. Today, the chance of success for a woman who seeks asylum via a gender-based claim is dependent on her ability to access quality lawyers and advocates.[13] To a surprising degree, it also depends on the individual decision maker to which the asylum seeker is assigned.

The American story began when the BIA handed down its decision in the *Matter of Acosta* in 1985. The case dealt with the question of whether members of a taxi drivers' collective in El Salvador who had been subject to extreme harassment from antigovernment guerillas constituted a particular social group. However, the details of that case matter less than the interpretation of the terms laid out in the decision, which have proved seminal for the jurisprudence of many nations. After remarking that Congress had neglected to define the term "particular social group" when they adopted the 1951 refugee definition into the 1980 Refugee Act, the BIA lamented that "the international jurisprudence interpreting this ground of persecution is sparse." The BIA then went on to explain that, in lieu of other guidance, it would rely on the doctrine of *ejusdem generis* (of the same kind), deducing that, like the other four grounds of race, religion, national origin, and political opinion, it is an immutable characteristic. The BIA then defined an immutable characteristic as one "that either is beyond the power of an individual to change, or is so fundamental to individual identity or conscience that it ought not be required to change." Finally, the decision mentioned in passing that gender or sexuality may be prototypical examples of such a characteristic, before concluding that Acosta's profession did not qualify.

Although the BIA's reasoning in *Acosta* set the stage for the interpretation of the particular social group clause in courts around the world, and was eventually influential in the United States as well, in the decade following the decision, the question of whether gender could be considered a particular social group remained very unsettled in American law.[14] The federal courts seemed generally reluctant to adopt the logic of *Acosta* wholesale, and by the time the INS published its gender "considerations" in 1995, three of the federal Courts of Appeals had handed down very different answers to this question. The 9th Circuit, in *Sanchez-Trujillo v. INS* (801 F.2d 1571, 1986) decided that members of a particular social group had to be cohesive and involve voluntary association, thus declining to extend the definition to women as a whole. Similarly, the 2nd Circuit, in *Gomez v. INS* (947 F.2d 660, 1991), found that "possession of broadly based characteristics such as youth and gender will not by itself endow individuals with membership in particular social group." In contrast, the 3rd Circuit, in *Fatin v. INS* (12 F.3d 1233, 1993), decided that a battered Iranian woman could, in theory, be considered a refugee "based solely on her gender." However, they concluded that in that particular case, the persecution occurred for a number of reasons, not necessarily gender, and thus denied refugee status.

Even when the INS issued its gender guidelines in 1995, the issue of whether gender could, on its own, constitute a particular social group was left unsettled. Despite the clear guidance of the UNHCR on this question and the strong stance outlined in the Canadian guidelines two years earlier, faced with a conflicted line of domestic jurisprudence, the INS decided to hedge. Their guidelines merely state that Asylum Officers should "be aware of the case law" and suggest that gender "might combine with other characteristics to define a particular social group" (Coven 1995). Because the INS embraced the notion that the issue of gender-based asylum claims was still being vetted by the RSD regime, the American guidelines did not really provide guidance to decision makers in the same sense that Canada's guidelines did.

Shortly after the memorandum was circulated, the BIA decided the *Matter of Kasinga* (Interim Decision #3278, 1996). Kasinga was a young woman who fled Togo to avoid forced genital mutilation prior to marriage. The BIA took note of the recently passed INS gender considerations and concluded that, based on those guidelines and the logic of its own *Acosta* decision, female genital mutilation was a clear example of persecution. The BIA also concluded that women who feared genital mutilation in Togo constituted a particular social group, concluding (in direct reference to *Acosta*) that "the characteristic of having intact genitalia is one that is so fundamental to the individual identity of a young women that she should not be required to change it." Refugee advocates considered Kasinga's success to be a huge victory, and such an expansive reading of the refugee definition by the BIA sparked hope that the memorandum on gender considerations would liberalize and unify American case law, bringing it in line with international standards.

In retrospect, Kasinga's story should be read more as an example of the importance of experienced counsel for making a strong case in the unsettled legal world of the American RSD regime. Kasinga was lucky enough to stumble onto the International Human Rights Law Clinic at American University, where a group of lawyers agreed to take her case pro bono (Center for Gender and Refugee Studies website). At that point, Kasinga's asylum claim had been denied by an IJ although the 1995 memorandum on female asylum claims had specifically listed genital mutilation as an example of persecution. Her attorneys were able to conduct detailed research on the issue of female genital mutilation in Togo, and presented the BIA with extensive documentation and expert testimony, including that of a cultural anthropologist from Duke University who had spent years doing fieldwork in northern Togo. Although it cannot be proven that Kasinga needed this high-quality legal assistance to eventually gain refugee status, it seems likely that, without it, the BIA would not have designated her case as precedent setting. This move enabled the BIA to use her well-documented case to take a clear stand on gender-based claims.

The *Kasinga* case puts several key features of the American RSD regime in sharp relief. First, it shows how a system that values thorough vetting is designed to rely more heavily on cases like Kasinga's, while other asylum claims get lost in the shuffle. Because the regime has so many moving parts, and so many different interpretations of the refugee definition are in circulation at any given time, a knowledgeable lawyer willing to dedicate time to a particular case can help give it additional weight. Second, the *Kasinga* case demonstrates the atomized way in which the American RSD regime resolves uncertainty. Unlike the Canadian approach, which viewed gender issues in a holistic manner, each subissue was treated separately in the United States. The BIA's decision in *Kasinga* resolved the particular issue of how cases of female genital mutilation should be treated, but its generosity in that case did not automatically extend to other forms of gender-based persecution. Most notably, the decision had not settled the issue of whether victims of domestic violence could be considered refugees in the United States.

That issue came to the forefront in the case of Rodi Alvarado, a Guatemalan woman who had been repeatedly and viciously beaten by her husband. The police had refused to step in and, after she fled, her husband told her sister that if he ever found her he would kill her. Initially, Alvarado's experience in seeking asylum was similar to that of Kasinga. She got legal assistance from the San Francisco Lawyers' Committee for Civil Rights, who presented her case to an IJ. The IJ granted her asylum, basing her decision on expert testimony about domestic violence and the 1995 considerations on gender (Center for Gender and Refugee Studies website).

The next phase of the story, however, is fraught with irony and, once again, illustrates the highly politicized nature of the American RSD regime. The INS announced that it disagreed with the IJ's interpretation of its own gender

guidelines, and appealed the decision to the BIA for reconsideration—a somewhat unusual move. Then, in one of the only documented instances of international borrowing by an American decision-making body in an asylum case, the
BIA examined a British House of Lords decision that granted asylum status to
a victim of domestic abuse and applied it to the case in front of them. However,
rather than use that case to justify its decision, the BIA declared its logic "too
broad," deciding instead that women who are victims of domestic abuse are not
a cohesive group in Guatemala (*In Re R-A-*, Interim Decision #3403, 1999).[15]
Assuming an almost sheepish tone, the BIA went on to explain why this decision did not contradict their landmark *Acosta* decision, which listed gender as an
example of an immutable characteristic: "We never declared ... that the starting
point for assessing social group claims articulated in *Acosta* was also the ending
point." This singular instance of American borrowing reveals that examination
of foreign precedent does not necessarily produce an expansion of international
norms or even a rise in cross-national judicial consistency in deciding similar
issues. This scenario bolsters Jacobsohn's (2004) claim that borrowing is often
much more strategic than systematic.

The BIA decision in *R-A* sparked an outcry among refugee advocates, as well
as immigrant rights and women's rights organizations more broadly. Some members of Congress began to take up her cause, sending letters lobbying Attorney
General Janet Reno to use her discretion in this case and asking her to address
the larger discrepancies and inconsistencies in gender-based asylum law.[16]
Meanwhile, Alvarado's lawyers appealed the BIA decision to the 9th Circuit Court
of Appeals. Then, in January 2001, before the case could be heard, and before
the Bush administration took over from the Clinton administration, Attorney
General Reno ordered the BIA to rehear the case, but put a stay on the rehearing
until after new regulations on gender-based asylum claims could be released.

Although the regulations that were drawn up by the Department of Justice
and the INS are a general statement on gender-based claims, they make specific reference to the case of Rodi Alvarado, and intimate that the case had been
wrongly decided. The proposed rule:

> [r]emoves certain barriers that the *In re R-A-* decision seems to pose to
> claims that domestic violence rises to the level of persecution of a per-
> son on account of membership in a particular social group. (INS 2000)

These regulations represented a major departure from the previous position
of both the INS and the Department of Justice on gender-based claims. However,
their expansiveness proved too much for the new Bush administration. Under
Attorney General Ashcroft, the Bush administration chose not to finalize the
rule, and the Alvarado case continued to be left open pending its finalization.

The Bush administration's willingness to leave Rodi Alvarado in legal limbo attracted protestations from a growing number of advocacy organizations, including the U.S. Conference of Catholic Bishops, Episcopal Migration Ministries, Lutheran World Relief, the Anti-Defamation League, the Leadership Conference on Civil Rights, the Hebrew Immigrant Advocacy Society, and the Washington Lawyers' Committee for Civil Rights and Urban Affairs (Center for Gender and Refugee Studies website). Despite this pressure, the INS under the Bush administration continued to defend strenuously the BIA's original logic in *R-A* as it litigated other cases. In a 2001 petition for rehearing of a case at the 9th Circuit, the INS wrote:

> Whether, and to what extent, the victims of domestic violence should be eligible for asylum in the United States involves policy judgments of the most sensitive nature that must be resolved in the first instance by the Executive Branch.[17]

Because the proposed regulations were never finalized, the stay that Attorney General Reno had placed on the Alvarado case remained in place throughout the Bush administration. In addition, because the outcome of her case had ramifications for other similar cases that had been appealed to the level of the BIA throughout the 2000s, by the time of the 2008 presidential election there were dozens of cases that had been left unresolved while the Alvarado case was pending.

The Bush administration finally took action on this issue in December 2008, when outgoing Attorney General Mukasey decided to lift the stay on all cases related to the *Matter of R-A* and allow the BIA to consider them. The Attorney General's order made it clear that the jurisprudence on the issue was in need of clarification:

> Insofar as a question involves interpretation of ambiguous statutory language, the Board is free to exercise its own discretion and issue a precedent decision establishing a uniform standard nationwide. (*Matter of R-A*, [Interim Decision #3624, A.G. 2008])

Because it had been a decade since the case was last decided, the BIA decided to send Alvarado's case back to the EOIR for a completely new hearing. An IJ in San Francisco granted her asylum in December 2009, 13 years after she first applied. The opinion made no grand pronouncement about gender-based claims, stating instead that "inasmuch as there is no binding authority on the legal issues raised in this case, I conclude that I can conscientiously accept what is essentially the agreement of the parties."[18]

The saga of Rodi Alvarado's asylum application is an extreme example, but it clearly illustrates the uncertainty, contentiousness, and the litigiousness of the American RSD regime. Even after Attorney General Reno placed a stay on the decision in 2001, according to lawyers who specialize in gender-based claims, many IJs still based their opinions in other asylum cases on the BIA decision to deny Alvarado asylum (Musalo and Knight 2003). Many of those cases led to deportations if the asylum seeker did not make an appeal to the BIA. Even now, after Rodi Alvarado has, finally, been granted asylum, the larger question of the place of gender-based asylum claims in American refugee law remains unsettled for several reasons. First, the decision granting her asylum was not precedent setting, applying only to her particular case. Second, the BIA has, on occasion, declined to follow its own precedent in *Kasinga*, denying asylum to a victim of female genital mutilation.[19] Third, although the Obama administration is more supportive of gender-based claims than the Bush administration, there is still a great deal of resistance among top policymakers to the idea of finding gender to be a particular social group. For example, a high-level official in the Department of Justice told me:

> It would be a total disaster, because it would be impossible to measure whether a discrimination is on account of gender, or for some other reason. Also, it would open us up for claims from men, such as Jewish men who have been circumcised, and people don't think it through, so they don't realize the consequences. (author interview, 2/12/2007)

Another top refugee policymaker also used the word *disaster*:

> If we were to do what some people suggested, which was to change the definition to add women to the nexus, this would be a disaster, and it would diminish attention from the people who we want to focus on. (author interview, 2/13/2007)

These officials were comfortable with prioritizing domestic immigration policy concerns over compliance with international guidance about how interpretation of the refugee definition should evolve.

In addition, a fourth barrier to a consistent, predictable response by the American RSD regime to gender-based claims is the high level of discretion, and thus variability, among IJs. Several studies have found cases in which IJ rejected asylum applicants based on the REAL ID Act, because they had not mentioned gender-based persecution in the initial airport interview. Inconsistency between the initial interview and later testimony is grounds to reject a claim, even if the applicant testifies that she did not know she could make a gender-based claim, or that she was afraid to speak about it to armed border agents (Fletcher 2006, Melloy 2007).

The underlying commitment of the American RSD regime to hearing a multiplicity of perspectives and allowing thorough vetting of issues as they arise meant that even when the United States issued guidelines for decision makers faced with gender-based asylum claims, they were treated as largely symbolic. The guidelines have been inadequate in achieving their stated goal of consistency and, instead, the jurisprudence on gender issues has been highly fragmented from the earliest cases with which the federal courts dealt, and the Supreme Court has not stepped in to resolve contradictions across the circuits. Attempts to achieve consistency through proposed regulations were stymied by political opposition within the Bush administration, and the BIA has proved itself ill equipped to fill the void by laying out clear precedent.

As a case study of judicial globalization, there is no evidence to suggest that an awareness of international soft law or expansionist foreign jurisprudence inspires RSD decision makers at any level to read the refugee definition in a particular way. Although the INS guidelines mentioned the guidance of the UNHCR, they were unsuccessful at bringing the United States in line with that guidance. In the sole instance that the BIA referred to a foreign decision, citing the generosity of a decision by the House of Lords when deciding *In Re R-A* in 1999, it used the case as an example of interpretation gone wrong. Thus, the commitment of the American RSD regime to considering a multiplicity of perspectives means that foreign precedent and international soft law are treated simply as competing views; they can be heard without being given any additional weight.

Australia

As a relative latecomer to domestic RSD, the rise of gender-based asylum claims came at an early stage in the development of Australia's RSD regime. Thus, when Australia followed the lead of Canada and the United States and released its own guidelines in 1996, the gender-based asylum issue was folded into the battle over shaping the regime that was developing between Parliament and the High Court at that time (Department of Immigration and Multicultural Affairs 1996). Although neither the Court nor Parliament have shown themselves to be particularly concerned with the international soft law guidance from the UNHCR, the Australian courts have sought legitimacy in their sparring with Parliament by making frequent reference to the decisions of other respected countries.

Like both the Canadian and American guidelines, the Australian gender guidelines are not binding on courts, but rather serve as a suggestion for RSD decision makers. However, in terms of content, the Australian guidelines are much more similar to the American memo than the Canadian policy document, because they were released by the immigration department, not the administrative tribunal, and do not answer the question of whether gender should be considered a particular social group. Rather, the guidelines state:

> Officers should bear in mind that there is no Australian jurisprudence on the issue of "women" as a particular social group .... Officers should consider this Convention ground on a case-by-case basis which takes account of the totality of an applicant's claims and the situation in the applicant's country of origin.

Because the larger landscape of Australian administrative law is still developing, there has been considerable confusion about the relationship between the RRT and the gender guidelines released by the DIAC. Officially, the guidelines do not apply to the tribunal, and a study of the RRT's handling of gender claims soon after the guidelines were released found that RRT decisions generally did not refer to them (Macklin 1998a). The perception that the guidelines apply only to frontline decision makers within the DIAC has significantly limited their impact on the RSD regime.

Because the regime was in its early stages in 1996, the immigration department released its guidelines into what it acknowledged was a jurisprudential void. Soon after their release, however, a case arose that enabled the judiciary to stake out a position in the battle over control of Australia's RSD regime. The case involved the asylum claim of a woman from Pakistan named Khawar, who had been repeatedly abused by her husband, including an attempt to burn her alive after pouring gasoline on her. She made multiple reports to the police that resulted in no intervention, and when her husband learned of her complaints, he beat her so badly that she was hospitalized for a week. She arrived in Australia in 1997 with her two children and filed a refugee claim with the Department of Immigration and Multicultural Affairs, which was unsuccessful. On appeal to the RRT, the tribunal member denied her claim, concluding that the violence against her was caused by an interpersonal dispute and the fact that she had not paid her husband a dowry.

In 1999, her luck changed when a judge in the Federal Court of Australia found the RRT had failed to determine whether Khawar was a member of a particular social group, and whether the country of Pakistan was able to provide protection from the type of persecution she had experienced (*Khawar v. Minister of Immigration and Multicultural Affairs*, [168 ALR 190, 1999]). The judge issued an opinion sending the case back to the RRT for a rehearing. However, the Immigration Minister, fearing the impact of a positive decision on future gender-based asylum claims, appealed to have the case heard by the full Federal

Court in the hopes that it would reverse the decision of the Federal Court judge and preclude a rehearing of the case at the RRT.

The full Federal Court heard Khawar's case, but it soon became clear that the Minister had been presumptuous in his confidence about the outcome. Instead of considering domestic policy developments, the Court looked outward, and engaged in a thorough review of particular social group precedent from foreign jurisdictions. In particular, the Court compared the American 9th Circuit decision in *Sanchez-Trujillo* that found particular social groups must be cohesive, with the more recent British decision in *Islam*. Judge Hill observed the two decisions contradicted each other directly:

> His Lordship [in the British case] was of the view that cohesiveness was not an indispensable requirement for the existence of a particular social group. In so doing, his Lordship disapproved the suggestion to this effect in *Sanchez-Trujillo*. (*Minister for Immigration and Multicultural Affairs v. Khawar* [101 FCR 501, 2000])

Ultimately, the Australian court agreed with the British assessment and the Federal Court judge's initial decision, and ordered Khawar's case to be remanded to the RRT for a rehearing and reassessment of the particular social group issue.

This time, Minister Ruddock took a two-pronged approach in response to a decision with which he disagreed. He applied for special leave for the case to be heard again at the High Court level, and simultaneously introduced legislation in Parliament that would dictate a restrictive interpretation of the refugee definition. Parliament quickly passed the Migration Legislation Amendment (Judicial Review) Act (2001) adding Section 91R to the Migration Act of 1958. The new section stated that refugee status can only be granted if

> a) the Convention reason is the essential and significant reason for the persecution; b) the persecution involves serious harm; and c) the persecution involves systematic and discriminatory conduct.

In a memorandum that accompanied the bill, the Minister explicitly stated that decision makers, especially in gender-based asylum claims, had been interpreting the definition of persecution too broadly and had been attributing persecution to people for reasons that were not central to the five Convention grounds:

> Over recent years the interpretation of the definition of a refugee by various courts and tribunals has expanded the interpretation of the definition so as to require protection to be provided in circumstances that

are clearly outside those originally intended. (Migration Legislation Amendment [Judicial Review] Act 2001, Explanatory Memorandum for the Bill)

Before the new act could take effect, the High Court issued its ruling in the *Khawar* case and, as the Minister feared, it agreed with the Federal Court that Khawar should be granted asylum. There was very little domestic jurisprudence about gender-based claims on which to base a decision, and the justices knew the Minister had actively opposed a decision in favor of the applicant. Nevertheless, the Court seemed convinced by the British House of Lords decision, which had also involved a battered woman from Pakistan. The High Court was faced with its own recent precedent in a different case, *Applicant A v. MIEA* (190 CLR 225, 1997), in which it had concluded that, for individuals to be considered members of particular social group, they must have a "common thread" linking them to each other personally. In making the *Khawar* decision, the High Court also backed away slightly from its own, more restrictive, "common thread" test in *Applicant A*, remarking that "some particular social groups are notoriously lacking in cohesiveness." On the issue of women as a particular social group, the justices were clear:

> Women in any society are a distinct and recognizable group; and their distinctive attributes and characteristics exist independently of the manner in which they are treated, either by males or by governments.

The High Court's opinion in *Khawar* does not refer to Australia's gender guidelines. Instead, it is a classic example of strategic borrowing. The opinion takes inspiration from the decision of a foreign court in the face of domestic legislation calling for a different interpretation.[20] This reference to precedent, even if it is from outside the national borders, can be seen as adding legitimacy to the decision, especially because the decision came from Britain, a country with which Australia maintains a very close connection. If one imagines the decision-making process as creating a ratio with the sources that contradict the judge in the numerator and the sources that support the judge in the denominator of the fraction, looking to foreign law increases the denominator and skews the balance of the ratio toward the desired outcome (Young 2005). However, in the case of *Khawar*, the High Court's attempt to add legitimacy did more to damage its reputation in Parliament than it did to influence political outcomes.

The inconsistency between the legislative directive and judicial precedent remains, and has led to confusion at the administrative level. A study conducted soon after the 2001 Act found that it had restricted women's ability to make successful gender-based claims (Hunter 2002). Another study of how the DIAC processes gender-based claims found there are still significant barriers to fair processing, but that the DIAC has worked to revise its gender guidelines in response to feedback from advocates. The authors of the study concluded that "in practice, the Guidelines are widely interpreted, and inconsistently applied" (McPherson et al 2011:343). Furthermore, a lawyer who frequently represents clients before the RRT explained that, in her experience, the RRT is very unpredictable when it comes to gender-based claims:

> One borderline issue is domestic violence against women. The way it's dealt with is quite inconsistent. Generally, the decision maker won't find a nexus, but they will find a lack of state protection. For example, I had two different Filipina cases in front of two different members. One was accepted and one rejected. (author interview, 11/19/2007)

The Australian story of adaptation to gender-based claims has placed Parliament and the Minister in direct conflict with the High Court. This collision has created confusion for the administrative agencies conducting the vast majority of RSDs, and has left the status of asylum seekers making gender-based claims in a tenuous position. The attempt by the High Court to bring Australian jurisprudence in line with the United Kingdom, Canada, and the UNHCR has not trickled down to influence administrative outcomes because Parliament continues to assert its sovereign prerogative to restrict. The administrative agencies do not have a clear enough sense of identity to adjudicate between the competing signals in a consistent way.

Conclusions

On the surface, the United States, Canada, and Australia all responded similarly to the global increase of gender-based asylum claims. All three made an initial nod to international standards by releasing guidance on the processing of gender-based asylum claims. Beyond that commonality, however, both the jurisprudence and the political responses to legal developments have diverged dramatically across countries. Taken together, these three distinct stories inspire skepticism about the idea that judicial globalization is a force inevitably pushing nations toward a common standard of justice. Instead, the trajectories of these three states on gender-based claims suggest that decision makers borrow international sources strategically to expand the sphere of conflict as well as their own power. Sometimes that strategizing results in compliance with international law, but just as often it does not.

The different tracks that gender-based asylum claims have taken in these three countries illustrate that the globalization of law is highly contingent on the domestic context, on the particular RSD regime in place in each country. In the United States, reference to international soft law has been minimal and symbolic, and the singular use of foreign precedent has been dismissive. The American RSD regime has largely ignored global legal developments, focusing in on its own domestic conflict and fragmentation, which provides more than enough perspectives to spark a vigorous debate about the direction gender-based asylum jurisprudence should take. The result, like the American RSD regime more generally, has been inconsistent, unpredictable, and politicized. In sharp contrast, the Canadian RSD regime has made a fairly uniform commitment to an internationalist response to gender-based asylum claims. Yet interestingly, the influence of UNHCR soft law has been from the bottom up, beginning in the administrative tribunal and then gradually being adopted by the federal courts, including the Supreme Court in the *Ward* decision. This story suggests that bureaucrats, as opposed to judges, can be agents of a judicial globalization that trickles up. In still another approach, the Australian RSD regime has turned gender-based asylum claims into the latest battle in a much larger war over judicial versus parliamentary power. The courts have been eager to seek legitimacy through judicial borrowing from respected foreign jurisdictions, rather than from the UNHCR. This tendency has revealed itself to be a strategic tool, rather than a nuanced review of international jurisprudence, and has not led to an increased acceptance of gender-based claims.

This case study illustrates how each distinct RSD regime has handled new claims that were not anticipated by the framers of the Convention. The responses of each receiving state are extremely significant for the women making asylum claims, and they are fascinating tests of the adaptability and flexibility of an RSD regime. However, gender-based asylum claims do not represent a large proportion of the RSD adjudications made in each state. In the next chapter, I examine the reaction of each RSD regime to claims from the biggest sending state in the world: the People's Republic of China. The two case studies combine to demonstrate that cross-national differences in RSD regimes are equally visible in state responses to common and uncommon types of claims.

Escaping the People's Republic of China: Chinese Asylum Claims in Three RSD Regimes

During the summer of 2008, the world turned its eyes to China. The most populous nation was playing host to the Olympic Games, and the stakes of making a good impression were very high; a dazzling opening ceremony and an impressive medal collection were key components in China's public relations campaign. Although the event may not have succeeded in convincing all observers that China is, in the words of President Hu Jintao, a "harmonious society."[1] there can be little doubt that China is in the midst of a momentous change on multiple fronts. The absolute power of the Communist Party has weakened in recent years, as the state has experienced the impact of a burgeoning civil society. Despite the global economic downturn that began in 2007, China's economy is still growing rapidly, and its trade relations with the West are robust. China is now an exporter of a vast proportion of the goods produced in the world.[2] Yet, despite China's changing global role, it also remains one of the top exporters of asylum seekers.

Worldwide, more than 24,000 citizens of the People's Republic of China filed asylum claims in 2012, making it the fourth most common source country for asylum seekers after Syria, Serbia, and Afghanistan (UNHCR 2013). Unlike many of the other countries that have been large-scale producers of asylum seekers over the years, China has remained steadily in the list of top source countries for several decades. Many of the people who flee China do so by leaving their homes on a business, student, or tourist visa and then filing an asylum claim after they reach their destination. Others are desperate enough to use more clandestine methods and pay exorbitant fees for smuggling or counterfeit documents.[3] Ironically, as the economic situation of many ordinary Chinese people has improved, fleeing to the West has become more possible. Snakeheads—organized crime rings that specialize in smuggling people out of China and into the West—have developed into a hugely profitable international black market that shows little signs of slowing (Keefe 2006, Kyle and Koslowski 2011).

Chinese asylum claims have been a dominant part of the refugee status determination regimes of the United States, Canada, and Australia for more than two decades (Table 8.1). Throughout the 1990s, China hovered in the top five source countries for asylum seekers in the United States, and for 13 of the past 14 years, China has been the number one source country for asylum applications (it sunk to second place for a year in 2001).[4] China was a top source country for asylum seekers in Canada during the late 1980s and early 1990s. After dropping behind Iran, Somalia, and Sri Lanka for several years, it reemerged again in 1998 and has been in the top five source countries every year since, usually coming second to Mexico, but reaching the top spot again in 2011 and 2012. Finally, China has been in the top four source countries for asylum seekers in Australia for well over a decade, and was the top source country for eight years during the 2000s. In sum, asylum seekers in the United States, Canada, and Australia are often, if not usually, Chinese. But, just because a country is a big producer of asylum seekers

Table 8.1 **Rank of China in Asylum Seeker Country of Origin, 1998 to 2012**

Year	United States	Canada	Australia
2012	1	1	4
2011	1	1	3
2010	1	2	2
2009	1	5	1
2008	1	5	1
2007	1	2	1
2006	1	2	1
2005	1	2	1
2004	1	3	1
2003	1	5	1
2002	1	4	1
2001	2	3	3
2000	1	3	3
1999	1	2	2
1998	3	3	2

Source: Compiled by author from UNHCR, *Asylum Levels and Trends in Industrialized Countries, 1998–2012*. Geneva: Switzerland.

does not mean that it produces large numbers of refugees in the eyes of receiving states. In other words, high application rates do not guarantee high success rates.

To be sure, some Chinese asylum seekers are high-profile journalists, activists, and dissidents with relatively clear-cut cases. According to human rights reports published by both the U.S. Department of State and independent monitoring organizations, the Chinese government still maintains tight restrictions on speech and press through intimidation, harassment, and arrest of those who are critical of the Communist party and its policies (Human Rights Watch 2008, 2012). Religious groups are heavily restricted and persecuted, and religious leaders frequently seek asylum in the West (U.S. Department of State 1999–2013). Since the Chinese government outlawed the popular spiritual movement Falun Gong in 1999, many practitioners have fled China, including the group's leader, Li Hongzhi, who now resides in New York City (Amnesty International 2000, Jacobs 2009). Ethnic minorities, such as Tibetans and Uighurs, are also subject to particular persecution. Further, the penal system is known for its rampant human rights abuses, including torture of prisoners and extrajudicial killings, and the government makes wide use of forced labor and reeducation camps. Thus, there are certainly asylum seekers from China whose experience fits neatly with the refugee definition.

However, a very large proportion of Chinese asylum seekers are ordinary people who have avoided these most oppressive tactics of the Chinese state. Their claims to refugee status are often very similar to one another and are based on experiences with policies of general application, rather than being targeted for specific individual characteristics. Many of these asylum seekers even come from the same towns (Zhang 2007, Liang and Ye 2011). The most notable example is the frequency of asylum claims based on the One-Child policy instituted by the Chinese government in 1979. This policy is enforced primarily through economic incentives (families with one child receive free education and health care) and propaganda campaigns (Hsu 1996, Greenhalgh 2010). However, as the 1980s progressed, the government in some regions began more aggressive strategies of enforcement, including compulsory birth control through intrauterine device insertion, forced sterilization and abortion, heavy fines, and intimidation by local officials. Experts estimate that during the 1980s and 1990s, the Chinese government forcibly sterilized millions of people per year, both male and female, as a punishment for having two children (Hsu 1996:322).[5] As China's economy has developed over the past two decades, the focus of the One-Child policy has shifted somewhat from a concern about pure quantity of births to a focus on producing "quality" babies; but, nevertheless, population control continues to be a key element of the invasive governance power of the Chinese state (Greenhalgh 2010).

Chinese asylum claims based on coercive population control represent a difficult dilemma for receiving states. On an abstract policy level, states must balance their obligation to protect those fleeing persecution, along with their powerful interest in controlling mass migration. At the level of individual RSD, the situation becomes much more complicated. First, there are several practical challenges. In such a vast country as China, there is a huge amount of local-level variation in the way the One-Child policy is implemented, including some methods that may constitute persecution and some that do not. In addition, because many claims are based on threats and a fear of future forced sterilization, they are almost impossible to corroborate.

Furthermore, as a matter of legal interpretation, it is not clear whether people who are affected by a general policy can be said to be refugees targeted for persecution on account of one of the five Convention grounds, even if that policy may violate broad human rights norms.[6] Ultimately, refugee status adjudicators must decide important legal questions about the difference between oppression and persecution, the standard for establishing that a fear of persecution is well-founded, and whether millions of people with little in common other than the desire to have more than one child can be considered a particular social group. In addition, they must determine credibility case by case with almost no evidence.

In Chapter 3, I argued that receiving states are becoming increasingly concerned about the use of asylum claims as a backdoor for economic migrants to gain access to the opportunities of advanced industrial democracies. This scenario puts pressure on RSD systems to sort through vast numbers of applicants who fall into the large gray area between those fleeing obvious persecution and those who are simply seeking a better life. Chinese asylum seekers fleeing the One-Child policy are a powerful illustration of the wide gray area between obvious Convention refugees and purely economic migrants. Unlike the question of how to handle gender-based claims, there is no specific guidance from international soft law via the UNHCR on where to draw the line on ambiguous cases, and so states vary widely in their response.

In Chapter 7, we saw that RSD regimes can differ significantly according to whether nations align their interpretations of the refugee definition with international soft law. We also saw that RSD regimes differ in terms of flexibility and responsiveness to innovative legal arguments. However, refugee claims based on domestic violence are relatively few and far between. The case study of Chinese coercive population control demonstrates that RSD regimes matter for very large numbers of asylum seekers. Furthermore, the Chinese story makes plain that the most challenging asylum claims do not necessarily become less challenging as they increase in frequency. Adjudicators must face these difficulties anew in each case, time and time again.

Linking Description to Numbers

It is not possible to provide hard numbers proving that different RSD regime types lead to drastically different outcomes in very similar cases, because when states report acceptance rates, they do not break them down by the type of claim made by the asylum seeker. In addition, acceptance rate is only one measure of the generosity of an RSD regime. Based on these numbers alone, we have no way of gauging the level of due process achieved in each country, or the accuracy of the process in verifying true claims versus detecting fraud. Nevertheless, the cross-national differences in asylum grant rate illustrated in Figure 8.1 suggest some notable trends. The first immediately apparent pattern is that the acceptance rates in the three countries run on three remarkably distinct tracks.

Overall, the Canadian picture is one that has always been more open to Chinese claims than other countries; Canada has accepted more than half the Chinese asylum seekers who have applied since 2000; in 2007, it accepted 65% of applicants (UNHCR Statistical Online Population Database). In the United States, the application volume and the acceptance rate have fluctuated quite a bit during the past decade and a half, and they seem to be unrelated to one another; the United States has decided between 10,000 and 18,000 Chinese cases each year, with a grant rate that has ranged from 16% in 1999 to a high of 42% in 2006. In Australia, the acceptance rate remained steady and incredibly low until

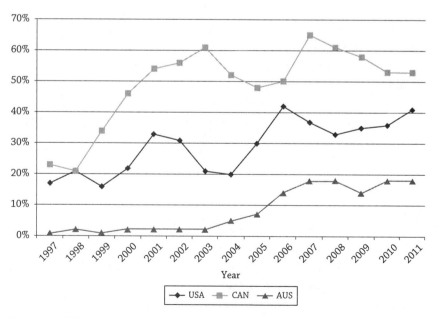

Figure 8.1 RSD Acceptance Rates for Chinese Applications (1997–2011).
Source: Compiled by author from the UNHCR Statistical Online Population Database.

very recently. It hovered between 1% and 2% from 1998 to 2003, then it began to climb slowly, and now seems to have plateaued around 18% (UNHCR Statistical Online Population Database). Despite the overall upward trend in acceptance rates, the three trajectories remain distinct and show no signs of convergence. These cross-national differences suggest that the RSD regime in which a claim is filed has a significant effect on the most important substantive outcome of an RSD regime: who gets to be a refugee.

In the remainder of this chapter, I use the empirical case of Chinese asylum seekers (and those who claim to be victims of China's coercive population control policies in particular) as a lens for examining how RSD regimes affect RSD outcomes. I illustrate why the United States, Canada, and Australia have each struck a different balance in the way that they adjudicate these types of claims based on the conceptualization of administrative justice in each place, and I examine the impact of three such different trajectories.

The United States

The position of the U.S. government on whether coercive population control is grounds for granting refugee status has changed over time according to the political winds. The ways in which this legal question has evolved across five different presidential administrations is illustrative of the institutional tug-of-war, adversarial legalism, and political wrangling that characterizes the American RSD regime. Initial reactions to the One-Child policy came from the political branches, but the issue has also been contested within the administrative agencies and the courts, illustrating the commitment the regime has made to hearing a multiplicity of perspectives.

In 1988, driven by ideological concerns about forced family planning, the Reagan Department of Justice issued a memorandum to the INS, instructing its RSD decision makers to give "careful consideration" to asylum seekers whose claims stemmed from fear of forced sterilization or abortion (Department of Justice 1988). However, in 1989, the BIA first considered the issue in a case called *Matter of Chang* (Interim Decision #3107, 1989), and in defiance of the DOJ memo, decided that, as a legal matter, coerced family planning did not amount to "persecution" under the refugee definition. The BIA also noted that such advisory memos were not binding on their agency. Thus, even from the earliest days of asylum claims making stemming from the One-Child policy, the American RSD regime issued contradictory decisions. The BIA and the EOIR began to deny asylum claims based on coercive population control, whereas the INS (a precursor to the Asylum Office) continued to follow the Department of Justice guidance to accept such claims.

After the Tiananmen Square massacre in 1989, the new administration of President George H.W. Bush became extremely active in encouraging defection from China, particularly by students. In fact, the Central Intelligence Agency was involved in helping some dissidents flee. As a way of making policy toward Chinese asylum seekers more internally consistent and more in tune with the generosity of the Bush administration's rhetoric toward those escaping China, President Bush issued an Executive Order in 1990 (No. 12,711 55 Fed. Reg. 13,897) that was even stronger than the memo issued by his predecessor. The order required refugee status adjudicators to give "enhanced consideration" to asylum seekers who expressed fear of persecution through forced sterilization or abortion.[7] Such an order had a more direct effect on the administrative agencies than the Reagan DOJ memo, especially after the Attorney General reiterated this order in a rule, known as the *1993 Final Rule*. This rule was issued days before the inauguration of President Clinton, and was presumably intended to cement the Bush administration's preferences before power switched hands. However, the new administration had a different position on the issue, and did not end up finalizing and publishing the rule in the Federal Register (Hsu 1996:341). Thus, the precedent of the BIA's *Matter of Chang* remained in place as President Clinton took office in January 1993.

The Bush rhetoric of openness toward Chinese immigration meant that hundreds of Chinese people were attempting entry into the United States each month by the early 1990s. However, the Clinton administration quickly made clear that it would be far less supportive of claims based on China's One-Child Policy.[8] When the *Golden Venture* freighter filled with 300 Chinese stowaways ran aground in New York harbor in spring 1993, and six people drowned in the freezing water while trying to swim to shore, INS officials were quoted as saying, "[T]he Bush Administration encouraged this. They sent a signal: If you get to the U.S., no matter in what manner, we'll accept your presence here."[9] In an attempt to discourage future smuggling, the INS decided to detain all the asylum seekers on the *Golden Venture* while their asylum claims were processed, the vast majority of which were based on fear of forced sterilization. The EOIR denied almost all of these applications, in sharp contrast to the high acceptance rates in previous years. For the most part, the federal courts upheld these decisions, finding that Bush's Executive Order had not overruled the BIA's decision in *Chang*, and that the 1993 Final Rule had not come into effect.[10]

At the time of the *Golden Venture* litigation, Congress was deep in the process of overhauling the asylum program as part of the Illegal Immigration Reform and Immigrant Responsibility Act of 1996. In contrast to the overall tenor of that legislation, which was highly restrictive, the Republican–controlled Congress wished to protect victims of forced abortion and sterilization for ideological reasons. To push past the Clinton administration's stonewalling on the issue,

Congress included a provision in the IIRIRA that overruled the BIA's *Chang* decision and the opinions of the federal courts. It amended the Immigration and Nationality Act's definition of a refugee to include explicit protection for victims of coercive population control policies, *and* those who feared such policies (Sicard 1999).[11] In a bizarre political compromise, however, the legislation limited the number of refugee visas that could be granted on this basis to 1,000 per year, far less than the overall demand (Immigration And Nationality Act, Section 101(a)(42), subsection (5)).

A few months after the passage of IIRIRA in 1996, the BIA addressed these legislative changes in their decision in the *Matter of X-P-T, Applicant* (Interim Decision #3299). The BIA concluded that the *Matter of Chang* had been "superseded by the new law," and granted asylum to a woman who had been forcibly sterilized by the Chinese government as a punishment for having two additional children beyond the one child limit. A few months later, the BIA also granted asylum to a male applicant whose wife had been sterilized, but who remained in China (*Matter of C-Y-Z, Applicant* [Interim Decision #3319, 1997]). In that case, the BIA interpreted the IIRIRA to include spouses of people affected by coercive population control measures. The decision had a huge impact on the number of people eligible for asylum, because the vast majority of Chinese asylum seekers were men who had fled alone in the hope of sponsoring their wives to come later. Since the *C-Y-Z* decision, the number of people seeking asylum each year based on coercive population control measures continued to far exceed the 1,000-person cap, leading the government to issue additional conditional asylum grants. By 2005, the backlog of people waiting for refugee visas based on coercive population control measures had grown so high that Congress removed the cap in the REAL ID Act of 2005.

The issue was not settled, however, because by 2006 the question of whether spouses could be granted asylum based on the persecution experienced by their partners had reached the federal courts. In the case of *Shi Liang Lin (et al.) v. Gonzales* (416 F.3d 184, 2007), the 2nd Circuit concluded that the wording of the IIRIRA provision was un ambiguous about whether it applied to partners. Because the statutory instructions to the administrative agency were clear, the court had the power to interpret the statute itself, rather than grant the agency deference under the *Chevron* standard.[12] The court, in an *en banc* (although not unanimous) opinion, concluded that the wording of a statute clearly did not extend to partners. The majority opinion analyzed the words of the amendment written by Congress and argued:

> This language refers to individuals who have failed or refused to undergo (i.e., "submit to") a procedure affecting *their own bodies*. Under the language used by Congress, having someone else, such as one's spouse,

undergo a forced procedure does not suffice to qualify an individual for refugee status. (*Shi Liang Lin (et al.) v. Gonzales* [2007])

Aside from the boldness of contradicting longstanding BIA precedent, this decision also created splits in the Circuits—subnational variation at the federal court level—on an important question of statutory interpretation. In contrast to the 2nd Circuit, which is based in New York state, the 5th, 6th, 7th, and 9th Circuits have all adopted the C-Y-Z standard of including spouses.[13] To complicate the matter even further, these Circuits are also split amongst themselves on whether nonmarried partners can be included in the C-Y-Z reasoning, something the BIA does not favor.[14] Thus, currently, an unmarried partner of a forced sterilization or abortion victim may be eligible for asylum in some parts of the country and not others. According to federal courts in the 2nd Circuit, where the majority of Chinese asylum claims are filed, only the victim herself is eligible. However, because the EOIR immigration courts still follow the BIA logic, which is more generous, many men who file claims in the New York region are still being granted asylum on the basis of their partner's persecution. This situation makes outcomes of asylum claims based on coercive population control extremely unpredictable and inconsistent, even among applications that were initially filed in the same office.

Although the 2nd Circuit took a more restrictive view of the refugee definition than the BIA in *Shi Liang Lin*, it engaged in another high-profile contradiction of the BIA by taking a much more inclusive stance on the issue of forced marriage in China. In the case of *Gao v. Gonzales* (440 F.3d 62, 2006), the 2nd Circuit Court of Appeals granted asylum to a young woman from China whose parents had sold her into an arranged marriage to pay off their debts. Her husband was abusive and, when she tried to leave him, he used his family connections in the local police department to force her to stay. The Court disagreed with the IJ and the BIA that her persecution was not based on one of the grounds listed in the refugee definition, and, in an interpretive move very much in line with Canadian gender jurisprudence, argued that she was a member of a particular social group—women in a part of China where the practice of forced marriage is common, and is enforced, or at least tolerated, by local authorities.

In March 2007, the Solicitor General filed a petition for *certiorari* with the Supreme Court, asking it to consider its third asylum case in five years. In the petition, the Solicitor General wrote:

> The 2nd Circuit here violated the same established principles of judicial review of agency action that supported summary reversal in *Thomas* and *Ventura*. The Court committed those errors, moreover, in the course of establishing a novel and potentially sweeping interpretation of the INA that could have far-reaching implications for the Executive Branch's

enforcement of immigration law in the highly sensitive context of culturally diverse approaches to marriage. (petition no. 06-1264: *Gonzales
v. Gao*. Paul D. Clement, Solicitor General)

In October 2007, the Supreme Court granted *certiorari* to the case, then called
Keisler v. Gao (128 S. Ct. 345, 2007), but chose not to hear arguments in the case.
Instead, the Supreme Court summarily vacated the decision of the 2nd Circuit,
remanding it for a rehearing in light of the *Thomas* decision. Such efforts on the
part of the Supreme Court to maintain some semblance of consistency on asylum
cases by reigning in activist circuit court decisions sends a message regarding the
particular issue at hand. However, they are unlikely to have an impact on the larger
problem of ongoing inconsistencies. Supreme Court decisions come few and far
between, whereas the Asylum Office, EOIR, and federal courts are constantly
deciding cases that raise new issues, and deciding them in contradictory ways.

The story of Chinese asylum claims based on coercive population control is
a very typical illustration of the character of the American RSD regime more
generally, as it was described in Chapter 4. Policy decisions and legal outcomes
are closely intertwined and highly variable. In a recent study conducted by the
Transactional Records Access Clearinghouse center at Syracuse University,
researchers found the grant rates of New York IJs deciding Chinese cases were
extremely similar to their overall grant rates for all cases. Judges' acceptance
rates varied widely, but Chinese cases did not seem to differ from the general
pattern that each individual judge had formed in his or her decision making
(TRAC 2005). These data suggest that Chinese cases tend to fall in the gray zone
between obvious yeses and obvious no's, allowing decision maker discretion to
kick in. High levels of discretion are also possible because the American RSD
regime leaves many legal issues unsettled, such that a person's chances of being
granted refugee status depend heavily on where they crossed the border, and can
also change from year to year. The Supreme Court has weighed in and resolved
splits in the circuits on matters of legal interpretation, but although it has been
actively involved in policing the institutional battles between the Courts of
Appeals and the administrative agencies, its involvement seems to have done
little to ease those tensions. Thus, RSD outcomes for Chinese asylum seekers are
as unpredictable as ever. The commitment to multiplicity has overwhelmed the
regime's capacity for achieving consistency across similar cases.

Canada

The Canadian response to asylum claims based on coercive population control contrasts with the American story for two main reasons. First, because

Canada's RSD regime is so centralized and the administrative agency is so powerful, there has been far less jurisprudence than in the United States. Canadian courts tend to defer to the expertise of the IRB, and usually decline to get involved. The second way in which the Canadian path is different is that, from the earliest days, the question of whether victims of forced sterilization can be considered refugees has been linked to Canada's pioneering stance on gender-based refugee claims. Despite the fact that many Chinese applicants are male, Canada's gender and China stories converged early on when the IRB subsumed the coercive population control issue under its gender guidelines. Canada's guidelines, in listing the particular forms of persecution women face, specifically mention forced abortion and sterilization, and protection from these forms of persecution was soon extended to men (IRB 1993). In contrast to this efficient linkage of related issues, the way in which coercive population control claims were initially handled in both the United States and Australia had almost nothing to do with the concurrent evolution of gender-based claims in those countries.

Only a few weeks after the IRB released Canada's gender guidelines in 1993, a case dealing with the issue of forced sterilization reached the Canadian federal courts for the first time. That case had been decided at the IRB before the gender guidelines had been conceived and before the controversy over the *Nada* case. It concerned a Chinese woman named Ting Ting Cheung, who chose to have a second baby in contravention of the One-Child policy, and who fled in secret when she discovered she would be forcibly sterilized and possibly imprisoned for her defiance. When in Canada, she also applied for refugee status for her baby daughter, who would be persecuted as an illegal child if they were forced to return to China. When her case was first heard, the decision maker at the IRB did not find her to be a Convention refugee, because the IRB found that as a general and logical law, the One-Child policy did not constitute persecution. As the board member put it:

> I do not read in the evidence a persecutory intent on the part of the Chinese government, simply a desperate desire to come to terms with the situation that poses a major threat to its modernization plans. It is not a policy born out of caprice, but out of economic logic. (quoted in *Cheung v. Canada* [Minister of Employment and Immigration] [2 F.C. 314, 1993])

By the time Cheung's case reached the Federal Court of Appeals, the IRB's gender guidelines had been issued. Although guidelines for administrative decision makers are not legally binding on courts, the Federal Court of Appeals showed great deference to both the tribunal and to international law. In its opinion in *Cheung v. Canada (Minister of Employment and Immigration)* (2 F.C. 314, 1993), the three-judge panel declared:

> The forced sterilization of women is a fundamental violation of basic human rights. It violates Articles 3 and 5 of the United Nations Universal Declaration of Human Rights...The forced sterilization of a woman is a serious and totally unacceptable violation of her security of the person. Forced sterilization subjects a woman to cruel, inhuman, and degrading treatment.

The Court found both Cheung and her daughter to be Convention refugees and stated, in an obvious reference to the words of the gender guidelines, that "sometimes the operation of a law of general application can constitute persecution."

Because the Federal Court of Appeals had relied so heavily on the gender connection in the *Cheung* case, when it was faced with a similar case involving a Chinese male who feared forced sterilization, it was in a difficult logical situation. In its opinion in the 1995 case of *Kwong Hung Chan v. Canada (Minister of Employment and Immigration)*, the Federal Court of Appeals confused the jurisprudence tremendously by ruling against Chan on the grounds that forced sterilization was a law of general application and did not constitute persecution under the Convention. On appeal to the Supreme Court of Canada, the Court did not find that Chan's fear of sterilization was "well founded." Because his persecution was unlikely, the Court declined to rule on the question of whether men who feared forced sterilization could be a particular social group (*Chan v. Canada (Minister of Employment and Immigration)* [3 S.C.R 593, 1995]).

In the aftermath of that decision, the question of whether males who faced forced sterilization should be considered Convention refugees was left wide open in Canada. But, instead of the continued litigation that characterizes the American RSD regime, the IRB acted as a typical professional judgment-style agency to fill the legal void and produce consistent outcomes. In 1997, the IRB published a precedent-setting decision in which they considered the application of a Chinese man who had violated the One-Child policy and feared persecution from local authorities as a result. The IRB considered his case in light of the *Cheung* case, which had granted asylum to a woman under similar circumstances. In its decision, the IRB argued that for it "to limit *Cheung* to women would have been to suggest that the reproductive rights of men were not on a par with those of women" (IRB decision no. U93-08191, Mora, April 21, 1997). Thus, they concluded the claimant was a member of a particular social group: men in China who face forced sterilization.

Since 1997, the issue has, amazingly, not returned to the federal courts for clarification, and the IRB has continued to consider male victims of forced sterilization to be members of a particular social group (IRB decision no. V99-03480, April 11, 2000). The deference shown by the Canadian federal courts to tribunal-level innovation means that each new issue is not litigated endlessly, as it is in the United States. Also notable is the deference shown to the tribunal by both Parliament and CIC. In sharp contrast to the American story, both of these political entities sat out and allowed the issue of coercive population control asylum claims to be handled as an administrative matter. Thus, the position of the Canadian RSD regime on coercive population control has remained extremely stable over time.

As we saw with the examples of the Czech Roma and Mexican asylum cases in Chapter 5, the professional judgment model of deference to administrative policymaking and the firm commitment to prioritizing efficiency does not always lead to generous outcomes. However, because the timing of the cases related to Chinese coercive population control linked them to the IRB's gender guidelines, the result was a line of decisions that is remarkably generous compared with other countries. The IRB had already chosen to base its gender policymaking on prevailing international human rights standards, and Chinese population control cases got swept along with gender cases more generally.

Australia

Chinese asylum claims have been central to the development of Australia's RSD regime, and have presented difficult dilemmas for politicians, decision makers, and judges from the regime's earliest days. The Australian government has been extremely conscious of China's large population and its proximity, and lawmakers have exhibited a constant concern about striking the right balance between fulfilling international protection obligations and discouraging mass migration. In other words, migration policy considerations have dominated the story of Chinese asylum claims in Australia. When strong parliamentary involvement is combined with a weak administrative agency and highly textualist court interpretations, the result is that very, very few people are successful in making asylum claims based on coercive population control.

At the time of the Tiananmen Square massacre in 1989, Australian Prime Minister Bob Hawke spoke openly in Parliament about his "outrage at the massive and indiscriminate slaughter" of innocent protesters (House of Representative, Parliamentary Debates, June 15 1989). However, the Australian government was somewhat uncertain about the proper policy response; it wanted to respond to public concern about the treatment of Chinese students, but without expanding the interpretation of the refugee definition to accommodate them. The Prime Minister initially announced that all Chinese people living in Australia on student or temporary work visas would be allowed to extend their visas for one year.[15] However, after several extensions of these temporary visas and years of uncertainty, the Australian government finally decided to grant all Chinese people who had been present in Australia prior to June 1989 permanent residence—approximately 40,000 people (DIMA 1997). Anyone who arrived after 1989 had to follow the normal channels.

This situation ran in parallel with, but was not directly connected to, the RSD system, which was just becoming established at that time. The same year that the Australian government was weighing its response to the thousands of Chinese students wishing to extend their visas, the High Court heard its first major case dealing with the refugee definition: *Chan Yee Kin v. Minister for Immigration and Ethnic Affairs* (HCA 62, 1989). In this decision, the Court stuck closely to the text of the refugee definition and made clear that to be eligible for refugee status, an individual has to have more than a fear of persecution. For that fear to be considered well-founded, they must have a "real chance" of persecution if they were returned to the home country. The test laid out in this case remains a foundational part of Australian refugee jurisprudence today, and establishes a higher bar for demonstrating that one's fear is "well-founded" than the standard in either the United States or Canada.

After the Tiananmen amnesty of 1993, a body of case law eventually developed around the issue of China's One-Child policy, leading up to the High Court's 1997 decision in *Applicant A v. Minister of Immigration and Ethnic Affairs* (HCA 4, 1997). The long and adversarial trajectory of the *Applicant A* case is very interesting—a Chinese couple applied for asylum because they feared forced sterilization by the Chinese government, but their initial application was rejected by the DIAC. The couple appealed to the RRT, which overturned the DIAC decision and granted them refugee status. Then, in an uncommon move, the Minister of Immigration appealed this positive decision to the Federal Court, presumably in the hope that the Federal Court would reverse the RRT and set a restrictive precedent on the matter. Instead, Justice Sackville of the Federal Court upheld the RRT decision, so the Minister appealed to the Full Federal Court, which reversed Sackville to support the DIAC's rejection of the couple (*Applicant A v Minister for Immigration and Ethnic Affairs*, FCA, 1994). The applicant then applied to the High Court for an appeal of this decision.

Meanwhile, the Federal Court decision in favor of the applicant had created such a public controversy that Parliament, in a move typical of its legislative activism on asylum issues more generally, drafted a bill in response. The proposed legislation was inspired by concerns among both the public and members of Parliament about opening the floodgates to a country with so many people in a similar situation (Crock 2004). Senator McKiernan, in urging passage of the bill, stated: "I would anticipate that hundreds of thousands of people from China and some other Asian countries will shortly be making plans to get to Australia" (quoted in Crock 2004).

The act was never put to a vote in Parliament because, by that time, the High Court ruled in *Applicant A v. Minister for Immigration and Ethnic Affairs* (190 CLR 225, 1997). The decision hinged on the fact that the couple in question had claimed that forced sterilization was widely practiced in their province, and if they returned to China, they would be targeted for this procedure. The majority of the Court concluded that because there were literally millions of Chinese people who would fall into the category of potential victims of forced sterilization, "to construe the term 'particular social group' in that way would make it an almost all-encompassing safety net" (*Applicant A*). In another strict textual reading of the refugee definition, the majority of the Court argued that it would be circular to call people who feared forced sterilization members of a particular social group. China's One-Child policy was a general law, and those who feared the policy were not persecuted on account of their fear. Thus, potential victims of forced sterilization in China lacked the critical nexus between fear and one of the five grounds for persecution that would make them eligible for refugee protection.

The logic of *Applicant A* is still dominant in Australian refugee law, but it has been tempered by a High Court decision on the eligibility for refugee status of so-called "black children"—children born in contravention of the One-Child policy (*Chen Shi Hai v. Minister for Immigration and Multicultural Affairs* [HCA 19, 2000]). In a similar path to the High Court as occurred in the *Applicant A* decision, the Minister of Immigration and Citizenship appealed a positive decision by the RRT. The Federal Court of Australia overturned the RRT decision, basing its opinion on the *Applicant A* decision. However, the child asylum seeker, Chen Shi Hai, appealed his case to the High Court. In April 2000, the High Court affirmed the decision of the RRT, that "black children" can be considered a particular social group in China because they are refused basic education and health case, and face social discrimination based on a characteristic they cannot change—their birth order. Although *Chen Shi Hai* is technically more generous than the *Applicant A* decision, both opinions rely heavily on a technical, textual reading of the refugee definition as it has been adopted into Australian law, and are logically consistent with one another.

The textualist approach of the Australian High Court is generally compatible with the concerns about floodgates, expressed so frequently by members of Parliament. The case of *Chen Shi Hai* illustrates, however, that the High Court is not simply bowing to the will of the legislative branch. In contrast to the proactive policymaking and legal interpretation of the Canadian IRB, and the bold precedent setting of the American BIA, it is noteworthy that the RRT is not a

key player in the Australian story. It is almost as if cases just pass through the
RRT on their way to court; if a decision is negative, it gets appealed by the applicant, and if it is positive (and potentially precedent setting), it gets appealed by
the Minister. In the story of Chinese asylum claims based on coercive population control measures, as in the Australian RSD regime more generally, the
administrative tribunal is a powerless fulcrum in a highly charged battle between
Parliament and the courts.

Conclusions

Many commentators, advocates, and scholars frequently observe that when it
comes to a particular subpolicy area of migration, such as refugee resettlement
or admission of asylum seekers, receiving states tend to fall on a spectrum ranging from inclusive to restrictive. However, without systematically examining the
way in which different states actually adjudicate very similar cases from the same
country of origin, it is not possible to determine whether cross-national variation in overall acceptance rates is due to the relative generosity of each receiving
state or some other factor related to the makeup of the asylum seeker population.
Because this chapter focuses on a specific group of asylum seekers from a single
country of origin, the asylum seeker population is held reasonably constant, as
is the basic definition used to identify refugees in the United States, Canada,
and Australia. Thus, this case study illustrates how and why—when it comes to
asylum, at least—countries fall where they do on the migration restrictiveness
spectrum. The concept of an RSD regime gives us a mechanism for explaining
this kind of variation. In fact, this chapter has demonstrated that, in a real sense
and on a large scale, who can be a refugee is literally different depending on the
country in which an asylum seeker lands.

   In a way, the Canadian story is the most counterintuitive, because an area
of asylum claims that is dominated by men came to be easily subsumed under
gender guidelines through an odd chain of events. The commitment to consistency, simplicity, and bureaucratic expertise that permeated the Canadian
case stands in sharp contrast to the total disconnect between the jurisprudence
around gender and coercive population control in the U.S. story. Consider, for a
moment, the U.S. 2nd Circuit Court of Appeals, which was activist to the point
of being sanctioned by the Supreme Court for linking a Chinese forced marriage
case to gender-based asylum jurisprudence, but made no connection between
forced abortion and the same line of gender-based asylum cases. In Australia, the
courts focused on the narrow question of a nexus between the persecution and
a Convention ground, so the issue of whether victims of such measures could be

considered a particular social group never came up, except in the case of a very particular group—so-called black children.

Political pressure to limit large-scale migration exists in all three countries, but in the United States that pressure has been eclipsed alternatively by political battles over the abortion issue, struggles over administrative agency authority, and conflicting court interpretations. In Canada, the political will to limit the number of refugees admitted each year was, in this case, overshadowed by the desire to be a pioneer and a leader in international human rights norm diffusion about gender. Then, the IRB's commitment to bureaucratic efficiency logically linked the population control issue to gender. In addition, deference to the administrative tribunal that is built into the system limits both political influence over, and court intervention into, the Canadian process. Finally, in Australia, political fears about unbridled Chinese migration have dominated the regime, but the power of the courts to temper that influence is not nonexistent. The High Court has shown that its commitment to legally consistent decision making is ultimately more powerful than its willingness to go along with government policy priorities in every instance.

The Chinese cases discussed in this chapter raise questions about the ways in which human rights law and refugee law may or may not be linked. The former was designed to protect people from degradation, even if it takes a generalized form, and the latter was originally designed to protect people who have been specifically targeted. These two approaches to protection have become blurred as the exilic model of defining a refugee becomes less dominant in the post-Cold War period. Lots of asylum claims are made by those who are not obvious Convention refugees, but who are nonetheless fleeing human rights violations, and similar countries have drawn the line distinguishing the two in different places. Lines get drawn in the way they do because each nation has struck its own balance between competing forces, and prioritizes a particular way of making decisions. In the next chapter, I extend this conclusion to examine the impact of RSD regimes on those whose requests for protection fall outside of the refugee definition, but whom the state may nonetheless wish to protect.

CHAPTER 9

Complementary Protection in a Complicated World

In the September/October 2008 issue of *Foreign Affairs*, the UN High Commissioner for Refugees, Antonio Guterres, reached out to the world's policy elites with an appeal. He wrote, "UNHCR confronts a disconnect between the limited formal mandate of protecting refugees and the immense scope of forced displacement around the world today" (Guterres 2008:91). He predicted that climate change, natural disasters, famine, and unstable states would be the main causes of displacement in the 21st century and asked receiving states to develop a new "humanitarian protection compact" to meet the needs of those migrants who are forced from their homes, but are beyond the scope of the 1951 Convention (Guterres 2008:92). As Guterres articulated, the practical reality of forced migration today is that, increasingly, people around the world are fleeing generalized violence and natural disaster rather than individualized persecution. To put it another way, many of the world's displaced people may look like refugees or feel like refugees to the average observer, but are not refugees in the technical sense of the word as it is used in international law. Thus, they may not be found eligible for refugee protection by the states in which they seek refuge.

In response to this shift in the causes of displacement, the UNHCR has expanded its own mandate over time, moving beyond Convention refugees to include under its purview assistance for a much broader range of displaced people (Martin 2010:29). Similarly, some asylum seeker destination states have responded to changing global circumstances and international calls to action by developing various forms of what is known as *complementary protection*. Complementary protection is not a precise legal term, and refers to a range of state practices, including granting permanent residency based on international agreements such as the Convention Against Torture, or providing protection from deportation for reasons that are purely domestic in origin and not based on international legal standards, or, lastly, offering temporary protection for those fleeing crisis, natural disaster, or war. In some states, the response to new and different requests for protection has been much more comprehensive, coordinated, and streamlined than in others. In these states, the divide between refugee law and other areas of international human rights law seems to be shrinking, as the various reasons for seeking protection are treated together. In other states, the divide continues to be very sharp, and Convention refugee protection remains the only significant form of permanent asylum available.

This chapter compares the ways in which the United States, Canada, and Australia have made complementary protection available to people within their borders who may not be eligible for refugee visas, but may still have a compelling need to avoid deportation to their home country. Perhaps not surprisingly, I find that the approach each state has taken to complementary protection is driven by the tenor of the larger RSD regime, which is a product of national conceptions of administrative justice. Because the complementary protection scheme is incorporated into the existing institutional landscape, the outcomes of protection decisions depend heavily on domestic variables such as centralization of policymaking, interbranch dynamics, and the insulation of administrative decision-making agencies from political tinkering and judicial review.

Chapter 7 examined the way different RSD regimes respond to new types of asylum claims; and Chapter 8 examined responses to the increasing number of ambiguous asylum claims. This chapter demonstrates how cross-national differences in RSD regimes have a broad impact on a state's entire protection system. In other words, RSD regimes matter for vast numbers of people—even those who are clearly not refugees in the official sense of the word. Just as the scope of the term *refugee* is dependent on national context, so is the scope of the larger category—persons deserving of protection from deportation.

Complementary Protection

The concept of complementary protection is controversial because it highlights the ways in which states and advocates alike have often treated refugee law as quite separate from (or even superior to) human rights law more generally. On one side of the debate are the proponents of complementary protection, who do not see an inherent tension between refugee law and human rights law. For example, McAdam (2010) views refugee law as a specialized area *within* human rights law, one that should complement other human rights instruments and be used in tandem with them. Her rich analysis of the historical record suggests that the original intent of the 1951 Convention's framers was to create a "dynamic, living human rights instrument" that would evolve and expand over time (McAdam 2007:37, 2010:4).

Goodwin-Gill, author of the indispensible reference book *The Refugee in International Law*, has also taken this unitary perspective. In the third edition of the book, McAdam joined Goodwin-Gill as a coauthor, and together they argue that complementary protection rests on several sources in international law (Goodwin-Gill and McAdam 2007:296–354). First, the 1976 International Covenant on Civil and Political Rights (ICCPR) and the 1948 Universal Declaration of Human Rights suggest that people should not be returned to places where they will be subject to inhumane treatment. Second, the 1984 Convention Against Torture (CAT) includes the commitment in Article 3 that states should not force people to return to a place where they are likely to be tortured. Finally, these treaties are linked to the Convention on the Status of Refugees via Article 33, which is the *nonrefoulement* provision—the prohibition of expelling or returning refugees to territories where their life or freedom would be threatened.

In addition, proponents of complementary protection point out that two major regional charters on refugees have adopted a much broader refugee definition than the 1951 Convention. The Organization of African Unity (OAU) Convention of 1969 defines refugees as people displaced by "external aggression, occupation, foreign domination or events seriously disturbing public order in either part or the whole of his country of origin" (Article 1.2). The Cartagena Declaration on Refugees of 1984 defines refugees as "persons who have fled their country because their lives, safety or freedom have been threatened by generalized violence, foreign aggression, internal conflicts, massive violation of human rights or other circumstances which have seriously disturbed public order" (Article 3.3). Proponents of complementary protection advocate that states incorporate processes to assess claims of this nature into their RSD regimes because "nonrefoulement under customary international law encompasses non-return to persecution *as well as* to cruel, inhuman, or degrading treatment or punishment" (Goodwin-Gill and McAdam 2007:351; emphasis in original).

For its part, the UNHCR has gradually come around to the idea that its mandate includes advocating for an international complementary protection regime. Although the Executive Committee has reaffirmed on a number of occasions that the 1951 Convention is the "foundation" and "cornerstone of the international refugee protection regime," in recent years the agency has also taken to insisting that "the human rights base of the Convention roots it quite directly in the broader framework of human rights instruments of which it is an integral part" (UNHCR 2001, 2009). In this way, the UNHCR seems to have adopted the Goodwin-Gill/McAdam unitary approach to the relationship between international refugee law and human rights law. Although some states have, historically, offered protection to people who fell outside the Convention definition of a refugee for a variety of reasons, by the 1990s the UNHCR began to push states to offer protection more consistently and expansively. Beginning in 1994, the UNHCR explicitly defined the people within its purview using the expansive OAU and Cartagena definitions, not the definition from Article 1 of the Convention (UNHCR 1994). Since 2005, UNHCR has recommended that states integrate their RSD systems to include complementary protection as part of one "comprehensive procedure" (UNHCR 2005).

This vision of complementary protection is based on the growing body of international human rights law described above, instead of a collection of ad hoc, strategically motivated protection decisions by states. Thus, as the High Commissioner's appeal in *Foreign Affairs* makes clear, states are increasingly expected to extend protection beyond Convention refugees in order to be considered to have met their protection obligations under international law. From the UNHCR's perspective, this stance does not conflict with its continued insistence on a clear conceptual distinction between refugees and other types of migrants (Feller 2005, Crisp 2008). Rather, the agency maintains the distinction between refugees and other migrants simply by encouraging an expansion of the refugee category. It is strategically necessary for the UNHCR to promote the distinction between categories to avoid being seen as interfering in migration policymaking, which is closely linked to sovereignty.

Nevertheless, not all states are equally receptive to arguments for complementary protection that are grounded in international law. Because of the connection between migration policy and sovereignty, when ideas about complementary protection were first articulated during the late 1980s and early 1990s, some forced migration scholars were skeptical about the possibilities for state-level compliance. As an early example of realist skepticism about international arguments, Hailbronner (1986) famously wrote that such an expansive view was "wishful legal thinking" and suggested that states would not be willing to offer such wide-reaching protection consistently. Almost 30 years later, this initial reaction remains an accurate assessment of the response of most states. Acceptance of complementary protection norms is an area in which state-level variation remains high, and protection options are likely to be adopted only if they are integrated into a domestic political context.

Because complementary protection statuses usually come with fewer rights and benefits, and reduced possibilities for naturalization compared with full refugee status, their increasing prominence raises an important empirical question (Hathaway 1991, Zetter 2007). Does the introduction of complementary protection measures divert potential refugees away from full protection and toward weaker, temporary measures? Or, does complementary protection allow for more displaced people to achieve protection than would have been possible in a system in which RSD is the only protection option? The following case studies suggest that, when states are interested in doing so, complementary protection can expand protection. Further, and somewhat ironically, complementary protection is most likely to do so in states in which the reading of the refugee definition itself is already expansive.

United States

Like its RSD regime, the American complementary protection regime is incredibly complex and multifaceted. There are almost a dozen different forms of relief from deportation that have been layered onto existing legislative frameworks over time, leading to an almost incomprehensible web of legal categories. Some forms of relief lead to permanent residency status; many do not. Some forms are connected to international legal obligations and others stem from domestic politics or foreign policy objectives. As with the American RSD regime, the broader world of humanitarian protection in the United States involves a lot of different players, is highly legalistic, and has varied over time and presidential administrations. As Kanstroom (2010:118) recently put it, "this patchwork quilt of specific protective measures evidences certain deep underlying humanitarian urges that have garnered specific political support." In other words, the complexity of the system is not the product of a holistic or coordinated vision for protection, but of the ad hoc nature of migration policymaking in a fragmented institutional landscape.

In fact, the United States has a major complementary protection avenue that predates its RSD system. Before the 1980 Refugee Act established an RSD process based on the Convention definition, American immigration law included a provision that would prevent deportation of anyone who could demonstrate a "clear probability of persecution" if returned to their home country (Immigration and Nationality Act, Section 243(h)). This provision is called *withholding of removal*, and prior to 1980, it was purely discretionary and was not linked to a path to permanent residency or eventual citizenship. When the Refugee Act inserted an RSD system based on the 1951 Convention definition into American law, it layered this new RSD process onto the existing framework, leaving the withholding of removal component intact. The only change the Refugee Act made to the withholding of removal category was to shift it from a discretionary form of relief to a mandatory form of protection. This change was made in order to comply with Article 33 of the UN Convention—the *non-refoulement* pledge.

The relationship between the new asylum provision and the old withholding provision in the law was the subject of confusion for several years after the 1980 Act was passed. There is no evidence in the historical record surrounding the passage of the Act to suggest that Congress deliberately intended to create two distinct forms of protection. Rather, this outcome seems to be an oversight; the asylum provision was barely discussed in the hearings on the bill because it was eclipsed by a focus on overseas resettlement issues—in particular, the immediate crisis in Southeast Asia (Martin 1990, Hamlin and Wolgin 2012). It took two separate Supreme Court decisions to resolve the question of whether the "clear probability of persecution" standard of proof for withholding of removal was different from the new "well-founded fear of persecution" standard the Act had created for RSD (*INS vs. Stevic*, [467 U.S. 407, 1984] and *INS vs. Cardoza-Fonseca*, [480 U.S. 421, 1987]). Initially, the BIA found that the two standards were "not meaningfully different and, in practical application, converge" (*Matter of Acosta* [Interim Decision #2986, 1985]). By this logic, withholding of removal had been subsumed into the new category of refugee protection. However, in *Cardoza-Fonseca*, the Supreme Court concluded (without reference to any supporting evidence) that because Congress had left the two forms of relief separate from one another when they passed the 1980 Act, they intended for them to be two distinct forms of relief.

Today, withholding of removal requests are considered at the same time as an asylum claim in the same hearing, but they have split standards. Withholding of removal has a greater burden of proof, and still does not result in a full legal status. Thus, it becomes relevant when it is used as a safety net for asylum seekers who do not meet the refugee definition but can show that they will be persecuted if deported. Most CAT claims come under the withholding of removal category, and today the CAT "is part of every U.S. refugee advocate's strategic arsenal" (Legomsky 2009:135). However, for those people who may not qualify for either refugee status or withholding (usually because they have a criminal record and thus are ineligible for other forms of relief), since 1998 it has been possible to make a direct application for a deferral of removal under the CAT. The United States became a party to the CAT in several stages, but eventually wrote it into law in 1998 (Foreign Affairs Reform and Restructuring Act of 1998 s. 2242). Deferral of removal is a temporary status that can be withdrawn, and still has some exceptions for those who have been involved in terrorist activities or persecution. However, its implementation has brought the United States very closely in line with its obligations under the CAT (Garcia 2004).

Beyond withholding of removal and the CAT, there are many other forms of relief available under U.S. law that are completely outside the RSD system and are not triggered by any international legal obligation. Prior to 1996, noncitizens in deportation proceedings could have their deportation suspended if they could show that their deportation would lead to extreme hardship for them or for their family. When the Republican Congress passed the IIRIRA in 1996, they changed the standard. Since that time, people may only apply for cancelation of removal, which is available to those who can show that their removal would cause "exceptional and extremely unusual hardship" to an American citizen or permanent resident family member (8 USC s.1229b). After this change in the law, the BIA soon found that this new standard was much more stringent, leading to a rapid reduction in the number of people who were eligible for this kind of relief (*In re Francisco Javier Monreal* [23 I. & N. Dec. 56, 2001]).

In contrast to this retraction of humanitarian protection, during the 1990s Congress also created two new forms of relief. First, in 1990, a Democratic–controlled Congress codified the new category of temporary protected status (TPS). This is not an individualized status, but a group-based safe haven for people from particular countries of origin that are in the midst of a conflict or natural disaster. It is a very powerful foreign policy tool because it can be exercised quickly to help large numbers of people. Prior to 1990, presidents used to offer something similar, known as Extended Voluntary Departure (EVD). However, EVD was a contentious program, with "a nagging separation of powers question," because Congress was not involved in deciding when to invoke it (Legomsky 2009:137). When Congress developed TPS in 1990, the relief was given a much more official standard. However, some controversies have arisen regarding TPS. First, some immigration restrictionists in Congress have opposed the granting of TPS to anyone from Central America for fear it "would serve as a magnet" and open the floodgates to potential new refugee flows (Legomsky 2009:5). Second, some refugee advocates have raised concerns that the United States has used TPS, which does not lead to citizenship, instead of conducting RSD (Martin et al. 1998).

Finally, in the cases of several national groups, TPS has been anything but temporary. For example, a large group of Liberians had their TPS renewed for decades with no pathway to permanent residency on the horizon, leaving them in a legal limbo (Wasem and Ester 2008). When their TPS finally expired in 2007, President Bush invoked his power of Deferred Enforced Departure (DED), which had been created to replace EVD as a discretionary presidential power to protect those who did not qualify for TPS (U.S. Department of Homeland Security 2007). The Liberians have continued to have their DED status renewed every 18 months since 2007, and although they can work legally in the United States and often have citizen children, they are not on the path to citizenship.

The second form of relief that Congress recently created are the T and U visa categories for victims and witnesses to crime who are willing to assist law enforcement officials by providing testimony (Victims of Trafficking and Violence Protection Act, October 2000). These visas were developed specifically for victims of human trafficking and sexual assault, and have helped some people in dire need of protection. However, there is also evidence that their implementation is highly subject to the discretion of local law enforcement and can vary widely by region in the United States.[1] As word spreads about these visa categories, it is likely the demand for them will increase; for now, the programs are quite new and it is difficult to predict what their long-term impact will be.[2]

Overall, the complementary protection system in the United States has been cast as a wide net, with many crisscrossing threads, but also some large holes. The RSD regime includes a channel for making CAT claims and complying with *nonrefoulement* obligations, but the rest of the protection avenues have not been integrated with that system. In addition, the long-term trend in the United States is unclear. Some beneficiaries of complementary protection, such as the Liberians with (not-so) temporary status, and the mostly female victims of human trafficking, have received protection that would not have been available to them 20 years ago. Others, such as Haitians, Central Americans, and undocumented immigrants who cannot prove extreme hardship to a U.S. citizen, are seeing their protection options contract. Thus, protection is not holistic and can be very inconsistent over time, depending on whether the individual or national origin group in question is politically sympathetic.

Compared with the Canadian commitment to internationalism, American policymakers, administrators, and judges tend to view migration policy and law as purely domestic concerns. Especially because there are so many moving parts and conflicting interpretations within the country, they see no need to look beyond its borders for yet more perspectives. America's position on international guidance is perfectly compatible with its assertion of sovereignty, and yet there have been moments of remarkable generosity driven by domestic political concerns. Thus, compliance with international guidance has been quite high at some moments and on some dimensions, but not consistently so—and perhaps even coincidentally—as opposed to being driven by a goal of internationalism. When domestic political support has formed around particular subgroups, opportunities for protection have developed.

There is no way to know for certain whether some of the people who have gained protection from deportation via complementary channels would have been granted refugee status and all the rights and privileges that go along with it if these additional forms of less comprehensive protection had not been developed as alternatives. It seems likely that this scenario applies to some individuals who were granted TPS. However, it also seems clear that many more people have avoided deportation through these channels than would have if RSD was the only option available. Thus, it is difficult to sustain the argument that these added forms of protection have reduced the overall level of protection available for displaced people. Rather, in the U.S. case, complementary protection has diversified (albeit inconsistently) the circumstances that are officially recognized as valid reasons for seeking protection.

Canada

The major characteristics of Canada's RSD regime—bureaucratic centralization, insulation from political tinkering, low levels of judicial review, and at least rhetorical support for international guidance—are also apparent in the way that Canada has come to provide complementary protection. In fact, Canada's complementary protection regime has been evolving steadily toward convergence with its RSD regime for the past two decades, providing further evidence of centralization as a core feature of Canadian administrative justice. Although Canada's protection procedures are not completely centralized, the reforms that came into effect in 2012 are designed to streamline and blend the complementary protection and RSD regimes even further. This step-by-step move toward a broad, holistic, and comprehensive protection system makes Canada the state that, currently, most closely resembles the UNHCR recommendations for how protection should be offered.

Canada has long offered multiple forms of protection beyond RSD, and in the early days, the different statuses were processed completely separately from one another. When the current RSD regime was established in 1989, the newly created IRB was given jurisdiction over Convention refugee claims only. Meanwhile, officials at the CIC conducted on-paper assessments of other protection requests—namely, the Pre-Removal Risk Assessment (PRRA) and Humanitarian and Compassionate (H&C) visa applications. Although the IRB was held to high standards of procedural justice, the decision making at the CIC was purely discretionary. There was no international legal obligation to provide H&C protection; the Minister granted it in cases where she was convinced that persons would face hardship if they were returned to their home country, much like the pre-1996 standard for cancelation of removal in the United States.

The first step toward the convergence of international human rights law and refugee protection in Canada occurred in 1999, when the departmental practices for conducting H&C assessments came under judicial scrutiny. The case before the Canadian Supreme Court involved an undocumented Jamaican woman, Mavis Baker, who had been living in Canada for more than a decade and had four Canadian citizen children. She was diagnosed with severe mental illness and was receiving financial assistance from the state. After her H&C application was denied and she was unsuccessful in Federal Court, the Supreme Court of Canada decided the landmark case *Baker vs. Canada,* in which it provided significant guidance for administrative decision makers in H&C cases (*Baker v. Canada* (*Ministry of Citizenship and Immigration*), [2 S.C.R. 817, 1999]). The Supreme Court reversed the previous negative decisions about Baker's case and found that H&C assessments must be made in compliance with the values of international human rights law. In particular, the Court opinion cited the 1990 Convention on the Rights of the Child. Canadian legal scholars have suggested that this case advances a unified vision of law, in which domestic and international law are interpreted harmoniously (Dyzenhaus 2004). The new-found influence of international human rights law over what was previously a purely discretionary visa was certainly a monumentally significant development in Canada's protection regime, and one that is unimaginable in the current American context. The timing of this development is also unsurprising given the UNHCR's growing advocacy for complementary protection during the 1990s.

This commitment to international law was tested in 2002, when the Supreme Court of Canada decided the controversial case of *Suresh v. Canada* (*Suresh v. Canada* (*Minister of Citizenship and Immigration*), [1 S.C.C, 2002]). The case was heard before September 11, 2001, but the decision was handed down after the terrorist attacks on the United States. It involved a refugee applicant who was a suspected member of the Tamil Tigers, an organization that many states consider to be a terrorist group. Suresh claimed that he would be tortured or killed if returned to Sri Lanka, but the Minister of Citizenship and Immigration concluded that he was a security risk and must be deported. In a unanimous decision attributed simply to "The Court," the justices concluded that Suresh's case must be reconsidered with more careful attention to the concept of procedural fairness.

Although the decision in the *Suresh* case was bold under the circumstances, the Court was not as aggressive in its advocacy for international human rights as it was in the *Baker* case, carefully balancing principles of fundamental justice and international law against the need to protect national security. The opinion of the Court made clear that Canada retains a sovereign right to return people to likely torture situations under extreme circumstances when the individual poses a significant national security risk. It also tempers its reading of international treaties that have not been officially ratified by Canada:

> In seeking the meaning of the Canadian Constitution, the courts may be informed by international law. Our concern is not with Canada's international obligations qua obligations; rather, our concern is with the principles of fundamental justice. We look to international law as evidence of these principles and not as controlling in itself. (*Suresh v. Canada* (*Minister of Citizenship and Immigration*), [1 S.C.C., 2002])

Although the *Suresh* case had a slightly more domestic orientation than the *Baker* case, it must be understood in the political context of the moment as well as the larger patterns in the way Canadian legislation, administrative agencies, and courts read international law (Macklin 2009a). In that light, the *Suresh* case is not a major aberration from the general Canadian jurisprudential pattern of compliance with international standards.

The next big step toward centralization occurred later in 2002, when a major piece of legislation was passed, overhauling the Canadian immigration system. Section 97 of the IRPA added a complementary protection element to the Canadian RSD regime by expanding the mandate of the IRB to include assessments beyond standard RSD. Since 2002, in cases where an asylum seeker is not found to be a Convention refugee, the IRB inquires whether they are "persons in need of protection." The grounds for gaining Section 97 protection are danger of torture under the CAT standard, risk to life, or threat of cruel and unusual punishment that is not faced generally in the home country, that is not a lawful sanction, and is not related to inadequate health care. A person who successfully gains Section 97 protection may apply for permanent residency in Canada, and eventual citizenship.

During an early analysis of the IRPA reforms, Dauvergne (2003:3) claimed the creation of Section 97 was not a major shift in Canadian law because those types of claims would have been heard previously under the H&C category. However, this conclusion assumes the institutional location has no impact on the way claims are assessed. In fact, Canadian immigration lawyers consistently told me that the change has been enormous because it has removed the need to make arguments that stretch the refugee definition to include new and unorthodox cases. One said Section 97 "really helps with victims of crime and victims of trafficking" (author interview, 5/22/2007). Another pointed out that "innovative arguments were a bigger deal before Section 97. Now it is more broad, no longer limited to the Convention definition. That is a major change which has expanded protection" (author interview, 5/24/2007). Another recalled that prior to the 2002 reforms, "we had to make arguments about the nexus [between persecution and the Convention grounds]. Usually it was a witness to corruption, and you had to argue that he fit into the definition…. Since Section 97, there is less need for innovative arguments. It has made a big difference, especially for victims of crime" (author interview, 5/18/2007). A 2006 study found that the shift to handling these types of claims within the IRB "contributed to a greater entrenchment and prominence of non-Convention refugee protection in Canada," because it meant that a formal jurisprudence had formed on these issues (Reekie and Layden-Stevenson 2006:38). In addition, subsuming these types of claims under the IRB mandate means that they are heard as part of an in-person assessment and are not discretionary grants by an officer of the CIC.

There is no evidence to suggest that Parliament considered this shift to be monumental when it discussed the IRPA before voting on it in 2002. In fact, the legislative debate was focused almost exclusively on the border security components of the Act in light of the September 11 terrorist attacks that had just occurred in the United States. When the bill was being debated, Minister of Citizenship and Immigration Elinor Caplan assured members of Parliament the IRPA "gives us the ability to streamline our procedures, so that those who are in genuine need of our protection will be welcomed in Canada more quickly and those who are not in need of protection will be able to be removed more quickly. That streamlining is extremely important" (remarks of Hon. Elinor Caplan, Minister of Citizenship and Immigration, 37th Parliament, 1st Session, no. 105; Tuesday, October 30, 2001). Immediately after IRPA went into force, the IRB Legal Services office produced a lengthy guide for decision makers on how to make Section 97 decisions. The guide states that these decisions were subsumed under the IRB mandate to avoid the "delays and inconsistencies" of the previous "fragmented" and "multilayered approach" (IRB 2002:3–4).

The Canadian commitment to streamlining its protection regime is powerful and durable. Parliament took another step in that direction with the BRRA of 2010, which transferred authority over the PRRA from the Minister to the IRB.[3] This further consolidation of the protection regime also represents a continued expansion of the IRB discretionary authority; H&C claims are now the only form of complementary protection still outside IRB jurisdiction. The *Baker* decision suggests even the H&C program is gradually being streamlined into a comprehensive protection regime. By any measure, then, Canada is more compliant with UNHCR guidance on complementary protection than any other state in the world.

The political motivation behind taking an internationalist position may have been, in part, to preserve Canada's symbolic reputation as a middle power. However, reform seems to have been just as driven by a deep-seated commitment to a streamlined bureaucratic process. Furthermore, this centralization is more than just symbolic; it has led to concrete and measurable results for asylum seekers with a variety of backgrounds and motivations. Today, both the Supreme Court of Canada and the IRB have, at least outwardly, embraced and routinized considerations of international law. Canada's generosity on complementary protection is a clear example of the diffusion of international human rights norms across multiple domestic institutions, and the closing gap between refugee law and human rights law.

Somewhat ironically, the country with the most expansive approach to reading the refugee definition is also the country with the most well integrated other options. These options are treated as alternative paths to protection, not inferior to refugee status. Their growth has not seemed to threaten refugee protection as some scholars have feared. If anything, it has preserved the concept of refugee status as one particular form of humanitarian visa without stretching the refugee definition to accommodate compelling claims that lie beyond it.

Australia

As with the Australian RSD regime, complementary protection in Australia is extremely contentious and uninsulated from political influence. Policy elites seem to view UNHCR guidance like unsolicited advice from a trying, moralistic relative; they are aware of it, but feel little pressure to comply. The Australian resistance to expanding its obligations beyond the refugee definition stems from an entrenched opposition within the DIAC, combined with a powerful parliamentary focus on tough border control. In contrast to the United States, where complementary protection is often generated as a practical means of dealing with people who are present in the territory, the Australian experience with unauthorized migration is still limited enough in numbers so that an illusion of control persists among policymakers. The advocacy community is also not well versed in political negotiations or savvy compromise. There has been a lot of grassroots interest group activity around reforming the system, but asylum seekers have few advocates in Parliament, and political passions about the issue run high. Thus, no reforms have been successful as yet.

To the extent that Australia offers complementary protection, it occurs via a process known as ministerial intervention. Since 1989, the Minister of Immigration and Citizenship has had the bureaucratic discretion under Section 417 of the Migration Act of 1958 to grant a protection visa, but in keeping with the fragmentation of the RSD regime, ministerial intervention is completely unintegrated with RSD. The administrative tribunal tasked with reviewing RSD decisions (the RRT) is not involved in these decisions at all. This system differs from the UNHCR's vision of complementary protection in a number of key ways. First, according to Australian law, ministerial intervention is "non-delegable, noncompellable, and nonreviewable," and so the process lacks basic transparency and predictability (DIAC 2011:ii). The decision is completely discretionary. The Minister can refuse any request, does not have to give reasons, and the outcome cannot be reviewed by a court. Thus, even if migrants' stories fit clearly within the framework of an international human rights compact such as the CAT, to which Australia became a signatory in 1989, they are not guaranteed to be successful. According to a UNHCR representative in Canberra: "Sometimes we will ask for ministerial discretion to implement the CAT or the ICCPR.... When we do this, the response by the Minister is quite high—60 to 70%" (author interview, 10/02/2007). This success rate decreases the likelihood that a person will be deported to torture or death, but is a very informal and nontransparent process compared with the automatic trigger of CAT protection in the United States and Canada. It is not based on any specific legal criteria or precedent, but on personal appeals by the UNHCR, which is not aware of every person who makes an application for ministerial intervention in Australia (Karlsen 2009:32).

To be eligible for ministerial intervention in Australia, people must first apply for refugee status, even if they are fairly certain their case does not fit the definition and they are unlikely to succeed. Because those who have applied for ministerial intervention are, by definition, failed asylum seekers, they are not thought of as potential refugees by the DIAC. A top asylum policymaker at the DIAC told me:

> You have to be careful about the term *asylum seekers*, because we don't consider them to be asylum seekers anymore once they have failed at the RRT. The term can be elastic when it is used by the advocacy community, but we tend to take a more purist approach to the term, and we believe it does not extend to the endgame of the process. (author interview, 10/05/2007)

Although this distinction is rhetorical, it illustrates the DIAC's view of people who are lodging intervention applications and its insistence on maintaining a clear distinction between those seeking refugee visas versus other forms of protection. Nevertheless, a very large proportion of rejected applicants view the intervention request as an essential step in the appeals process. In 2010/2011, approximately 8,000 people applied for refugee status in Australia (UNHCR 1980–2013). That same year, more than 3,000 people filed applications for ministerial intervention regarding their protection visa requests, and the Minister intervened favorably on behalf of about 400 people, either to grant a visa or to grant another hearing for the applicant (DIAC 2011).

In 2003, the ministerial intervention power was tainted by scandal when members of the opposition accused Immigration Minister Ruddock of granting visas in exchange for donations to the Liberal Party.[4] In response to these charges, the Senate conducted an official inquiry into both the accusations of impropriety and the ministerial intervention system in general. However, because the DIAC refused to provide the committee with full case files, the committee was not able to resolve the issue of the specific allegations. It is final report, it stated that it "can only conclude that the present Minister's unwillingness to provide the detailed information necessary to conduct a full and thorough investigation of relevant cases suggests a reluctance to expose the decision-making process to close scrutiny" (Senate Select Committee on Ministerial Discretion in Migration Matters 2004:xii). The investigation concluded "the current Australian practice of relying solely on ministerial discretion places it at odds with emerging international trends" (quoted in Karlsen 2009:28). The committee recommended reform of the system, but it was sharply divided along party lines about what those reforms should include.

There have been regular attempts at reform ever since the parliamentary committee called for a change to the system in 2004, but political divisions have stalled the process each time. Charges of corruption as well as the advocacy of human rights groups and Australian experts in international law such as Jane McAdam have moved the issue onto the Labor Party agenda. However, there is still strong opposition among the Liberals in Parliament to expanding the system, and because the Labor Party is reluctant to seem soft on migration issues in the public eye, it never goes far enough to satisfy the vocal migrant advocacy community.

The first attempt came in September 2006, when Senator Andrew Bartlett of the minor Australian Democrat Party introduced a bill that would have added a complementary protection visa class to protect those who fear "a substantial threat to his or her personal security, human rights or human dignity on return to his or her country of origin" (Migration Legislation Amendment (Complementary Protection) Bill 2006, Proposed subsection 36A(2)). The bill would have inserted a list of specific guidelines the Minister would have to follow when assessing applications under this visa class, thus reducing the discretionary component of the intervention power. Bartlett's proposal proved to be too generous for Parliament. The coalition government under Prime Minister Howard "expressed the view that Australia already effectively had a system of complementary protection in place" (Karlsen 2009). Similarly, DIAC defended the current system, noting that it provides a "safety net for the exercise of migration laws which are generally fair but may, in certain exceptional cases, lead to an unintended harsh result"(Submission No. 24, Senate Select Committee on Ministerial Discretion in Migration Matters, 2004:22). At other times during that period, the DIAC noted they preferred the "flexibility" of the "case-by-case" approach to protection (Kneebone 2009:207). Despite some support from the Green Party, the bill did not pass the Senate, and Senator Bartlett, the Australian government's biggest champion of complementary protection, was defeated when Parliament held elections in late 2007.

Despite this defeat, public dissatisfaction with the Howard government's handling of immigration policy became a central issue in the 2007 elections, helping Kevin Rudd's Labor Party to sweep into power. In February 2008, the new Labor Immigration Minister announced a desire to reform the ministerial intervention process, stating: "I have formed the view that I have too much power. I am uncomfortable with [the current system], not just because of concern about playing God, but also because of the lack of transparency and accountability for those ministerial decisions."[5] Minister Evans directed the DIAC to design a complementary protection proposal, which was introduced into Parliament in September 2009.

This second attempt at reform alienated constituents on both ends of the political spectrum. The Liberal Party opposition decried complementary protection as a backdoor for illegal immigrants, denouncing the bill as "yet another softening of Australia's immigration laws that sends a clear message to people smugglers and unlawful noncitizens seeking entry that Australia is an easy target" (Migration Amendment [Complementary Protection] Bill 2009; dissenting report by Liberal Senators). Conversely, the advocacy community expressed frustration with both the lack of "broader consultation" in developing the proposal and the narrow scope of the protection scheme it outlined (Field 2008, see also Australian Human Rights Commission 2009).

Immigration Minister Evans maintained his support for the bill, saying: "I see it as an important measure. Out of the immigration legislation that is outstanding, I see that as the most important."[6] However, the shadow Immigration Minister Morrison was very vocal in opposing the bill and it eventually stalled.

To date, complementary protection reform has gone nowhere in Parliament, and appeals to the Minister remain the last resort for failed asylum seekers in Australia.[7] Even if the proposed reform is eventually implemented, Australia's protection regime will still be far less integrated and more limited than its counterparts in the United States and Canada. In Australia, refugee protection is given pride of place above any other form of protection, leaving the worlds of refugee law and human rights law quite separate from one another. However, the privileged and unique position given to refugee status in Australia has not led the Australian RSD regime to be more expansive than states with potentially distracting alternative paths to protection. In fact, Australia has the most narrow and textualist reading of the refugee definition of the three countries in this study (Hamlin 2012b). It seems the desire to limit protection to a narrow band of refugee claims drives both the interpretation of the refugee definition within the RSD regime and the resistance to creating alternative avenues to protection.

Conclusions

Many modern asylum seekers fall into categories that were unanticipated by the framers of the 1951 Convention, but are nonetheless compelling. These claims are often supported by a thick web of international law or by organized domestic advocacy suggesting that the individual deserves protection. Thus, receiving states are forced to find a balance between powerful competing pressures when deciding the scope of their international human rights obligations. Some protection regimes, such as Canada's, have made a commitment to comply with the expansive generosity outlined in international soft law guidance of the UNHCR, and have created proactive policy designed to embrace an evolving concept of a refugee. Other states, such as the United States and Australia, have been much less receptive to international appeals. The level of internationalism that a protection regime achieves is linked to larger historical and geopolitical developments regarding the role of each nation in the global community. However, although it is certainly a significant predictor of generosity, it is only one part of the reason why the United States, Canada, and Australia approach complementary protection issues in such different ways.

The other aspects of a protection regime that matter for explaining cross-national differences are more structural and institutional, stemming from both the degree of centralization in the process and the relative power of each actor in the regime. Protection regimes vary in their ability to adapt to change in a clear and consistent manner; the more centralized Canadian system has evolved much more quickly and unidirectionally on this issue than the United States and Australia. The American system has sprouted new components almost randomly and layered them on top of one another in ways that highlight some powerful contradictions and tensions in the system. The Australian system has maintained stasis even in the face of increasing pressure to change, revealing the deep entrenchment of the interests on opposing sides of this issue.

Complementary protection has also played a very different role in the larger migration politics of each state. In Australia, it has been used to maintain a strict and narrow reading of the Convention definition, but still grants some protection under the CAT. In Canada, it has been used to supplement and blur the boundaries between refugee law and human rights law; in the United States, it has been used both to supplement existing protection schemes and to replace those options at different times for different reasons. The irony is, the state with the most comprehensive complementary protection regime is also the state that arguably needs complementary protection the least, because its RSD regime usually reads the refugee definition so expansively. The centralization of Canada's RSD regime means that almost all potential avenues for protection are considered simultaneously. America's politicized and fragmented system leads some particular groups to be protected whereas others are not. Australia's high-profile conflicts combined with a narrow textual reading of the refugee definition have led to a firm distinction between refugees and other migrants that has kept all nonrefugees completely out of the protection regime. These particularities reveal that it is difficult to understand an RSD regime without looking at its context within a larger protection system and, conversely, it is difficult to understand cross-national variation in complementary protection options without understanding the RSD regime with which it must interact.

Academic study has tended to perpetuate distinctions between migrants rather than challenging them or acknowledging gray areas. This three-country comparison illuminates some of the ways that migrant categories are undeniably blurred, just as the motivations of migrants often are cumulative. It shows that migration politics vary by domestic context, not by constructed migrant category. Only by observing the wide range of reactions to international legal arguments by otherwise similar receiving states can we understand that migrant categories depend greatly on where the migrant lands.

CONCLUSIONS

CHAPTER 10

Asylum Seeker Blues and the Globalization of Law

Today, refugee status determination regimes around the world are under pressure. They are under pressure from high application rates and a lack of political support for the expense of processing them. They are under pressure from new and unanticipated types of claims of persecution, and an increasing number of claims that are outside the refugee definition but are nonetheless compelling. These claims are often supported by international law suggesting that the individual deserves protection, and thus, they directly challenge the notion that refugee and migrant are obviously distinct categories. In other words, it is becoming increasingly clear that the 1951 Convention definition is out of date, inadequate for the task at hand.

This is not an unfamiliar dilemma. What to do about a text that does not get us where we want to go is a question that is as old as legal text itself. It is the central question of American constitutional law and is often the subject of heated, painful political debate. For example, many books have been written about whether the U.S. Constitution can and should be read to include the notion of privacy, and what that shift would mean for democracy. Similarly, RSD raises the questions of how far the refugee definition should expand to accommodate on-the-ground realities, and what those new interpretations would mean for both human rights and state sovereignty.

Because asylum seekers raise such questions, they are the human embodiment of the globalization of law. As they cross borders, they invoke international human rights protections, often access the RSD regimes of host nations, and sometimes gain the right to stay permanently in those states. The existence of domestic RSD regimes is a testament to the power of international human rights. However, the quality of an RSD regime depends not just on the degree to which those rights have permeated the state, but also the extent to which they are compatible with existing domestic rights frames. Thus, asylum seekers do not simply cross physical borders between states; as they work their way through an RSD regime, asylum seekers also cross borders between areas of law. It is not always clear which type of law is governing the process at any given moment. For example, when an asylum seeker shows up uninvited without legal documentation, files a claim, and pursues that claim through various levels of administrative and judicial review, this series of events is possible because a complex blend of domestic and international human rights have been activated.

Understanding the different ways in which these areas of law can be woven together with one another, and the core values that underlie each combination, is essential to explaining how RSD regimes vary. International human rights law is always a key component; it is fundamentally concerned with human dignity and the substantive protection of individual rights. But, the values at the heart of domestic law vary greatly depending on the place. Administrative law is always concerned with protecting the proper procedure granted to individuals and regulating relationships between the various institutional players. However, it can prioritize efficiency and expediency, well-researched expert judgment, centralization and consistency of outcomes, or thorough vetting and a multiplicity of perspectives. Constitutional law can prioritize various individual rights, procedural rights, and institutional design features, depending on the constitution. The logic of administrative justice, the arrangements of the bureaucratic state, the relative power of the courts, and the existence of textual rights protections are of central importance for understanding divergence across RSD regimes, because the players in an RSD regime often assert themselves or hold back according to the constitutional and administrative framework that has developed in each country independent of migration policy. These factors affect the way states draw the line between refugee and nonrefugee.

The Difference an RSD Regime Makes

Once potential refugees access the unique sorting process that each host country has developed, they discover that the differences between RSD regimes matter, both procedurally and in terms of raw acceptance rates. For asylum seekers with obvious cases—those whose stories fit neatly within the definition and can be easily corroborated—the difference an RSD regime makes may only be in the experience of the process, not the outcome. However, variations in the way RSD is conducted are significant, because they can have an impact on refugees' outlook about their new country, and may affect naturalization rates down the road (Bloemraad 2006). For example, an obvious refugee in Canada may find the process to be expedient and humane, whereas in the United States the same asylum seeker may have trouble hiring a lawyer or may feel badgered by aggressive questioning during the RSD hearing. An obvious refugee is more likely to be kept in detention in Australia, and may feel demoralized by fears of having to reargue his case in a few years, as asylum seekers were forced to do until 2008 in order to keep their refugee visas. For obvious refugees, the outcome of being granted refugee status may be the same in all three countries, but the psychological impact on potential new citizens, many of whom are already traumatized, may vary widely.

For asylum seekers whose claims do not fit clearly within the Convention definition, the RSD regime effect is much more stark. The claims of many modern asylum seekers fall into categories that were unanticipated by the framers of the 1951 Convention. As the exilic model (in which refugees are typically political dissidents) becomes less dominant during the post-Cold War period, many asylum claims fall into the more ambiguous middle zone between obvious UN Convention refugees and economic migrants. As the example of Chinese victims of coercive population control clearly illustrates, RSD regimes can have a particularly powerful effect on asylum seekers with more ambiguous claims, in part because regimes vary widely in their ability to adapt to change in a clear and consistent manner.

In general, an RSD regime with high levels of administrative insulation results in questions about the refugee definition being more settled, either in a generous or restrictive direction, than they are in other, less centralized regimes. The centralized Canadian system has evolved much more quickly and unidirectionally than that of the United States or Australia. Because Canada has high levels of administrative insulation, the IRB develops detailed guidance for its decision makers that is less likely to be contradicted later. In contrast, both the Australian Parliament and the U.S. Congress have acted to narrow or specify the refugee definition; this type of legislative intervention has not happened in Canada.

The fact that Canada has a highly unified system centered on an independent administrative tribunal has some major implications for RSD outcomes. Most important, in Canada, key questions about the interpretation of the refugee definition get settled in a way they do not in less centralized regimes. Because relatively few cases are reconsidered by courts, decision makers process most asylum claims on an individual, case-by-case basis without concern that the outcome will be precedent setting for other applications down the road. RSD may well be decided in contradiction of the logic of other similar applications on a regular basis in Canada, but these contradictions do not often bubble up into the courts as they do in the United States.

In addition, because the Canadian system has low levels of intervention from either courts or the political branches, the administrative tribunal is able to develop and provide detailed guidance to its decision makers that is not contradicted later. Policy guidance from the IRB is not always used to push for more generosity, as it did in the gender case, but sometimes for less generosity, as in the case of the Roma and Mexican persuasive decisions. Of course, this system puts a great deal of pressure on the one hearing, requiring the tribunal to invest resources into fact-finding and training, to ensure decision makers have as much information at their disposal as possible. The fact that Canada's IRB members are political appointees who often lack professional legal training pushes against other concerted efforts by the IRB to achieve consistency and uniformity. However, research by scholars focused on variation *within* RSD regimes confirms that the Canadian RSD regime has lower levels of variation by individual decision makers than other regimes (Macklin 2009b, Ramji-Nogales et al. 2009).

What makes the development of asylum law in the American case so particularly messy is that *every* player in the RSD process is powerful and involved. This dynamic institutional landscape is almost the polar opposite of Canada; the judicial and legislative branches, the president, the Department of Justice, and the administrative agencies all regularly assert their authority, and weigh in with competing interpretations and policies, leaving the development of legal interpretation very uncertain. The courts are not just extremely active in reviewing administrative decisions in the United States, they are active across a fragmented judicial landscape. Once cases reach the federal court level, case law develops across multiple circuits that have yet to be reconciled with each other on many important legal questions. Even when the BIA has issued precedent-setting cases at the administrative level, the federal courts often ignore those decisions, and the Supreme Court weighs in only rarely to check the most egregious cases of judicial activism and set the record straight.

Unlike in Canada, where both Parliament and the CIC tend to sit back and allow the IRB to develop innovative policy, American asylum policy is developed in a highly politicized manner. In rare instances, such as the protection of victims of coercive population control that was codified in the 1996 IIRIRA, Congress steps in and dictates specifics on how the refugee definition is to be interpreted. More often, policy is generated from within the immigration bureaucracy in the executive branch (formerly the INS, now the Department of Homeland Security). As a result, these policies get linked to particular presidents and are often stalled, blocked, or openly defied by later administrations—as was the case in both the gender and Chinese stories.

If the Canadian RSD regime is centered around one institution, the IRB, and the American RSD regime is fragmented across multiple competing agencies, the bureaucratic adversarialism of the Australian RSD regime puts it somewhere in the middle. Not every player in the process is as activated as they are in the United States, but the most powerful political actors are. Because both Parliament and the High Court are invested in the way asylum law—and administrative law more generally—develops, their contention for control overshadows the actions of the administrative agency, the independent tribunal, and the federal courts. This bifurcation of power turns the Australian RSD regime into a tug-of-war.

The rhetoric in Australia about the battle for asylum policy between Parliament and the courts is very heated, but the forcefulness of the High Court should not be overstated. Although there is certainly an increasingly level of back-and-forth between the two, the High Court continues to be fairly cautious in asserting itself, especially on policy matters that are very important to Parliament. Parliament has varied its policies at the margins over time, but has tended toward restriction regardless of which party is in control. This restrictionism is not just aimed at the border, but at the domestic rights of asylum seekers and the ability of courts to review RSD decisions. The response of the High Court has evolved, as both the Court and Parliament have adjusted to the idea of a more powerful judiciary. Even as recently as 2005, the Court upheld the controversial Pacific Solution, which was eventually ended through political channels. It also allowed the policy of mandatory detention of asylum seekers in the 2004 *Al-Kateb* case despite powerful evidence that the conditions in detention centers were shockingly inhumane. In another recent example, the High Court found, contra to developments in the United States and Canada, that victims of China's One-Child policy did not qualify for refugee protection.

When the High Court has pushed back against Parliament on matters of interpretation of the refugee definition, it has shown that it must walk a fine line. In the 2000 case of *Chen Shi Hai*, when the court granted refugee protection to "black children" victims of the One-Child policy, the case was decided through the lens of careful textualism. However, the High Court's attempt to bring legitimacy to its 2001 decision in the *Khawar* domestic violence case by linking it to a similar case in the United Kingdom, a jurisdiction with close ties to Australia, backfired. Parliament issued a major revision of the law in response—a clear sign the court had overstepped its bounds. Although the High Court is still feeling its way on how to handle high-profile interpretive and policy questions, there is no doubt that it has become more aggressive in protecting its ability to review decisions. There is a also snowball effect; because the administrative RSD process in Australia is so underdeveloped and lacking in resources, each time the High Court weighs in on questions of procedural fairness, more and more cases are able to capitalize on that and seek judicial review. In this sense, the High Court has turned the federal courts into yet another layer of administrative review.

If RSD regimes make a huge difference for nonobvious refugees, they also make a major impact on the experience of nonrefugees. The degree of administrative insulation, adaptability to change, and commitment to following international guidance of each particular RSD regime trickles over to affect the level of complementary protection each state tends to offer to those beyond the limits of the refugee definition. The centralization of Canada's RSD regime means that almost all potential avenues for protection are considered simultaneously. America's politicized and fragmented system leads some particular groups to be protected whereas others are not. Australia's high-profile conflicts combined with a narrow textual reading of the refugee definition has led to a firm distinction between refugees and other migrants that has kept all nonrefugees completely out of the protection regime.

Migration Policy Convergence and Divergence

Migration scholarship is far from reaching consensus about the determinants of asylum policy. Nevertheless, the international convergence, exclusionary convergence, and domestic divergence camps all tend to generalize about how states will react to asylum seekers. International convergence theories, coming mostly from the political science subfield of international relations, speculate about the erosion of national sovereignty, the diffusion of international human rights norms, and the emergence of a renewed postnational citizenship. Scholars in this vein tend to assume that expansive forces will eventually permeate the state from the outside and lead to a wide array of rights for migrants. These theories often view states as uniformly exclusionary black boxes, without recognizing that expansionist trajectories are also in play within states. International convergence theories also sometimes ignore the role that those domestic trajectories have played in designing international human rights norms in the first place, and gloss over the Cold War history of documents like the 1951 Convention Relating to the Status of Refugees, which are themselves the result of political compromises between states.

The single biggest weakness of international convergence theories is the substantial body of evidence put forward by exclusionary convergence scholars. This disciplinarily diverse group of migration scholars has illustrated the ways in which states have joined a race to the bottom, trying to find innovative strategies for keeping asylum seekers and other migrants out of their territories. The United States, Canada, Australia, and many other liberal democracies share a lack of regard for international standards when it comes to establishing border control policy. Politicians take firm public stands on border control issues, and assume (to the extent they are concerned) that "real refugees" are either waiting patiently overseas in camps or will find some way to rise like cream to the top of domestic RSD processes.

Scholars who are focused on deterrence tend to share the view held by international convergence theorists of the state as a unitary actor resistant to admitting asylum seekers. However, in contrast to those theories, they deny that the concept of state sovereignty has lost any real authority. In fact, they view states as achieving increasing levels of success in keeping people out. The stories of the three countries in this study certainly support the claim that receiving states share a disregard for international standards and a commitment to deterrence when it comes to establishing border control policy. However, what scholars who focus on these policies often do not acknowledge is the fact that deterrence measures affect different RSD regimes in very different ways.

In response to both lines of convergence scholarship, the domestic divergence line of argument recognizes that each state will react differently to the rise of global governance institutions and the human rights norms they perpetuate. However, this line of thinking falls too often into a binary view of domestic politics as a struggle between exclusionary legislators and inclusive courts. The three-country comparison outlined in this book suggests that state responses to irregular migration flows are much more internally complex, and tell an interesting story about the legal and political institutions of each receiving state.

Certainly, exclusionary politics can lead to institutional design changes that are systematically less inclined to generosity, but their specific nature depends on the institutions involved. For example, in the United States, deterrence policies have meant that, since 1996, there are far fewer administrative RSD hearings held, because whole categories of asylum seekers are now diverted away from the Asylum Office and straight into the more adversarial immigration court. In a more extreme way, Australia's policy-based distinction between onshore and offshore migrants is a clear-cut example of how restrictionist politics can affect RSD and strip away administrative insulation. So-called offshore asylum seekers (those who have been diverted from making a claim within Australian territory) never access the same RSD processes as other asylum seekers and are vulnerable to summary exclusion. Even in Canada, a system that prides itself in administrative insulation from the politics of deterrence, the new visa requirement for Mexico screens out the majority of potential claimants from that country before they ever arrive in Canada to make a claim. Ironically, this development will probably increase Canada's annual acceptance rate and strengthen the IRB's reputation for generosity. It is worth noting that none of these examples show deterrence politics operating at the level of the individual decision maker who feels a personal pressure to deny claims as a way of patrolling the border from within. Rather, deterrence politics can become much more institutionally embedded and can influence the type of process the asylum seeker experiences.

A central goal of this book has been to encourage migration scholars to move beyond bold claims of convergence and divergence. However, to the extent that states are each following their own distinct tracks, I suggest three important additions to domestic divergence theory. These theoretic contributions stem from my public law approach, which places great significance on the role of legal institutions. First, I argue that domestic struggles over asylum policy are only partially about how generous to be to immigrants. The dynamics of RSD regimes are also about protecting institutional turf, such as asserting the right to review administrative decisions or reemphasizing the position of administrative agencies as expert specialists. In many interbranch conflicts, international human rights norms are not part of the conversation. In others, they are used strategically to shore up power for one player. For example, when the Australian High Court refused to acknowledge the privative clause that Parliament had issued in an attempt to strip the Court of its jurisdiction over RSD, it was not because the Court had a preference for a more expansionist migration policy. Rather, the Court was protecting its power. Further, in the United States, the RSD regime has been subsumed at different moments by political battles over abortion, struggles over administrative agency authority, and conflicting court interpretations. Political pressure to limit large-scale migration certainly exists in these countries, but power struggles are often unrelated to the desired migration policy outcome held by a particular actor. Nevertheless, the outcomes of power struggles have unintended consequences that affect the rights of migrants.

Second, I find that courts are not always a strong counterbalance to the immigration restrictionism that often dominates the elected branches. Courts must be strategic about when they push against strong political will, and they need ammunition to shore up their legitimacy when taking bold stances. The United States, Canada, and Australia all have strong courts relative to other countries, but even among these three powerful judiciaries, there is a lot of variation in the level and style of court involvement in policymaking. American courts have a much longer tradition of judicial activism and are more involved in reviewing the substance of RSD, sometimes even granting refugee status to individual asylum seekers. Canadian courts were empowered by the passage of the Charter of Rights and Freedoms in 1982, but beyond a few landmark decisions, such as the *Singh* case, which guaranteed asylum seekers a hearing, Canadian courts are still reluctant to become involved in the substance of RSD. Australian courts also pick their battles. They are willing to protect their turf, and they step in when political interference in the administrative process has gone too far, but they exhibit no obvious eagerness to push for an expansionist reading of the refugee definition.

As a third insight into domestic divergence theory, this study illustrates that international norms can bubble up into an RSD regime via administrative agencies; they need not always trickle down from courts. Thus, courts need not be the only forces of expansion and rights protection in an RSD regime, just as the political branches are not the only force of restriction. Administrative agencies are frequently left out of debates about international convergence and domestic divergence, but they are the frontline interpreters of international law as well as the frontline enforcers of migration policy. They must constantly respond to new types of claims and the innovative legal arguments supporting them. They may decide to push the boundaries of protection and offer relief to groups, such as homosexuals, whose civil rights remain in question even in the nations offering asylum, and whose situation could not possibly have been foreseen by the draft-ers of the 1951 Convention (Walker 2003). Eventually, they must set limits to what can be an incredibly elastic definition and, in essence, enforce the borders from within.

In this sense, it is often individual, low-level bureaucrats who are the agents of legal globalization, not judges or politicians. For example, the Canadian IRB was the innovative actor that pushed the overall tenor of the Canadian RSD regime in line with UNHCR standards on handling gender-based asylum claims. Canada's generosity on gender-based claims, and the extension of the gender logic to include victims of coercive population control, are clear examples of the diffusion of international human rights norms within a domestic context. This expansion was, initially, extrajudicial, but it percolated up to influence courts via the deferential attitude toward the expertise of administrative tribunals. The political motivation behind taking an internationalist position may have been, in part, to preserve Canada's symbolic reputation as a middle power. This position certainly grates against the extreme border control measures that Canada has taken despite international guidance to the contrary. Yet, in the case of Canada's adoption of the UNHCR gender guidance, internationalism is more than just symbolic; it has led to concrete and measurable results for asylum seekers. Of course, insulated bureaucracies do not always look to international norms for guidance, as the IRB's handling of Mexican and Roma claims illustrates. Like all the institutional players in an RSD regime, they are strategic about when they synch up with international legal guidance and when they do not.

The United States has had a very different level of official commitment to inter-nationalism than Canada. American policymakers, administrators, and judges tend to view asylum policy and law as a purely domestic concern. Especially because there are so many moving parts and conflicting interpretations within the country, they see no need to look beyond its borders for yet more perspec-tives. America's position on international guidance is perfectly compatible with its assertion of sovereignty when it comes to border control issues such as inter-diction at sea and the expedited removal program. The United States is very clear that it need not consult other countries or international institutions when gen-erating migration policy.

By contrast, Australian decision makers and judges are highly attuned to international developments, and regularly cite and borrow from the opinions of courts in other countries. Nevertheless, this commitment to understanding the diversity of approaches worldwide seems to stem not from a desire to be seen as a team player in global governance, but from a dearth of jurisprudence within the country, combined with a need to legitimate their decisions. By the time the question of how to define the Convention term "membership in a particular social group" reached the Australian High Court in 1997 in the case of *Applicant A v. MIEA* (190 CLR 225, 1997), the justices stated with some consternation and a good deal of accuracy that "courts and tribunals in the United States and Canada have given many decisions which cannot be reconciled with each other." This international confusion allowed the judges the freedom to go ahead and decide the case based on their own preferred logic. Australian judges often pick and choose among foreign opinions and highlight contradictions among them, but they neglect to relate this analysis back to the guidance of the UNHCR. Thus, the Australian case suggests that judicial cross-fertilization and borrowing is a distinct phenomenon from the internationalism of Canada, one with very different motivations and results. The outward-looking perspective of Australia's High Court is both exploratory and self-serving; it is not designed to lead to the diffusion of international human rights norms.

Lessons for Public Law

Much of this book has been focused on highlighting the ways in which a public law approach can inform migration scholarship. However, the reverse is also true; migration policy can be a helpful case study for informing some of the central debates within the field of public law. In particular, this comparison of RSD regimes suggests three specific insights into our understanding of law and courts. First, this study makes clear that the relationship between administrative law and asylum law is not just unidirectional, with national conceptions of administrative justice shaping RSD regimes. Rather, asylum cases have also frequently prompted courts in the United States, Canada, and Australia to examine the contours of procedural fairness more generally. Thus, to a surprising degree, asylum seekers have become the engines that drive larger scale administrative law reform. In Australia, migration and asylum cases have forced new clarifications of the Administrative Decisions (Judicial Review) Act of 1977, and fueled the longstanding and heated debate about the need for a Bill of Rights (Williams 2000). In Canada, asylum cases have forced the Canadian Supreme Court to rework and clarify the reasonableness standard of judicial review that applies to all administrative decisions. In the United States, migration decisions are, regularly, the means by which the federal courts and administrative agencies work out the limits of the general *Chevron* deference doctrine.

The frequency with which asylum cases have become jurisprudentially significant beyond their area may simply be attributed to the fact that these cases are so numerous today. However, because it is a common phenomenon across the years and across all three jurisdictions in this study, it seems likely that there is something particularly challenging about asylum questions that inspires the reevaluation of old doctrines and practices. Because they weave multiple areas of law together, Dyzenhaus (2004:1) has suggested that decisions about asylum claims illustrate the challenges that lie in the future of the "legal relationship between individual and state." As asylum seekers continue to arrive and make complex claims, decision makers must figure out how flexible the text of the internationally based refugee definition is within their particular domestic context. Thus, the case of asylum helps public law scholars think through questions about the relationship between various levels of law—whether administrative, constitutional, and international law must be in competition with one another, or whether it is possible for them to eventually coexist as a unified public law.

The second lesson that asylum cases can offer is for those public law scholars interested in the phenomenon known as judicialization. All three countries in this study have very high levels of asylum cases appealed to their federal courts, and thus are often construed as experiencing a judicialization of asylum policy. However, a closer look reveals that the judiciary plays a very different role in each place. Judicial deference to administrative agencies is an important legal concept in all three states, but the standard is completely different in each. In Australia, the High Court has become a big player in asylum policy, but without much impact on the expansion of individual rights. As with its administrative agencies, the role of courts in Australian politics is far less settled than in the United States or Canada, and asylum seekers frequently bring the cases that are being used to sort out these larger constitutional questions.

Thus, the case study of asylum supports those who claim that judicialization does not always mean automatic rights expansion. In Canada, the relatively powerful courts have actively resisted getting involved in asylum decision making, declining to review the vast majority of cases that are appealed out of the administrative agency. However, the courts maintain a significant degree of authority to weigh in and change the RSD regime if they deem it necessary. This contrast between Australia and Canada illustrates that one should be very careful not to measure judicialization purely quantitatively. Australia's heavy asylum caseload suggests more power than the judiciary actually has, and Canada's lower caseload belies the power of the federal courts in this area. Ultimately, because the judicialization of RSD does not look remotely the same everywhere it happens, even in very similar states, the concept becomes unhelpful. At the very least, it needs much more elaboration in future scholarship.

Finally, asylum cases are useful to public law because the conundrums inherent in making life-and-death decisions based on the refugee definition help illuminate major questions in constitutional theory about the difficulties of textual interpretation. In many ways, the 1951 Convention is an artifact of a particular historic moment, drafted with a specific vision of a refugee in mind. Countries such as the United States, Canada, and Australia ratified the Convention before they were really asylum seeker destinations, and so in many ways they are only now seeing the consequences of these past commitments come home to roost. Each country seems to have either chosen, or haphazardly fallen into, distinct approaches to handling this interpretive dilemma. Canada has adopted more of a "living Convention" approach, allowing the meaning of the refugee definition to expand and incorporate new claims quite fluidly. Australia's approach is much more text based. The interpretation still evolves, but in a very slow and measured fashion, always making reference to the words on the page. In yet a third way, the U.S. approach is highly politicized, leading the meaning of the refugee definition to expand and contract in fits and starts. It is not predictable or consistent for one type of claim over time or across analogous claims.

Asylum cases do not just require interpretation of the refugee definition; they also regularly invoke questions of constitutional interpretation. Looking at the way that courts in each state have treated vulnerable noncitizens reveals the ways in which protection of their rights may be dependent on the existence of textual entry points, such as the 5th and 14th Amendments' due process rights in the United States, and the Section 7 rights in Canada's Charter of Rights and Freedoms. Court decisions about the rights of noncitizens, such as *Zadvydas v. Davis* (533 U.S. 678, 2001) in the United States and *Singh v. Minister of Employment and Immigration* (1 S.C.R. 177, 1985) in Canada have demonstrated that enumerated rights are important sources of power for courts in these two countries.

Because rights protections are not enumerated in Australia, it is much more difficult for courts to transfer them and apply them to areas for which they were not originally designed. Instead, Australian courts work much more by drawing analogies, even if the cases they cite come from other nations—a technique that has met with mixed success. The Australian case reveals that, even in a system with no enumerated rights and low levels of administrative insulation, text can be hugely significant. Australia's constitutional quirk—the High Court's right to review decisions by commonwealth officers—was not drafted with migration in mind, but has become the key tool that empowers the Court in this area.

In these three ways, public law can benefit from taking asylum more seriously. It is a significant driver of developments in administrative, constitutional, and international law. More importantly, it provides a prototype for understanding the various ways in which these three areas of law might interact in the future.

The Future of Asylum

Categorizing migrants is an important part of border control policy for receiving states, and because they defy categorization, asylum seekers represent an inconvenient truth for policymakers and refugee advocates alike. Recent decades have ushered in a global panic about unauthorized, uncontrollable migration, and asylum seekers have often been the poster children for that panic (Steiner 2000, Dauvergne 2008). They bring confusion to debates about how to weigh the sovereign right of nations to police their borders against the moral obligation of states to provide refuge to people fleeing oppression. Policymakers in the United States, Canada, and Australia have resolved this dilemma by enacting policies that weed out not just obvious economic migrants, but also the poor, old, sick, weak, and unlucky. The logic seems to be that because it is so expensive to process asylum seekers who successfully arrive, it is worth spending a great deal of effort to prevent them from arriving. Thus, the moment of actually crossing the border remains crucial to the process of asylum seeking.

Many scholars of forced migration, aware of domestic political concerns about "opening the floodgates" to uncontrolled entry, are often incredibly reluctant to acknowledge any ambiguity in the motivations behind the migration of those seeking refugee status. For example, academics are often concerned that "by contending that the distinctions between voluntary and forced migration are blurred...researchers run the risk of preparing the ammunition for governments or other actors who will not recognize the legitimate claims of refugees" (Stepputat 1999:416–417). Assuming that states have a finite tolerance level for offering protection, many refugee scholars insist that a clear divide between refugees and other displaced people is important, both theoretically and politically (Hathaway 2007, Price 2009). This approach to scholarship reifies the refugee as a concept and falsely portrays RSD as a positivist truth-seeking activity. In contrast, the stories in this book make clear that migrant categories are blurred, just as the motivations of migrants often are cumulative. Policymakers know this, and it does migrants no favors for scholars to pretend otherwise.

In many ways, the international refugee regime has been remarkably durable. States continue to conduct RSD for large numbers of migrants each year, despite the end of the Cold War and major shifts in both the types of claims being made and the most frequent countries of origin. International convergence scholars point to the fact that receiving states all use the same textual standard for assessing refugee status as evidence that international human rights are globalizing, a glimmer of hope in the face of widespread noncompliance with other international norms. However, when we take into account the shapes that RSD regimes can take, the fact that all three countries are using the same basic test for RSD can become irrelevant quite rapidly. In all three countries, if asylum seekers can cross the border, they can access their right under international law to seek asylum. But, once this happens, we do not see international human rights following migrants across borders. We see migrants accessing different sets of rights, depending on which borders they cross. RSD regimes make a big difference, and the difference an RSD makes is only going to become more significant as the numbers of nonobvious refugees continue to increase.

Appendix

LIST OF INTERVIEWS

Organization/Role	Date
U.S. Citizenship and Immigration Services, Asylum Office	2/05/2007
UNHCR, D.C.	2/06/2007
Human Rights First	2/07/2007
Refugee Council USA	2/07/2007
U.S. Conference of Catholic Bishops	2/07/2007
Human Rights Watch	2/08/2007
International Rescue Committee	2/08/2007
Women's Commission for Refugee Women and Children	2/08/2007
American Immigration Lawyers Association	2/09/2007
Amnesty International, D.C.	2/09/2007
Migration Policy Institute	2/09/2007
Refugees International	2/12/2007
U.S. advocate	2/12/2007
Office of Immigration Litigation, Department of Justice	2/12/2007
Office of Immigration Litigation, Department of Justice	2/12/2007
Board of Immigration Appeals	2/13/2007
State Department, Bureau of Population, Refugees, and Migration	2/13/2007
American Bar Association, Committee on Immigration	2/14/2007
U.S. advocate	2/15/2007
Lutheran Immigration and Refugee Services	2/16/2007

(*Continued*)

Appendix: List of Interviews (Continued)

Organization/Role	Date
Immigration and Refugee Board, Operations	3/29/2007
Citizenship and Immigration Canada, Asylum Policy	3/30/2007
Citizenship and Immigration Canada, Refugee Branch	3/30/2007
Citizenship and Immigration Canada, International Coordination	3/30/2007
Former Immigration Refugee Board member	4/02/2007
Amnesty International, Montreal	4/03/2007
UNHCR, Ottawa	4/03/2007
Citizenship and Immigration Canada, Senior Counsel	4/03/2007
Canadian Council for Refugees	4/07/2007
Canadian advocate	5/09/2007
Canadian advocate	5/09/2007
Immigration and Refugee Board, Regional Director	5/10/2007
Immigration and Refugee Board, Legal Services	5/10/2007
Canadian advocate	5/11/2007
Canadian advocate	5/11/2007
Immigration and Refugee Board, Training	5/14/2007
Canadian advocate	5/14/2007
Immigration and Refugee Board, Coordinating Member	5/15/2007
Canadian advocate	5/15/2007
Canadian advocate	5/15/2007
Canadian advocate	5/18/2007
Canadian advocate	5/22/2007
Canadian advocate	5/22/2007
Canadian advocate	5/23/2007
Canadian advocate	5/24/2007
Department of Justice, Canada	5/25/2007
Canadian advocate	5/25/2007
Canadian advocate	5/28/2007
Canadian advocate	5/28/2007
Canadian advocate	5/28/2007
Canadian advocate	5/29/2007

(*Continued*)

Appendix: List of Interviews (Continued)

Organization/Role	Date
Canadian advocate	5/29/2007
Refugee Law Office, Toronto	5/30/2007
Canadian advocate	5/30/2007
Canadian advocate	5/31/2007
U.S. advocate	8/23/2007
U.S. advocate	8/23/2007
U.S. advocate	8/24/2007
U.S. advocate	8/27/2007
U.S. advocate	8/28/2007
U.S. advocate	8/29/2007
U.S. advocate	9/12/2007
U.S. advocate	9/13/2007
U.S. advocate	9/14/2007
U.S. advocate	9/15/2007
UNHCR, Canberra	10/02/2007
Federation of Ethnic Communities Australia	10/03/2007
Department of Immigration and Citizenship, Legal Policy	10/05/2007
Department of Immigration and Citizenship, Legal Officer	10/05/2007
Department of Immigration and Citizenship, Protection Policy	10/05/2007
Department of Immigration and Citizenship, Litigation	10/05/2007
Department of Immigration and Citizenship, Onshore Protection Branch	10/05/2007
Refugee Action Committee	10/08/2007
Australian advocate	10/15/2007
A Just Australia	10/16/2007
Australian advocate	10/16/2007
Australian advocate	10/16/2007
Refugee Council of Australia	10/18/2007
Edmund Rice Center	10/18/2007
Jesuit Refugee Services	10/19/2007
Refugee Advice and Casework Service	10/22/2007

(*Continued*)

Appendix: List of Interviews (Continued)

Organization/Role	Date
Asylum Seeker Center	10/22/2007
Bar Association of New South Wales	10/23/2007
Australian advocate	10/24/2007
Australian advocate	10/25/2007
Australian advocate	10/25/2007
Australian advocate	10/26/2007
Legal Aid Office, Sydney	10/29/2007
Australian advocate	10/31/2007
Australian advocate	10/31/2007
Australian advocate	11/01/2007
Refugee Review Tribunal, Registrar	11/02/2007
Refugee Review Tribunal, Legal Services	11/02/2007
Australian advocate	11/05/2007
Federal Court of Australia, Registrar's Office	11/05/2007
Federal Court of Australia, Registrar's Office	11/05/2007
Australian advocate	11/06/2007
Australian advocate	11/06/2007
Australian advocate	11/07/2007
Australian advocate	11/08/2007
Australian advocate	11/09/2007
Australian advocate	11/13/2007

NOTES

Chapter 1

1. The UNHCR estimates that this number represents only about 60% of the 45.2 million displaced people in the world (UNHCR 2013).
2. The United Nations Population Fund estimates there are 214 million migrants worldwide, comprising about 3% of the total global population (UNFPA 2014).
3. China has been the top source country for asylum applications in the United States every year since 1999 except 2001, when it was second. In Canada, China was in the top three source countries from 1998 to 2007 and has since been number five. China has been the top source country in Australia since 2002 (UNHCR 1980–2012).
4. See also: Nicholas Keung, "Canadian refugee decisions hinge on presiding judge, says report," *The Toronto Star*, March 12, 2012 and Marina Jimenez, "Refugee Approval Rates Vary Widely: Some Board Members Reject All Applicants," *The Globe and Mail*, July 24, 2004.
5. Salehyan and Rosenblum (2008) attempt to measure public salience of asylum policy by counting the number of *New York Times* articles that mention "immigration" or "refugee" in any given year. They found that increased media attention was correlated with greater admissions rates of asylum seekers during the 1980s, but found no statistically significant relationship for the 1990s. I find this measure to be unsatisfactory; it is too blunt, and the mixed results suggest a much more complicated relationship between public opinion, media coverage, and policy action than their measure can capture.

Chapter 2

1. See also Holmes and Keith (2010) and Rottman, Fariss, and Poe (2009) for international relations studies that use quantitative data to confirm that both humanitarian and strategic concerns influence RSD.
2. See, for example, the American case of *Campos-Guardado v. INS* (1987) in which the 5th Circuit Federal Court of Appeals found that when soldiers raped the relatives of high-profile political activists, it was not due to the political opinion of the women who were raped, but the "sexual desire" of the soldiers. Thus, the women did not qualify for protection under the Convention.
3. The head of the U.S. Asylum Program told me: "It is a game of catch-up. Strategies for fraud are always improving, and so are detection strategies" (author interview, 2/05/2007).
4. RSD agencies in many countries make heavy use of U.S. State Department reports.

5. See Bohmer and Shuman (2007) and Showler (2006) for rich descriptions of these hearing room dynamics, many of which I have witnessed personally.
6. The difficulty of recounting memories of extreme trauma in a clear narrative was expertly demonstrated in psychiatrist Judith Herman's landmark *Trauma and Recovery: The Aftermath of Violence* (1992). Many lawyers described their difficulty in getting their clients' stories straight. One American lawyer described the process to me as being like "peeling an onion."
7. In response to this argument, scholars such as B.S. Chimni (1998) have asserted that there is nothing new about the new asylum seekers save the fact that large numbers of them are more likely to make wealthy western democracies their nations of first asylum rather than waiting patiently to be selected from camps.
8. Because Price (2009) combines rates for all industrialized states into one over-time figure, his data tell us nothing about the relationship between application rates and acceptance rates in any given state.
9. For detailed histories of migration policy and refugee resettlement see Zucker and Zucker (1987), Loescher and Scanlan (1986), Tichenor (2002) on the United States; Kelley and Trebilcock (1998) on Canada; Hawkins (1989) on Canada and Australia; Tavan (2005) on Australia; and Freeman and Jupp (1992) on Australia and the United States.
10. To calculate these numbers, I compared the UN asylum application statistics for the years 2006 to 2010 with the 2010 census estimates for the population of each country.
11. For a defense of multisite fieldwork in comparative migration studies, see FitzGerald (2012).

Chapter 3

1. Although the U.S. Senate ratification of the Protocol in 1968 was, by all accounts, intended as a symbolic gesture, there is good evidence to suggest that the action nonetheless laid the groundwork for the eventual adoption of the UN Convention standard in the 1980 Refugee Act (see Hamlin and Wolgin 2012).
2. U.S. Constitution Article I, Section 8 states that "the Congress shall have power to…establish a uniform rule of naturalization…[and] to make all laws which shall be necessary and proper for carrying into execution the foregoing powers."
3. The 1980 Act codified the UN definition into law almost verbatim. Section 101(a)(42) of the Immigration and Nationality Act, as amended by the Refugee Act of 1980 states: "The term 'refugee' means (A) any person who is outside any country of such person's nationality or, in the case of a person having no nationality, is outside any country in which such person last habitually resided, and who is unable or unwilling to return to, and is unable or unwilling to avail himself or herself of the protection of, that country because of persecution or a well-founded fear of persecution on account of race, religion, nationality, membership in a particular social group, or political opinion."
4. See also, for example, Marjorie Hyer, "U.S. policy on Central America opposed by mainline Christians," *Washington Post*, July 3, 1983; George Volsky, "U.S. churches offer sanctuary to aliens facing deportation," *New York Times*, April 8, 1983; Robert Reinhold, "Churches and U.S. clash on alien sanctuary," *New York Times*, June 28, 1984.
5. Marvin Howe, "Study asks for new safeguards for refugees asking asylum," *New York Times*, March 16, 1990.
6. Editorial, "The refugee panic act of 1993," *New York Times*, July 23, 1993.
7. Al Kamen, "Bush Defends Policy on Return of Haitians," *Washington Post*, November, 21, 1991; Barbara Crossette, "U.S. Transfers Haitians to Base in Cuba," *New York Times*, November 2, 1991.
8. Michael Wines, "Switching Policy, U.S. will return refugees to Haiti," *New York Times*, May 25, 1992.

9. Deborah Sontag, "Reneging on refuge: The Haitian precedent," *New York Times*, June 27, 1993.

10. Seth Faison, "A flicker of empathy for 110 Chinese," *New York Times*, October 21, 1993.

11. Tim Weiner, "Pleas for asylum inundate system for immigration," *New York Times*, April 25, 1993.

12. Michael S. Arnold, "Calls to change asylum system gain urgency," *Washington Post*, June 13, 1993.

13. Although detention of noncitizens is recognized by international law as a legitimate exercise of sovereignty, the UN has called repeatedly on governments to use it as sparingly as possible, and only in extreme circumstances. The UNHCR declares: "detention is only permissible when there is an intention to mislead or a refusal to cooperate with authorities. Asylum seekers who arrive without documentation because they are unable to obtain any in their country of origin should not be detained solely for that reason" (UNHCR 1999:4).

14. *American Immigration Lawyers Association, et al. v. Janet Reno, Attorney General of the United States, et al.* 199 F.3d 1352 (D.C. Cir. 2000). The IIRIRA states that all lawsuits must be "filed no later than 60 days after the date the challenged section, regulation, directive, guidance, or procedure ... is first implemented" (1 8 U.S.C. s 1252(e)(3)(A)-(B)); William Branigin, "INS's 'Expedited Removal' Attacked," *Washington Post*, April 4, 1998.

15. Mirta Ojito, "Inconsistency at I.N.S. complicates refugees' asylum quest," *New York Times*, June 22, 1998; Barbara Crossette, "In the Secret Detentions Club," *New York Times*, August 11, 2002.

16. Dora Schriro, *Immigration Detention Overview and Recommendations.* ICE Report. Washington, DC: 2009; National Immigration Forum, *Backgrounder: The Math of Immigration Detention.* Washington, DC: 2009.

17. This provision came at the behest of asylum advocates who had been prioritizing an end to the one-year bar for more than a decade. In particular, Human Rights First's End the Deadline campaign conducted extensive lobbying on this issue throughout the reform process.

18. In Canada, the term *inland refugee status determination* is used instead of *asylum seeking*, but because they are equivalent, and because the United States and Australia both use the more concise term, I refer to the *asylum program* in Canada at times.

19. Victor Malarek, "Give refugee claimants welfare, report urges," *Globe and Mail*, June 18, 1985.

20. Victor Malarek, "Smear tactics cited India pressing Canada on refugees, Sikhs say," *Globe and Mail*, July 23, 1985.

21. Peter Edwards, "Another refugee boat is off our coastline," *Toronto Star*, August 1, 1987.

22. Patricia Poirier, "Hoping to stay, Turks begin walk to Ottawa," *Globe and Mail*, April 5, 1988.

23. Elaine Carey, "Immigration system on verge of collapse," *Toronto Star*, April 2, 1988.

24. William Angus and James Hathaway, "Ominous overkill in Ottawa's refugee bill," *Globe and Mail*, August 25, 1987; Bruce McLeod, "Why the refugee bill embarrasses Canadians," *Toronto Star*, August 18, 1987; Michael Schelew, "Misguided bills pose a threat to true refugees," *Globe and Mail*, August 13, 1987.

25. Lorne Waldman, "A refugee system teetering on the brink," *Toronto Star*, May 31, 1990; Christie McLaren, "Jammed at the door: Refugee-backlog plan in a mess: Scheme to resolve thousands of cases mired in delays, inequalities," *Globe and Mail*, February 23, 1991; Michele Landsberg, "Canadian refugee system is torturing Iranian family," *Toronto Star*, October 21, 1991; Paul Watson, "Refugee boards accept Tamil, reject brother," *Toronto Star*, November 25, 1991.

26. Dorothy Lipovenko, "Refugee law satisfies Charter, judge rules," *Globe and Mail*, January 5, 1989.

27. Canadian Press, "Immigration legislation receives royal assent," *Globe and Mail*, December 18, 1992.

28. Paulette Peirol, "Panel to review immigration law: Lawyers not pleased with selections for Robillard committee," *Globe and Mail*, November 26, 1996.

29. Allan Thompson, "Talk of scuttling refugee board worries critics," *Toronto Star*, December 18, 1997.

30. "Canada Planning Human Smuggling Crackdown," *Toronto Star*, July 22, 1999.

31. Campbell Clark, "Coderre to delay plan for Refugee Appeal Division," *Globe and Mail*, April 29, 2002; Allan Thompson, "Ottawa scraps refugee reforms," *Toronto Star*, April 27, 2002.

32. Allan Thompson, "Flow of refugees at heart of deal: Bilateral accord would let U.S., Canada return refugee claimants," *Toronto Star*, October 26, 2001. The policy was modeled on a similar agreement outlined in the Dublin Convention, which restricts the ability of asylum seekers to lodge claims in multiple European countries.

33. *Canadian Council for Refugees, Canadian Council of Churches, Amnesty International and John Doe vs. Her Majesty the Queen*, FCC 1262 (2007).

34. Nicholas Keung, "Refugee deal with U.S. back in force. Asylum-seekers at border will continue to be rejected until 'Safe Third Country' pact reviewed," *Toronto Star*, February 1, 2008; Jim Brown, "Refugee pact survives court challenge," *Globe and Mail*, February 5, 2009.

35. Arch MacKenzie, "U.S. refugee crackdown boosts exodus to Canada," *Toronto Star*, January 15, 1987.

36. Debra Black, "Canada's immigration system lacks heart, critics say," *Toronto Star*, June 28, 2013.

37. "Hawke jumps the queue." *Sydney Morning Herald*, Editorial, June 8, 1990.

38. Elizabeth Wynhausen, "Champion of the Boat People, Snooping Around," *The Sunday Herald*, June 26, 1994.

39. *Weekend Australian*, July 21–22, 1990. There may be a double meaning to this statement, because the phrase "Bob's your uncle" is a common expression in Commonwealth countries, and the Prime Minister's first name was Bob. Thus, he may have also been implying that he was personally unwilling to offer help.

40. Helen Signy, "Committee to assess policy on boat people," *Sydney Morning Herald*, May 29, 1993.

41. Paola Totaro, "Photios backs UN Villawood inquiry," *Sydney Morning Herald*, July 5, 1994.

42. Moira Rayner, "Nobody's child deserves to grow up behind razor wire," *The Age*, July 24, 1995.

43. Michael Magazanik, "Tougher laws on 'refugees'," *The Age*, December 31, 1994.

44. Stephen Hutcheon, "China tour points to refugees' return," *The Age*, April 8, 1995.

45. David Lague, "Timor refugees test Jakarta ties," *Sydney Morning Herald*, October 11, 1995.

46. Karen Middleton, "Asylum policy turnabout on East Timorese," *The Age*, August 16, 1996.

47. Louise Williams, "Reject refugees or risk flood, Australia warned," *Sydney Morning Herald*, May 7, 1997.

48. Steve Butcher, "Ruling lifts Timor asylum hope," *The Age*, October 31, 1998.

49. Cynthia Banham, "East Timorese draw a blank after pleas for refugee status," *Sydney Morning Herald*, September 26, 2002.

50. Helen Signy and Cynthia Banham, "Timorese asylum claims blocked by secret freeze," *Sydney Morning Herald*, November 18, 2002.

51. Meaghan Shaw and Andra Jackson, "Win for Timorese asylum seekers after 10-year battle," *The Age*, June 4, 2003.

52. Mark Metherell and Lindy Edwards, "Influx packs detention centers," *Sydney Morning Herald*, June 17, 1999.

53. Mike Seccombe, "'Queuejumpers' may be genuine," *Sydney Morning Herald*, December 28, 1999.

54. Janine MacDonad, "Barriers go up for illegal immigrants," *The Age*, October 14, 1999.

55. In 2002, the UNHCR awarded the Nansen Award to Captain Arne Rinnan and the crew of the *MV Tampa*.

56. Louise Dodson, Simon Mann, and Kerry Taylor, "Refugees stranded at sea: Boat people get refuge in containers, PM sends a message to the world," *The Age*, August 28, 2001.
57. Louise Dodson, Simon Mann, and Kerry Taylor, "Tension in Coalition as stalemate deepens," *The Age*, August 29, 2001.
58. Kerry Taylor and Mark Forbes, "Pacific Solution refugees in Australia," *The Age*, July 31, 2002.
59. Brendan Nicholson, "More patrols to deter smugglers," *The Sunday Age*, September 2, 2001.
60. Russell Skelton, "Channels open in a no-go zone," *The Age*, August 3, 2002.
61. Cynthia Banham, "Islands wiped off map in boat people mix-up," *Sydney Morning Herald*, December 18, 2002.
62. Margo Kingston, "Asylum boat sank 'in search area'," *Sydney Morning Herald*, June 15, 2002.
63. Phillip Hudson and Russell Skelton, "Minister rules out apology to 'Anna,'" *Sunday Age*, February 6, 2005.
64. "The truth overboard," Editorial, *The Age*, August 10, 2004.
65. "Extra police sent after Christmas Island detention centre riots," *The Australian*, March 18, 2011.
66. Yuko Narushima and Kirsty Needham, "Abbott to talk to Nauru on reopening camp," *The Age*, August 7, 2010.
67. "Gillard announces Malaysian solution," *Sydney Morning Herald*, May 7, 2011.
68. "UN refugee agency condemns Nauru detention centre," *The Australian*, December 14, 2012.
69. Bianca Hall and Daniel Flitton, "Fire tears through Nauru centre as detainees riot," *Sydney Morning Herald*, July 20, 2013.
70. Greg Sheridan, "Popular sense trumps policy and media elite," *The Australian*, October 5, 2013.
71. Greg Sheridan, "Abbott in Indonesia: The adventure begins," *The Australian*, October 3, 2013.
72. For more on the bifurcation of Australia's asylum seekers into legal and illegal arrivals, see Stevens (2002) and Schloenhardt (2003).

Chapter 4

1. Adam Liptak, "Fed courts criticize judges' handling of asylum cases," *New York Times*, December 26, 2005.
2. There are eight Asylum Offices across the United States. Together, they hear approximately 40,000 cases per year.
3. If asylum applicants bring a lawyer, their counsel may make some brief closing remarks at the end of the hearing.
4. There are about 250 IJs in 58 EOIRs across the United States. They currently hear between 40,000 and 60,000 asylum cases per year, in addition to thousands of other immigration matters.
5. For an assessment of problems with access to legal counsel in the American RSD regime, see Schoenholtz and Jacobs (2002). The Department of Homeland Security lawyers who represent the government interest before the Immigration Judge are from a separate subdivision of the Department of Homeland Security than the Asylum Office, although they do have access to the notes of the Asylum Officer from the initial hearing. The time delay for Freedom of Information Act requests means that lawyers representing asylum applicants rarely see this file prior to the EOIR hearing.
6. From 1995 to 1999, the average grant rate was 24.4%; from 2000 to 2004, the average grant rate was 36.8% (Office of Immigration 2004). Unite States Citizenship Immigration Services has not reported this statistic since 2004, but in recent research, Ramji-Nogales et al. (2007, 2009) claim the affirmative grant rate was approximately one in three.

7. Amy Goldstein and Dan Eggen, "Immigration Judges often picked based on GOP ties law forbids practice; courts being reshaped," *Washington Post*, June 11, 2007.

8. Lynne Marek, "Posner blasts immigration courts as 'inadequate' and ill-trained," *The National Law Journal*, April 22, 2008.

9. Liptak, "Fed Courts Criticize Judges' Handling of Asylum Cases."

10. The EOIR statistical yearbooks update numbers each year. Therefore, the number of cases completed in a given year can be reported as a slightly different number in the following yearbook. I made every effort to report the most recent figures for each year. In addition, the BIA does not report in its statistics a breakdown of its completed cases by topic. Because there is no statistic for the number of asylum cases completed by the BIA per year, the total number is reported here.

11. The American Immigration Lawyers Association testified before the Senate Judiciary Committee in February 2002 in vigorous opposition to the BIA reform proposals. See AILA Issue Paper entitled "The Importance of Independence and Accountability in Our Immigration Courts."

12. The Court upheld the right of Congress to exclude in a series of three cases, known as the Chinese Exclusion cases: *Chan Chae Ping vs. U.S.* (1889), *Eiku v. U.S.* (1892), *and Fong Yue Ting v. U.S.* (1893).

13. In a recent decision outlawing the death penalty for minors, Justice Kennedy wrote: "the opinion of the world community, while not controlling our outcome, does provide respected and significant confirmation for our own conclusions." In dissent, Justice Scalia scathingly declared that although "the views of our own citizens are essentially irrelevant to the Court's decision today, the views of other countries and the so-called international community take center stage" (*Roper v. Simmons*, 543 U.S. 551 [2005]). Similarly, U.S. Supreme Court Justice Steven Breyer has heralded the benefits of "learning" in a debate with Justice Scalia at American University Law School, Constitutional Relevance of Foreign Court Decisions, January 13, 2005. These are two fairly isolated incidents, however.

14. Data compiled by author from Administrative Office of U.S. Courts, *Judicial Business*, 1996–2012.

15. These numbers of administrative appeals do not reflect the simultaneous dramatic increase in the number of people being charged with immigration-related crimes, such as trafficking or use of fraudulent documents. The increase of immigration cases in the criminal law context is beyond the scope of this book, but is noteworthy because it adds to the impact on federal judges of immigration as a policy issue. For data on this topic, see the Transactional Records Access Clearinghouse (TRAC).

16. I made repeated attempts to request this information from the U.S. Administrative Office of the U.S. Courts, Statistics Division, and from individual circuit courts, but in each instance I have been told the data do not exist.

17. Karin Brulliard, "Law students rush to meet needs in booming field of immigration," *The Washington Post*, July 7, 2008

Chapter 5

1. Peter Showler, "Proposed refugee reforms may be a step towards a faster, fairer system," *News Release*, March 30, 2010.

2. The Protecting Canada's Immigration System Act received royal assent on June 28, 2012, and went into effect on December 15, 2012.

3. As the *Singh* decision suggests, the supremacy of the border as a delineation of rights eligibility is less clear in Canada than in the Unites States. On the one hand, the Supreme Court decided in the *Singh* decision that the Charter applied to noncitizens in the Canadian territory even if they are still officially outside Canada and are seeking entry. Five years later, the Court backtracked from that position in the case of *Canadian Council of Churches v. Canada* (Minister of Employment and Immigration) (1 S.C.R. 236, 1992) which

suggests that noncitizens that are completely outside of Canada are "beyond the scope of the Charter."

4. The justices were split on whether the Charter or its precursor, the Canadian Bill of Rights, applied to this case, but when that issue was settled, the judges agreed unanimously that if the Charter applied, than fundamental justice required a hearing.

5. If the CIC is informed by the Canadian Border Services Agency that a particular claimant may be a security risk or may be undesirable for some other policy reason, the Minister of Citizenship and Immigration may choose to send a representative to sit in on the hearing. That representative may or may not make a submission arguing for the denial of the refugee claim. Intervention by a Minister's representative occurs only in a small minority of cases.

6. According to a 2008 report, the Toronto office of the IRB processes two-thirds of the total national caseload (Pricewaterhouse Coopers 2008).

7. In December 2003, the IRB chairperson issued a document, known as *Guideline 7*, titled *Concerning Preparation and Conduct of a Hearing in the Refugee Protection Division*. In the interest of expediency, this guideline reversed the longstanding practice of opening a hearing with counsel's questions before allowing the IRB to question the refugee claimant. Guideline 7 has been challenged in court, and the order of questioning is now up to the discretion of the board member in each case (see *Canada (Citizenship and Immigration) v. Thamotharem* [FCA 198, 2007]).

8. Personal correspondence with Paul Aterman, Director, IRB Operations Branch, 7/10/2007. The IRB does not distinguish in their statistics between legal counsel and immigration consultants.

9. Immigration and Refugee Board annual reports 2002–2010. See also Sean Rehaag, "2012 refugee claim data and IRB member recognition rates." Report for the Canadian Council for Refugees. May 13, 2013.

10. Source: Internal statistics provided by the IRB Operations Branch, July 2007.

11. Ibid.

12. Lesley Ciarula Taylor, "Refugees seek avenue for appeal; Critics push Parliament on passing legislation to reform system for failed applicants," *Toronto Star*, August 20, 2008.

13. "Tories reach deal with NDP, bloc on refugee reform; Abuses of immigration system addressed in legislation," *Toronto Star*, June 11, 2010.

14. Campbell Clark, "Tories 'let's-make-a-deal' approach good politics," *Globe and Mail*, June 11, 2010.

15. IRB statistics presented in the case at the federal court. Corroborated by the UNHCR statistical database. *Kozak v. Canada (Minister of Citizenship and Immigration)* (FCA 124, 2006). For a detailed discussion of this controversy, see Kernerman (2008).

16. Although Epp (1998) discusses the shift in the Supreme Court of Canada's docket away from economic matters and toward individual rights between 1960 and 1990, he makes no mention of administrative law or the relative proportion of the Court's docket it represented during that period.

17. On this topic, see Cartier (2004) for a rich discussion of *Slaight Communications Inc. v. Davidson* (1 S.C.R. 1038, 1989) and *Ross v. New Brunswick School District No. 15* (1 S.C.R. 825, 1996).

18. The American standard of *Chevron* deference is probably most similar to the middle Canadian standard of simple reasonableness; it defers to the administrative agency unless the agency decision is unreasonable.

19. The leave rate for refugee cases was 12% in 2004, 15% in 2005, 14% in 2006, 18% in 2007, 15% in 2008, 13% in 2009, 14% in 2010, 14% in 2011, and 14% in 2012 (Federal Court of Canada statistical reports).

20. This attitude, that legal expertise is not necessary for RSD, was prevalent among all staff members with whom I spoke with at the IRB, with the exception of those in the Legal Services Department.

21. Kim Bolan, "Vacancies 'poisoning' immigration board," *Vancouver Sun*, May 2, 2008.

22. Bora Laskin was one of Canada's most famous legal minds. As Chief Justice of the Canadian Supreme Court from 1973 to 1984, he presided over the transition to the Charter of Rights and Freedoms in 1982.

23. These decisions were edited for spelling and grammar on November 28, 2006, after they were identified as Persuasive Decisions.

24. "Canada defends visa change for Mexicans, Czechs," CBC News, July 14, 2009.

25. "Mexico doesn't merit safe label," Op-Ed by Axelle Janczur, *Toronto Star*, February 20, 2013.

Chapter 6

1. George Williams, "PM would be wise not to play catch-up with High Court," *Sydney Morning Herald*, November 24, 2010.

2. When the interbranch turf wars between Parliament and the High Court first emerged, they seemed like a reaction to the aggressive politics of deterrence that the Liberal Party pursued under Prime Minister Howard from 1996 to 2007. However, after the Labor Party took control in 2007, both parties seem to agree on maintaining the basic framework of that approach. Yuko Narushima, "Parties Row in the Same Direction Over Boat Arrivals: Decision 2010," *Sydney Morning Herald*, August 10, 2010.

3. Commonwealth of Australia Constitution Act of 1901, Section 75(v): Original Jurisdiction of High Court. The text gives original jurisdiction over writs or injunctions, but has been interpreted to mean all orders made by an officer of the Commonwealth.

4. Chris Bowen, Minister for Immigration and Citizenship, "Government announces faster, fairer refugee determination process." Press release, January 7, 2011.

5. This discretion is outlined in Section 46A of the Migration Act, which was added via the Migration Amendment (Excision from Migration Zone) Act of 2001.

6. According to the head of the RSD program, the DIAC conducts interviews "if there is a credibility issue or for client facilitation reasons, like if the person has major obstacles to expressing themselves on paper" (author interview, 10/05/2007).

7. Ibid.

8. The RRT has more than 90 members, but the vast majority of them are part-time. In addition, all members are cross-appointed to the Migration Review Tribunal, and spend some of their time hearing other migration cases.

9. Author interviews with RRT Registrar and head of Legal Services, 11/02/2007; see also MRT/RRT 2011:39).

10. The RRT upheld the DIAC decision 88% of the time for unrepresented applicants compared with 65% of the time for represented applicants (MRT/RRT 2011:40).

11. See also Glendenning et al. (2006) for a detailed criticism of the DIAC by the Edmund Rice Center for Justice and Community Education.

12. Michael Pelly, "Judge blasts 'biased' refugee tribunal," *The Australian*, September 28, 2009.

13. In 2009/2010, the RRT upheld the DIAC 71% of the time, in 2010/2011 it was 70%, and in 2011/2012, it was 69% (MRT/RRT, 2010, 2011, 2012).

14. Philip Ruddock, "Immigration reform: Unfinished agenda" (speech delivered at the National Press Club, Canberra, March 18, 1998).

15. The "real chance" test was created by the High Court in the case *Chan v. Minister of Employment and Immigration* (HCA 62, 1989). This test is designed to guide decision makers in how to evaluate whether the applicant has an objective basis for fearing persecution.

16. Margaret Easterbrook, "Outcry over boat people clamp," *The Age*, May 6, 1992.

17. Parliament revised the Migration Act via the Migration Amendment (Review Provisions) Act of 2007.

18. Section 91R of the Migration Act was amended by the Migration Legislation Amendment Bill (No. 6) 2001 to limit the definition of persecution. The specifics of this are discussed in more detail in the case studies in Part III of this book.

Chapter 7

1. This story is a hybrid inspired by the testimony in *Mayers v. Canada (MEI)* (97 D.L.R [4th] 729, 1992), involving a Trinidadian woman; *Narvaez v. Canada* (2 FC 55 [T.D.], 1995), involving an Ecuadorian woman; the *Matter of R-A-* (Interim Decision #3403, 1999), involving a Guatemalan woman; and *MIMA v. Khawar* (FCA 1130, 2000), involving a Pakistani woman.

2. UNHCR website: "Refugee Women." http://www.unhcr.org/pages/49c3646c1d9.html

3. See Chimni (1998:351) who argues that the "exilic bias" in the refugee definition makes it difficult to extend refugee protection to women. See also Musalo (2003).

4. Kneebone (2005) argues that the subsuming of women under the particular social group category perpetuates the image of the refugee woman as a helpless victim, rather than a political actor who has taken a stand by fleeing an oppressive situation. She argues that gender-based claims should be conceptualized more frequently under the political opinion ground of the definition. However, this position has not been the dominant approach to gender-based refugee claims. See also MacIntosh (2005) for more discussion on how gender claims may be framed.

5. Thanks to Rachel VanSickle-Ward for this particular framing.

6. For examples of recent UNHCR guidance, see "Position Paper on Gender-Related Persecution." UNHCR January 2000; "Guidelines on International Protection: Gender-Related Persecution within the context of Article 1A(2) of the 1951 Convention and/or its 1967 Protocol relating to the Status of Refugees." UNHCR May 2002; "Sexual and Gender Based Violence Against Refugees, Returnees, and Internally Displaced Persons: Guidelines for Prevention and Response." UNHCR, May 2003.

7. Edward Broadbent, "Prisoners in their own homes," *The Globe and Mail*, December 21, 1992; Michele Landsberg, "To Valcourt, raped, beaten women aren't refugees," *The Toronto Star*, January 19, 1993; Andrew Cardozo, "Refuge for abused women Panel has dragged its heels on refugee status," *The Toronto Star*, February 17, 1993; Tim Harper, "Groups plead cause of female refugees," *The Toronto Star*, February 3, 1993.

8. Allan Thompson, "Women fleeing abuse to qualify as refugees," *The Toronto Star*, February 11, 1993; Geoffrey York, "Domestic abuse accepted for refugee status: Experts hail new guidelines recognizing persecution of women," *The Globe and Mail*, March 10, 1993.

9. A former IRB member told me: "The gender expansion is a source of pride for the government now, but they certainly didn't champion it. That came from within the Board—some women members in particular in the '90s. It's notable that the things the CIC boasts about come from the Board" (author interview, 4/03/2007).

10. Interviews with Canadian Council for Refugees and Amnesty International, plaintiffs, April 2007.

11. Jim Brown, "Refugee pact survives court challenge," *The Globe and Mail*, February 5, 2009.

12. Among the expert witnesses used by the Canadian government were Kay Hailbronner, Chair of Public Law, Public International Law, and European Law at the University of Konstanz, and Director of the Centre for International and European Law on Immigration and Asylum; and David Martin, Professor of International Law, University of Virginia School of Law.

13. The state of gender-based asylum jurisprudence up until 2002 was remarkably well laid out in a letter from the Center for Gender and Refugee Studies at University of California, Hastings School of Law to the Immigration Minister of Canada, Denis Coderre. April 2, 20002. Much of the following analysis is informed by the legal research conducted by the Center for Gender and Refugee Studies, hereafter referred to as the Coderre letter.

14. In fact, as I discuss in the sections on Canada and Australia, *other countries* have been more willing to adopt the logic of the BIA in *Acosta* relating to gender than the United States itself.

15. See the BIA decision *In re R-A-* (Interim Decision #3403, 1999), citing *Islam v. Secretary of State for Home Department* (House of Lords, March 25, 1999).

16. See, for example, letter from the Congressional Hispanic Caucus to Attorney General Reno, July 22, 1999; letter from a group of Senators to Attorney General Reno, December 2, 1999; letter from Senators Leahy, Brownback, Jeffords, Kerry, Kennedy, Feingold, and Schumer to Attorney General Janet Reno, February 14, 2000; and letter from members of both the House and Senate to Attorney General Janet Reno, September 2000.

17. INS Petition for Rehearing en banc, *Aguirre-Cervantes v. INS.* 9th Circuit Court of Appeal (2001). [Cited in Coderre Letter].

18. "Documents and information on Rodi Alvarado's claim for asylum in the U.S: Current update." *Center for Gender and Refugee Studies*, University of California, Hastings, IJ opinion quoted in Musalo (2010:47).

19. *In re A-T-* (September 27, 2007) BIA. This decision has since been vacated by the Attorney General. See also, Trymaine Lee, "Mukasey Vacates Panel's Decision Denying Asylum to Malian Woman," *New York Times*, September 23, 2008.

20. Justices Gummow and McHugh remarked, "the appeal is to be determined by reference to the legislation as it stood before the commencement of the Migration Legislation Amendment Act (No. 6) 2001."

Chapter 8

1. Jim Yardley, "China's leaders try to impress and reassure world," *The New York Times*, August 8, 2008.

2. David Barboza, "Big recalls don't slow exports from China," *The New York Times*, October 13, 2007; Sharon LaFraniere, "Chinese exports grow, but imports show signs of weakening," *The New York Times*, January 10, 2012.

3. In Fujian Province, in southeastern mainland China, it is very common for women to live alone for years while they wait for word that they can join their husbands who have immigrated to the West. These women are known as the *eighteen-thousanders wives* because of the typical price (in U.S. dollars) that their spouses paid to be smuggled into a city like New York, Vancouver, or Sydney (Zhang 2007:81).

4. In order to calculate these rankings, I used UNHCR Reports: 1980–2012, "Asylum Levels and Trends in Industrialized Countries – Statistical Overview of Asylum Applications Lodges in Europe and Selected Non-European Countries."

5. The coercive population control measures used in China today run against traditional notions of family, especially in rural areas, and because of the cultural preference for male children, are thought to exacerbate problems with gender-selective abortion and female infanticide (Matthew 1997).

6. The five grounds are race, religion, nationality, membership of a particular social group, or political opinion (Convention Relating to the Status of Refugees, Article 1, Section 1).

7. Andrew Rosenthal, "Bush to formalize shield for Chinese in U.S.," *The New York Times*. April 7, 1990. Executive Order No. 12,711 55 Fed. Reg. 13,897 (April 11, 1990).

8. INS spokesman Richard Kinney is quoted as saying: "The best way is to actually hold the people in detention, and word will get back" (Arnold 1993).

9. Tim Weiner, "Smuggled to New York: Fixing Immigration," *The New York Times*, June 8, 1993.

10. Seth Faison, "A Flicker of Empathy for 110 Chinese," *The New York Times*. October 21, 1993. See, for example, *Chang Lian Zheng v. INS, Zhang Xin-Jie v. INS, Yu Bao Chun v. INS,* and *Chen Yee Wang v. INS* (44 F.3d 379, 1995).

11. The text added by IIRIRA is as follows: "A person who has been forced to abort a pregnancy or to undergo involuntary sterilization, or has been persecuted for failure or refusal to undergo such a procedure, or for other resistance to a coercive population control program, shall be deemed to have been persecuted on account of political opinion, and a person who

has a well-founded fear that he or she will be forced to undergo such a procedure or subject to persecution for such failure, refusal, or resistance shall be deemed to have a well-founded fear of persecution on account of political opinion" (8 U.S.C. § 1101(a)(42)).

12. In *Chevron U.S.A., Inc. v. Natural Resources Defense Council, Inc.* (467 U.S. 837, 1984), the Supreme Court concluded: "If the intent of Congress is clear, that is the end of the matter; for the court, as well as the agency, must give effect to the unambiguously expressed intent of Congress."

13. See, for example, *Zhang v. Gonzales* (434 F.3d 993, 7th Cir. 2006), *Huang v. Ashcroft* (113 F. App'x 695, 6th Cir. 2004) (unpublished opinion), *He v. Ashcroft* (328 F.3d 593, 9th Cir. 2003), and *Li v. Ashcroft* (82 F. App'x 357, 5th Cir. 2003) (unpublished *per curiam* opinion).

14. *Zhu v. Gonzales* (465 F.3d 316, 7th Cir. 2006) and *Ma v. Ashcroft* (361 F.3d 553, 9th Cir. 2004) both show support for claims of partners who are officially unmarried but who have been married in traditional ceremonies, a common practice resulting from age restrictions on official marriage. The 3rd Circuit recognizes official marriages only (*Chen v. Gonzales*, [434 F.3d 212, 3rd Cir. 2005]). The remaining circuits have not ruled on these questions.

15. Mark Chipperfield and Tracey Aubrey, "Hawke's haven for frightened Chinese," *The Australian*, June 17, 1989.

Chapter 9

1. Katherine Ellison, "A Special Visa Program Benefits Abused Illegal Immigrants," *The New York Times*, January 8, 2010.

2. Paloma Esquivel, "U-visas gaining momentum," *The Los Angeles Times*, September 26, 2011.

3. The PRRA occurs as the last step before deportation. Failed asylum seekers as well as anyone else who has been given a removal order is eligible for this assessment.

4. Mark Riley, "Ruddock's cash-for-visa quagmire deepens," *Sydney Morning Herald*, June 18, 2003.

5. Mark Metherell, "I should not play God: Evans," *Sydney Morning Herald*, February 20, 2008.

6. Yuko Narushima, "ALP push to widen asylum," *The Age*, September 22, 2010.

7. Scott Morrison, "Plan won't help asylum seekers," *The Australian*, March 9, 2011.

REFERENCES

Adelman, H., and S. McGrath. 2007. To date or to marry: That is the question. *Journal of Refugee Studies* 20 (3):376–380.

Adelman, H. 1991. Canadian refugee policy in the postwar period. In *Refugee policy: Canada and the United States*, ed. H. Adelman, 170–221. Toronto: York Lanes Press.

Adler, M. 2003. A socio-legal approach to administrative justice. *Law & Policy* 25 (4):323–352.

Administrative Office of U.S. Courts. *Judicial business: Annual reports*, 1990–2012. http://www.uscourts.gov/Statistics/JudicialBusiness/2013.aspx.

Alford, W. 1986. On the limits of grand theory in comparative law. *Washington Law Review* 61:945–956.

American Bar Association. 2003. *Seeking meaningful review: Findings and recommendations in response to Dorsey & Whitney study of Board of Immigration Appeals procedural reforms.* Chicago, IL: American Bar Association.

American Immigration Lawyers Association. N.d. *The Importance of Independence and Accountability in our Immigration Courts.* Washington, D.C.: American Immigration Lawyers Association.

Amnesty International. 2000. *The crackdown on Falun Gong and other so-called heretical organizations.* Washington, D.C.: Amnesty International.

Anker, D., and M. Posner. 1981. The forty-year crisis: A legislative history of the Refugee Act of 1980. *San Diego Law Review* 19 (9):9–89.

Arbel, E., and A. Brenner, 2013. Bordering on failure: Canada-U.S. border policy and the politics of refugee exclusion. *Harvard Immigration and Refugee Law Clinical Program*, Cambridge, MA.

Arnett, A. K. 2005. One step forward, two steps back: Women asylum-seekers in the United States and Canada stand to lose human rights under the Safe Third Country agreement. *Lewis & Clark Law Review* 9:951–979.

Auden, W.H. 1939 [2007]. "Refugee Blues," in *Selected Poems*, New York: Vintage International.

Australian Human Rights Commission. 2009. Submission to the Senate Standing Committee on Legal and Constitutional Affairs: Inquiry into the Migration Amendment (Complementary Protection) Bill 2009, Canberra, September 30.

Bagaric, M., K. Boyd, J. Vrachnas, P. Dimopoulos, and S. Tongue. 2006. *Migration and refugee law in Australia: Cases and commentary.* Cambridge, UK: Cambridge University Press.

Benson, L. B. 2006. Making paper dolls: How restrictions on judicial review and the administrative process increase immigration cases in the federal courts. *New York Law School Law Review* 51:37–74.

Betts, A. 2009. *Forced migration and global politics.* Sussex, UK: Wiley-Blackwell.

Betts, A., and G. Loescher, eds. 2010. *Refugees in international relations.* Oxford UK: Oxford University Press.

Betts, K. 2005. Cosmopolitans and patriots: Australia's cultural divide and attitudes to immigration. *People and Place* 13 (2):29–40.

Beyer, G. 1992. Establishing the United States Asylum Officer Corps: A first report. *International Journal of Refugee Law* (4):455–486.

Birrell, R. 1992. Problems of immigration control in liberal democracies. In *Nations of immigrants: Australia, the United States and international migration*, ed. G. Freeman and J. Jupp, 23–40. Oxford: Oxford University Press.

Black, R. 2001. Fifty years of refugee studies: From theory to policy. *International Migration Review* 35 (1):57–78.

Bloemraad, I. 2006. *Becoming a citizen: Incorporating immigrants and refugees in the United States and Canada*. Berkeley, CA: University of California Press.

Bohmer, C., and A. Shuman. 2007. *Rejecting refugees: Political asylum in the 21st century*. London: Routledge.

Bon Tempo, C. J. 2008. *Americans at the gate: The United States and refugees during the Cold War*. Princeton, NJ: Princeton University Press.

Borjas, G. J. 2001. *Heaven's door: Immigration policy and the American economy*. Princeton, NJ: Princeton University Press.

Bosniak, L. 2008. *The citizen and the alien: Dilemmas of contemporary membership*. Princeton, NJ: Princeton University Press.

Bowen, C. 2011. *Government announces faster, fairer refugee determination process*. Canberra: Department of Immigration and Citizenship Press release, January 7.

Brennan, F. 2003. *Tampering with asylum: A universal humanitarian problem*. Queensland: University of Queensland Press.

Brubaker, W. R. 1995. Comments on Freeman. *International Migration Review* 29 (4):903–908.

Burnside, J. 2007. *Watching brief: Reflections on human rights, law, and justice*. Carlton North, VIC: Scribe Publishers.

Camp Keith, L., J. S. Homes, and B. P. Miller. 2013. Explaining the divergence in asylum grant rates among Immigration Judges: An attitudinal and cognitive approach. *Law & Policy* 35 (4):261–289.

Canadian Association of Refugee Lawyers. 2012. *Designated country of origin scheme is arbitrary, unfair, and unconstitutional*. Press Release. Toronto.

Canadian Bar Association, 2010. *CBA expresses appreciation for amendments to Bill C-11, Balanced Refugee Reform Act*, Press Release, Ottawa.

Canadian Council for Refugees. 2006. *Less safe than ever: Challenging the designation of the U.S. as a Safe Third Country for refugees*, Montreal.

Canadian Council for Refugees. 2010. Open letter (Bill C-11), Montreal.

Carens, J. H. 1988. Nationalism and the exclusion of immigrants: Lessons from Australian immigration policy. In *Open borders, closed societies*, ed. M. Gibney, 41–60. Santa Barbara, CA: Greenwood Press.

Carp, R. A., and R. Stidham. 2001. *The federal courts*. 4th ed. Washington, D.C.: Congressional Quarterly Press.

Cartier, G. 2004. The Baker effect: A new interface between the Canadian Charter of Rights and Freedoms and administrative law: The case of discretion. In *The Unity of Public Law*, ed. D. Dyzenhaus, 61–86. Portland OR: Hart Publishing.

Castles, S., and E. Vasta. 2004. Australia: New conflicts around old dilemmas. In *Controlling immigration: A global perspective*, ed. W. A. Cornelius, T. Tsuda, P. L. Martin, and J. F. Hollifield, 2nd ed., 141–173. Stanford, CA: Stanford University Press.

Center for Gender and Refugee Studies. 2002. *Letter to the Immigration Minister of Canada, Denis Coderre*. San Francisco: University of California, Hastings School of Law, April 2. http://cgrs.uchastings.edu/about/kasinga.php">

Center for Gender and Refugee Studies, "Fauziya Kassindja and the struggle for gender asylum," http://cgrs.uchastings.edu/about/kasinga.php.

Center for Gender and Refugee Studies, "Rodi Alvarado's story." http://cgrs.uchastings.edu/our-work/matter-r.

Chapnik, A. 2000. The Canadian middle power myth. *International Journal* 55 (2):188–206.

Chen, M. H. 2007. Explaining disparities in asylum claims. *Georgetown Public Policy Review* 12 (1):29–48.

Chimni, B. S. 1998. The geopolitics of refugee studies: A view from the south. *Journal of Refugee Studies* 11 (4):354–374.

Chin, G. 2004. Is there a plenary power doctrine? A tentative apology and prediction for our strange but unexceptional constitutional immigration law. *Georgetown Immigration Law Journal* 14:257–288.

Chin, G. 2005. Chae Chan Ping and Fong Yue Ting: The origins of plenary power. In *Immigration stories*, ed. D. A. Martin and P. H. Schuck, 7–30. New York: Foundation Press.

Cole, D. 2002. In aid of removal: Due process limits on immigration detention. *Emory Law Journal* 51:1003–1039.

Congressional Research Service. 2004. *Immigration-related detention: Current legislative issues.* Washington, D.C.

Cornelius, W., T. Tsuda, P. Martin, and J. Hollifield. 2004. *Controlling immigration: A global perspective.* 2nd ed. Palo Alto, CA: Stanford University Press.

Coven, P. 1995. *Considerations for asylum officers adjudicating claims from women.* Memorandum from P. Coven, Office of International Affairs, Immigration and Naturalization Service to all INS asylum officers, May 26.

Creyke, R. 2007. Administrative tribunals. In *Australian administrative law: Fundamentals, principals, and doctrines*, ed. M. Groves and H. P. Lee, 77–99. Cambridge: Cambridge University Press.

Creyke, R., and J. McMillan. 2004. The operation of judicial review in Australia. In *Judicial review and bureaucratic impact: International and interdisciplinary perspectives*, ed. M. Hertogh and S. Halliday, 161–189. Cambridge, UK: Cambridge University Press.

Crisp, J. 2008. Beyond the nexus: UNHCR's evolving perspective on refugee protection and international migration. Geneva: UNHCR research paper no. 155.

Crock, M. 1998. *Immigration and refugee law in Australia.* Annandale: Federation Press.

Crock, M. 2000. Fortress Australia and castles in the air: The High Court and judicial review of migration decisions. *University of Melbourne Law Review* 24:190–217.

Crock, M. 2004. Judging refugees: The clash of power and institutions in the development of Australian refugee law. *Sydney Law Review* 51 (26):51–74.

Crock, M., and R. McCallum. 1994. Australia's federal courts: Their origins, structure, and jurisdiction. *South Carolina Law Review*, 46:719–757.

Crock, M., and B. Saul. 2002. *Future seekers: Refugees and the law in Australia.* Annandale: Federation Press.

Cross, F. B., and E. H. Tiller. 1998. Judicial partisanship and obedience to legal doctrine: Whistleblowing on the federal Courts of Appeals. *Yale Law Journal* 107:2155–2176.

Damaska, M. R. 1986. *The faces of justice and state authority.* New Haven, CT: Yale University Press.

Dauvergne, C. 1998. Chinese fleeing sterilization: Australia's response against a Canadian backdrop. *International Journal of Refugee Law* 10 (1/2):77–96.

Dauvergne, C. 2003. Evaluating Canada's new Immigration and Refugee Protection Act in its global context. *Alberta Law Review* 41:725–744.

Dauvergne, C. 2005. *Humanitarianism, identity, and nation: Migration laws in Canada and Australia.* Vancouver: UBC Press.

Dauvergne, C. 2008. *Making people illegal: What globalization means for migration and law.* Cambridge, UK: Cambridge University Press.

Dench, J. 1999. *A hundred years of immigration to Canada 1900–1999: A chronology focusing on refugees and discrimination.* Report by the Canadian Council for Refugees. http://www.web.net/~ccr/history.html.

Department of Citizenship and Immigration Canada. 2002. *Refugee Appeal Division implementation delayed.* CIC press release, Ottawa, April 29.

Department of Homeland Security. 2013. *Refugees and asylees 2012.* Washington, D.C.: Office of Immigration Statistics Policy Directorate annual flow report.

Department of Immigration and Citizenship. 2011. *Ministerial intervention statistics—Australia 2010–11.* Canberra: Department of Immigration and Citizenship.

Department of Immigration and Multicultural Affairs. 1996. *Refugee and humanitarian visa applicants: Guidelines on gender issues for decision-makers.* Canberra: Department of Immigration and Multicultural Affairs.

Department of Immigration and Multicultural Affairs. 1997. *People's Republic Permanent Entry Visa Class 815.* Annual Report. Canberra: Department of Immigration and Multicultural Affairs (1996–7).

Department of Justice. 1988. *Memorandum from the Office of Attorney General Meese to Alan Nelson.* Washington, D.C.: Department of Justice, August 5.

Dirks, G. E. 1977. *Canada's refugee policy: Indifference or opportunism?* Montreal: McGill-Queen's University Press.

Dirks, G. E. 1985. Canadian refugee policy: Humanitarian and political determinants. In *Refugees and world politics,* ed. E. G. Ferris, 120–135. New York: Praeger Special Studies.

Dirks, G. E. 1995. *Controversy and complexity: Canadian immigration policy during the 1980's.* Montreal: McGill-Queen's University Press.

Dyzenhaus, D., ed. 2004. *The unity of public law.* Portland OR: Hart Publishing.

Epp, C. R. 1998. *The rights revolution: Lawyers, activists, and supreme courts in comparative perspective.* Chicago, IL: University of Chicago Press.

Erdos, D. 2010. *Delegating rights protection: The rise of bills of rights in the Westminster world.* Oxford, UK: Oxford University Press.

Executive Office of Immigration Review. 2013. *Statistical yearbook, FY 2012.* Falls Church, VA: Executive Office of Immigration Review.

Feen, R. 1985. Domestic and foreign policy dilemmas in contemporary U.S. refugee policy. In *Refugees and world politics,* ed. E. Ferris, 105–119. New York: Praeger Publishers.

Feller, E. 2005. Refugees are not migrants. *Refugee Survey Quarterly* 24 (4):27–35.

Ferejohn, J. 2002. Judicializing politics, politicizing law. *Law and Contemporary Problems* 65:41–68.

Field, N. 2008. *Playing God with sanctuary: A study of Australia's approach to complementary protection obligations beyond the Refugee Convention.* Report by A Just Australia and Oxfam, Glebe, NSW.

FitzGerald, D. 2012. A comparativist manifesto for international migration studies. *Ethnic & Racial Studies* 35 (10):1725–1740.

Flaherty, M. S. 2006. Judicial globalization in the service of self-government. *Ethics & International Affairs* 20 (4):477–503.

Fletcher, A. 2006. "The REAL ID Act: Furthering gender bias in U.S. asylum law. *Berkeley Journal of Gender Law and Justice* 21:111–131.

Freeman, G. 1995. Modes of immigration politics in liberal democratic states. *International Migration Review* 19 (4):881–902.

Freeman, G., and J. Jupp, ed. 1992. *Nations of immigrants: Australia, the United States and international migration.* Oxford, UK: Oxford University Press.

Frelick, B. 2004. Abundantly clear: Refoulement. *Georgetown Immigration Law Journal* 19 (2):245–275.

Friedman, L. M. 1985. *Total justice.* New York: Russell Sage Foundation.

Fullerton, M. 1993. A comparative look at refugee status based on persecution due to membership in a particular social group. *Cornell International Law Journal* 26:505–563.

Galligan, B. 1995. *A federal republic: Australia's constitutional system of government.* Cambridge, UK: Cambridge University Press.

Gammeltoft-Hansen, T. 2011. *Access to asylum: International refugee law and the globalisation of migration control.* Cambridge, UK: Cambridge University Press.

Garcia, M. J. 2004. *The U.N. Convention Against Torture: Overview of U.S. implementation policy concerning the removal of aliens.* Congressional Research Service Report, Washington, D.C.

Gelber, K., and M. McDonald. 2006. Ethics and exclusion: Representations of sovereignty in Australia's approach to asylum-seekers. *Review of International Studies* 32:269–289.

Gibney, M. 2004. *The ethics and politics of asylum: Liberal democracy and the responses to refugees.* Cambridge, UK: Cambridge University Press.

Gibney, M. 2006. "A thousand little Guantanamos": Western states and measures to prevent the arrival of refugees. In *Displacement, Asylum, Migration,* ed. K. E. Tunstall, 139–169. Oxford, UK: Oxford University Press.

Ginsburg, T. 2003. *Judicial review in new democracies: Constitutional courts in Asian cases.* Cambridge, UK: Cambridge University Press.

Glazer, N. 1998. *We are all multiculturalists now.* Cambridge, MA: Harvard University Press.

Glendenning, P., C. Leavey, M. Hetherton, and M. Britt. 2006. *Deported to danger: The continuing study of Australia's treatment of rejected asylum seekers.* Sydney: Edmund Rice Center for Justice and Community Education.

Gonzales, A. 2006. *Memorandum from Attorney General Gonzales to Immigration Judges in the Executive Office of Immigration Review.* Washington, D.C.: Department of Justice, January 9.

Goodwin-Gill, G., and J. McAdam. 2007. *The refugee in international law.* 3rd ed. Oxford, UK: Oxford University Press.

Gould, J., C. Sheppard, and J. Wheeldon. 2010. A refugee from justice? Disparate treatment in the Federal Court of Canada. *Law & Policy* 32 (4):454–486.

Government Accounting Office. 1987. *Report on the immigration and naturalization service.* Washington, D.C.: Government Accounting Office.

Grahl-Madsen, A. 2001. *The land beyond: Collected essays on refugee law and policy.* The Hague, Netherlands: Martinus Nijhoff Publishers.

Greenhalgh, S. 2010. *Cultivating global citizens: Population in the rise of China.* Cambridge, MA: Harvard University Press.

Groves, M., and H. P. Lee, eds. 2007. *Australian administrative law: Fundamentals, principles and doctrines.* Cambridge, UK: Cambridge University Press.

Guiraudon, V. 2000. The Marshallian triptych reordered: The role of courts and bureaucracies in furthering migrants' social rights. In *Immigration and welfare: Challenging the borders of the welfare state,* ed. M. Bommes and A. Geddes, 72–89. London, UK: Routledge.

Guterres, A. 2008. Millions uprooted: Saving refugees and the displaced. *Foreign Affairs* September/October, 87 (5):90–98.

Hailbronner, K. 1986. Non-refoulement and humanitarian refugees: customary international law or wishful legal thinking? *Virginia Journal of International Law* 26 (4):857–896.

Hamlin, R. 2012a. Illegal refugees: Competing policy ideas and the rise of the regime of deterrence in American asylum politics. *Refugee Survey Quarterly* 31 (2):33–53.

Hamlin, R. 2012b. International law and administrative insulation: A comparison of refugee status determination regimes in the United States, Canada, and Australia. *Law and Social Inquiry* 37 (4):933–968.

Hamlin, R., and P. E. Wolgin. 2012. Symbolic politics and policy feedback: The United Nations Protocol Relating to the Status of Refugees and American refugee law during the Cold War." *International Migration Review* 46 (3):586–623.

Hammerstad, A. 2010. UNHCR and the securitization of forced migration. In *Refugees in international relations,* ed. A. Betts and G. Loescher, 237–260. Oxford: Oxford University Press.

Hathaway, J. 1991. *The law of refugee status.* Charlottesville, VA: Lexis Law Publishing.

Hathaway, J. 2007. Forced migration studies: Could we agree just to "date?" *Journal of Refugee Studies* 20 (3):349–369.

Hawkins, F. 1989. *Critical years in immigration: Canada and Australia compared.* Montreal, Quebec: McGill-Queen's University Press.

Heckman, G. 2008. Canada's refugee status determination system and the international norm of independence. *Refuge* 25 (2):79–102.

Hein, J. 1993. Refugees, immigrants and the state. *Annual Review of Sociology* 19:43–59.

Helton, A. C. 1991. The detention of asylum seekers in the United States and Canada. In *Refugee policy: Canada and the United States*, ed. H. Adelman, 253–267. Toronto: York Lanes Press.

Helton, A. C. 2002. *The price of indifference: Refugees and humanitarian action in the new century.* Oxford, UK: Oxford University Press.

Herman, J. 1992. *Trauma and recovery: The aftermath of violence.* New York, NY: Basic Books.

Hirschl, R. 2002. Resituating judicialization of politics: Bush v. Gore as a global trend. *Canadian Journal of Law and Jurisprudence* 15 (2):191–218.

Hirschl, R. 2004. *Towards juristocracy: The origins and consequences of the new constitutionalism.* Cambridge, MA: Harvard University Press.

Hohl, D. 1978. The Indochinese refugee: The evolution of United States policy." *International Migration Review* 12 (1):128–132.

Holland, K. M. 1991. *Judicial activism in comparative perspective.* New York: St. Martin's Press.

Hollifield, J. 2001. The emerging migration state. *International Migration Review* 38 (3):885–912.

Holmes, J. S., and L. Camp Keith. 2010. Does the fear of terrorists trump the fear of persecution in asylum outcomes in the post-September 11 era? *PS: Political Science* 43: 431–436.

Houston, A., P. Aristotle, and M. L'Estrange. 2012. *Report of the expert panel on asylum seekers.* Canberra: Australian Government, August.

Howard, J. 2001. *Prime Minister's speech delivered on October 28, 2001.* Sydney, NSW. http://electionspeeches.moadoph.gov.au/speeches/2001-john-howard.

Hsu, W. 1996. The tragedy of the *Golden Venture*: politics trump the Administrative Procedures Act and the Rule of Law. *Georgetown Immigration Law Journal* 10 (3):317–370.

Human Rights First. 2004. *In liberty's shadow: U.S. detention of asylum seekers in the era of homeland security.* Washington, D.C.: Human Rights First.

Human Rights First. 2009. *U.S. detention of asylum seekers: Seeking protection, finding prison.* Washington, D.C.: Human Rights First.

Human Rights Watch Report. 2008. "China's Forbidden Zone: Shutting the Media Out of Tibet and Other 'Sensitive Stories.'" Washington, D.C.: Human Rights Watch. July.

Human Rights Watch Report. 2012. "China 2012." Washington, D.C.: Human Rights Watch. January.

Hunter, C. 2002. Khawar and Migration Legislation Amendment Bill (No. 6): Why narrowing the definition of a refugee discriminates against gender-related claims. *Australian Journal of Human Rights* 8 (1):107–120.

Hurrell, A. 2010. Refugees, international society, and global order. In *Refugees in international relations*, ed. A. Betts and G. Loescher, 85–104. Oxford: Oxford University Press.

Hurwitz, P. 1989. The new detention provisions of the Immigration Act: Can they withstand a Charter challenge?" *University of Toronto Faculty Law Review* 47:587–606.

Immigration and Customs Enforcement. 2011. *Immigration enforcement actions: 2012 report.* Washington, D.C.: Department of Homeland Security.

Immigration and Naturalization Service. 1994. *Statistical yearbook, FY 1994.* Washington, D.C.: Department of Justice.

Immigration and Naturalization Service. *Statistical yearbook FY 1996.* Table 27: "Asylum Cases Filed with INS District Directors and Asylum Officers, FY 1973–96." Washington, D.C.: Department of Justice.

Immigration and Naturalization Service. *Asylum and withholding definitions.* Proposed Rule. [INS No. 2092–00; AG Order No. 2339– 2000] Federal Register/Vol. 65, No. 236/Thursday, December 7, 2000. Washington, D.C.: Department of Justice.

Immigration and Refugee Board. *Guideline four: women refugee claimants fearing gender based persecution*, February 1993 (updated in 1996 and 2003), Toronto.

Immigration and Refugee Board. 2002. *Consolidated grounds in the Immigration and Refugee Protection Act: Persons in need of protection: Risk to life or risk of cruel and unusual treatment or punishment.* Toronto: Legal Services Branch.

Immigration and Refugee Board. 2002. *Consolidated Grounds in the Immigration and Refugee Protection Act: Persons in Need of Protection – Danger of Torture*. Toronto: Immigration and Refugee Board.

Immigration and Refugee Board. 2014. *2013–14 Report on plans and priorities*. Toronto: Immigration and Refugee Board.

Jacobsohn, G. 2004. Borrowing: The permeability of constitutional borders. *Texas Law Review* 82:1763–1818.

Jacobson, D. 1996. *Rights across borders: Immigration and the decline of citizenship*. Baltimore, MD: Johns Hopkins University Press.

Jacobson, D., and G. Benarieh Ruffer. 2003. Courts across borders: The implications of judicial agency for human rights and democracy. *Human Rights Quarterly* 25:74–92.

Joppke, C. 1998a. Asylum and state sovereignty: A comparison of the United States, Germany and Britain. In *Challenge to the nation-state: Immigration in Western Europe and the United States*, ed. C. Joppke, 109–152. Oxford: Oxford University Press.

Joppke, C. 1998b. Why liberal states accept unwanted immigration. *World Politics* 50 (1):266–293.

Joppke, C. 2001. The legal–domestic sources of immigrant rights: The United States, Germany, and the European Union. *Comparative Political Studies* 34 (4):339–366.

Kagan, R. 2001. *Adversarial legalism: The American way of law*. Cambridge, MA: Harvard University Press.

Kanstroom, D. 2010. Loving humanity while accepting real people: A critique and a cautious affirmation of the "political" in U.S. asylum and refugee law.: In *Driven from home: Protecting the rights of forced migrants*, ed. D. Hollenbach, 115–146. Washington, D.C.: Georgetown University Press.

Karlsen, E. 2009. Complementary protection for asylum seekers: Overview of the international and Australian legal frameworks. *Parliament of Australia*, Research paper no. 7, Canberra.

Keefe, P. R. 2006. The snakehead: The criminal odyssey of Chinatown's Sister Ping. *The New Yorker*, April 24, 68–85.

Kelley, N., and M. Trebilcock. 1998. *The making of the mosaic: A history of Canadian immigration policy*. Toronto: University of Toronto Press.

Kennedy, E. M. 1981. The Refugee Act of 1980. *International Migration Review* 12 (1/2):141–156.

Kernerman, G. 2008. Refugee interdiction before heaven's gate. *Government and Opposition* 43 (2):230–248.

Kitching, A. 2007. *Past statements and committee recommendations regarding implementation of the RAD*. Ottawa: Law and Government Department, Library of Parliament, House of Commons Standing Committee on Citizenship and Immigration.

Klug, H. 2000. *Constituting democracy: Law, globalism and South Africa's political reconstruction*. Cambridge, UK: Cambridge University Press.

Kneebone, S. 2003. *Bouncing the ball between the courts and the legislature: What is the score on refugee issues?* Paper presented at Human Rights 2003: The Year in Review, Castan Centre for Human Rights Law, Monash University, Melbourne, Australia. December 4.

Kneebone, S. 2005. Women within the refugee construct: "Exclusionary inclusion: in policy and practice: The Australian experience. *International Journal of Refugee Law* 17 (1):7–42.

Kneebone, S. 2009. *Refugees, asylum seekers and the Rule of Law*. Cambridge, UK: Cambridge University Press.

Kyle, D. and R. Koslowski, eds. 2011. *Global human smuggling: comparative perspectives*. Baltimore, MD: Johns Hopkins University Press.

Lane, P. H. 1994. *An introduction to the Australian Constitution*. 6th ed. Sydney: The Law Book Company Limited.

Law, A. O. 2010. *The immigration battle in American courts*. Cambridge, UK: Cambridge University Press.

Legomsky, S. H. 1996. The new techniques for managing high-volume asylum systems. *Iowa Law Review* 81:671–706.

Legomsky, S. H. 2009. Refugees, asylum and the Rule of Law in the USA. In *Refugees, asylum seekers and the Rule of Law: Comparative perspectives*, ed. S. Kneebone, 122–170. Cambridge, UK: Cambridge University Press.

Legomsky, S. 1998. Refugees, administrative tribunals, and real independence: Dangers ahead for Australia. *Washington University Law Review* 76:243–254.

Liang, Z., and W. Ye. 2011. From Fujian to New York: Understanding the new Chinese immigration. In *Global human smuggling: Comparative perspectives*, ed. D. Kyle and R. Koslowski, 187–215. Baltimore, MD: Johns Hopkins University Press.

Loescher, G. 2003. UNHCR at fifty: Refugee protection and world politics. In *Problems of protection: The UNHCR, refugees, and human rights*, ed. N. Steiner, M. Gibney, and G. Loescher, 3–18. New York: Routledge.

Loescher, G., and J. Scanlan. 1986. *Calculated kindness: Refugees and America's half-open door, 1945 to the present*. New York: The Free Press.

Loughran, A. 2004. Congress, categories and the Constitution: Whether mandatory detention of criminal aliens violates due process. *Georgetown Immigration Law Journal* 18 (4):681–696.

MacIntosh, C. 2005. When 'feminist beliefs' became credible as 'political opinions': Returning to a key moment in Canadian refugee law. *Canadian Journal of Women and the Law* 17 (1):135–150.

Macklin, A. 1998a. Cross-border shopping for ideas: A critical review of United States, Canadian, and Australian approaches to gender-related asylum claims. *Georgetown Immigration Law Journal* 13 (35):25–71.

Macklin, A. 1998b. Truth and consequences: Credibility determination in the refugee context. In *The realities of a refugee determination on the eve of a new millennium: The role of the judiciary*, 3rd Conference, 134–140. Ottawa: International Association of Refugee Law Judges.

Macklin, A. 2009a. Asylum and the Rule of Law in Canada: Hearing the other (side). In *Refugees, asylum seekers and the Rule of Law: Comparative perspectives*, ed. S. Kneebone, 78–121. Cambridge, UK: Cambridge University Press.

Macklin, A. 2009b. Refugee roulette in the Canadian casino. In *Refugee roulette: Disparities in asylum adjudication and proposals for reform*, ed. J. Ramji-Nogales, A. I. Schoenholtz, and P. G. Schrag, 135–163. New York: New York University Press.

Mandel, M. 1994. *The Charter of Rights and the legalization of politics in Canada*. Toronto: Canada. Thompson Educational Publishing.

Manfredi, C. P. 1993. *Judicial power and the Charter*. Norman: OK. University of Oklahoma Press.

Marek, L. Posner blasts immigration courts as "inadequate" and ill-trained. *The National Law Journal*, April 22. http://www.law.com/jsp/article.jsp?id=1208861007986.

Mares, P. 2003. *Borderline: Australia's response to refugees and asylum seekers in the wake of the Tampa*. Sydney: University of New South Wales Press.

Markus, A. 1994. *Australian race relations: 1788–1993*. St. Leonards: Allen & Unwin.

Martin, D. A., ed. 1988. *The new asylum seekers: Refugee law in the 1980's*. Dordrecht: Netherlands. Martinus Nijhoff.

Martin, D. A. 1990. Reforming asylum adjudication: On navigating the coast of Bohemia. *University of Pennsylvania Law Review* 138 (5):1247–1381.

Martin, S., A. Schoenholtz, and D. Waller Meyers. 1998. Temporary protection: Towards a new regional and domestic framework. *Georgetown Immigration Law Journal* 12:543–588.

Martin, S. 2010. Rethinking the international refugee regime in light of human rights and the global common good. In *Driven from home: Protecting the rights of forced migrants*, ed. D. Hollenbach, 15–35. Washington, D.C.: Georgetown University Press.

Mashaw, J. L. 1985. *Due process in the administrative state*. New Haven, CT: Yale University Press.

Matthew, P. 1997. Case note: *Applicant A v. Minister for Immigration and Ethnic Affairs*: The High Court and particular social groups: Lessons for the future. *Melbourne University Law Review* 21:277–330.

Matthew, P. 2003. Safe for whom? The Safe Third Country concept finds a home in Australia. In *The Refugee Convention 50 years on: Globalization and international law*, ed. S. Kneebone, 133–172. Surrey, UK: Ashgate Publishing.

McAdam, J. 2007. *Complementary protection in international refugee law.* Oxford, UK: Oxford University Press.

McAdam, J. 2010. Status anxiety: Complementary protection and the rights of non-convention refugees. *University of New South Wales Faculty of Law Research Series,* working paper 1, University of New South Wales, Sydney.

McMillan, J. 2011. *Regulating migration litigation after plaintiff M61.* A report to the Minister for Immigration and Citizenship. Canberra: Department of Immigration and Citizenship.

McPherson, M., L. S. Horowitz, D. Lusher, and S. DiGiglio. 2011. Marginal women: Impediments to gender-based persecution claims by asylum-seeking women in Australia. *Journal of Refugee Studies* 24 (2):232–347.

Melloy, K. E. 2007. Telling truths: How the REAL ID Act's credibility provisions affect women asylum seekers. *Iowa Law Review* 92 (2):637–676.

Migration Review Tribunal/Refugee Review Tribunal. 2001–2013. Annual Reports, Sydney.

Mill, J. S. [1843]. 2002. *A system of logic.* Honolulu, HI: University Press of the Pacific.

Morton, F. L. 1987. The political impact of the Canadian Charter of Rights and Freedoms. *Canadian Journal of Political Science* 20 (1):31–55.

Morton, F. L., and R. Knopff. 2000. *The Charter revolution and the court party.* Ontario: Broadview Press.

Motomura, H. 2005. Immigration law and federal court jurisdiction through the lens of habeus corpus. *Cornell University Law Review* 91 (13):101–136.

Musalo, K. 2003. Revisiting social group and nexus in gender asylum claims: A unifying rationale for evolving jurisprudence. *DePaul Law Review* 52:777–808.

Musalo, K. 2010. A short history of gender asylum in the United States: Resistance and ambivalence may very slowly be inching towards recognition of women's claims. *Refugee Survey Quarterly* 29 (2):46–63.

Musalo, K., and S. Knight. 2003. Asylum for victims of gender violence: An overview of the law, and an analysis of 45 unpublished decisions. *Immigration Briefings.* San Francisco, CA: Center for Gender and Refugee Studies.

National Immigration Forum. 2009. *Backgrounder: The math of immigration detention.* Washington, D.C.: National Immigration Forum.

Neuman, G. L. 2006. On the adequacy of direct review after the REAL ID Act of 2005. *New York Law School Law Review* 51:133–160.

Ngai, M. 2004. *Impossible subjects: Illegal aliens and the making of modern America.* Princeton, NJ: Princeton University Press.

Office of Immigration. 2004. *Statistical Yearbook.* Washington, D.C.: Department of Justice.

Ozdowski, S. 2002. *A report on visits to immigration detention facilities by the Human Rights Commissioner 2001.* Sydney: Australia Human Rights Commission.

Palmer, J. R. B. 2006. The nature and causes of the immigration surge in the federal Courts of Appeals: A preliminary analysis. *New York Law School Law Review* 51:13–36.

Palmer, J. R. B, S. W. Yale-Loehr, and E. Cronin. 2005. Why are so many people challenging Board of Immigration Appeals decisions in federal court? An empirical analysis of the recent surge in petitions for review. *Georgetown Immigration Law Journal.* 20 (1):1–100.

Pellerin, H. 2008. The politics of migration regulation in the era of globalization. In *Globalization: Theory and practice,* ed. E. Kofman and G. Youngs. 3rd ed., 175–190. London, UK: Continuum Press.

Plaut, G. W. 1985. *Refugee determination in Canada: Proposals for a new system.* A Report to the Honorable Flora MacDonald, Minister of Employment and Immigration, Ottawa.

Posner, R. A. 1996. *The federal courts: Challenge and reform.* Cambridge, MA: Harvard University Press.

Pratt, C. 1990. *Middle power internationalism: The north–south dimension.* Montreal: McGill-Queen's Press.

Price, M. E. 2009. *Rethinking asylum: History, purpose, and limits.* Cambridge, UK: Cambridge University Press.

PricewaterhouseCoopers. 2008. *Audit of Immigration and Refugee Board of Canada regional offices.* Prepared for Corporate Management and Services Branch, Immigration and Refugee Board, Toronto.

Przeworski, A., and H. Teune. 1970. *The logic of comparative social inquiry.* New York: Wiley.

Ramji-Nogales, J., P. Schrag, and A. Schoenholtz. 2007. Refugee roulette: Disparities in asylum adjudication. *Stanford Law Review* 60 (2):295–412.

Ramji-Nogales, J., P. Schrag, and A. Schoenholtz. 2009. *Refugee roulette: Disparities in asylum adjudication and proposals for reform.* New York, NY: New York University Press.

Reekie, J., and C. Layden-Stevenson. 2006. *Complementary refugee protection in Canada: The history and application of Section 97 of the Immigration and Refugee Protection Act (IRPA).* Paper presented at the International Association of Refugee Law Judges' 7th World Conference, Mexico City, Mexico, November 6–9.

Refugee Review Tribunal. 2006. *Guidance on the assessment of credibility.* Sydney: RRT.

Refugee Review Tribunal. 2007. *Members of the Refugee Review Tribunal.* Sydney: Brochure, RRT.

Refugee Review Tribunal. 2014. *Fact Sheet 61: seeking protection in Australia.* http://www.immi.gov.au/media/fact-sheets/61protection.htm.

Rehaag, S. 2008. Troubling patterns in Canadian refugee adjudication. *Ottawa Law Review* 39:335–366.

Rehaag, S. 2013. *2012 Refugee claim data and IRB member recognition rates.* Report for the Canadian Council for Refugees, Montreal.

Reitz, J. G. 1998. *The warmth of the welcome: The social causes of economic success for immigrants in different nations and cities.* Boulder, CO: Westview Press.

Rottman, A. J., C. J. Fariss, and S. C. Poe. 2009. The path to asylum in the US and the determinants for who gets in and why. *International Migration Review* 43 (1):3–234.

Ruddock, P. 1998. *Immigration reform: Unfinished agenda.* Speech delivered at the National Press Club, Canberra, Australia, March 18.

Ruddock, P. 2003. *Speech delivered in the Australian Parliament.* Reported in the *Senate Hansard*:11353, Canberra, June 16.

Sadrehashemi, L. 2011. *Gender persecution and refugee law reform in Canada,* Response to the Balanced Refugee Reform Act (Bill C-11), Battered Women's Support Services. Vancouver, B.C., Canada, April.

Salehyan, I., and M. R. Rosenblum. 2004. Norms and Interests in US asylum enforcement. *Journal of Peace Research* 41 (6):677–697.

Salehyan, I., and M. R. Rosenblum. 2008. International relations, domestic politics, and asylum admissions in the United States. *Political Research Quarterly* 61 (1):104–121.

Sassen, S. 1996. *Losing control? Sovereignty in an age of globalization.* New York: Columbia University Press.

Schauer, F. 1993. Constitutional positivism. *Connecticut Law Review* 25 (797):824–825.

Scheppele, K. L. 2003. The agendas of comparative constitutionalism. *Law & Courts* 13 (2):5–22.

Schloenhardt, A. 2002. To deter, detain and deny: Protection of onshore asylum seekers in Australia. *International Journal of Refugee Law* 14 (2/3):302–328.

Schloenhardt, A. 2003. *Migrant smuggling: Illegal migration and organised crime in Australia and the Asia Pacific region.* Leiden, Netherlands: Martinus Nijhoff Publishers.

Schoenholtz, A. I., and J. Jacobs. 2002. The state of asylum representation: Ideas for change. *Georgetown Immigration Law Journal* 16 (1):739–772.

Schrag, P. 2000. *A well-founded fear: The congressional battle to save political asylum in the America.* New York: Routledge.

Schriro, D. 2009. *Immigration detention overview and recommendations.* Report for Immigration and Customs Enforcement, Department of Homeland Security, Washington, D.C.

Schuck, P. 1998. *Citizens, strangers and in-betweens: Essays on immigration and citizenship.* Boulder, CO: Westview Press.

Schuck, P. H., and E. D. Elliott. 1991. To the Chevron station: An empirical study of federal administrative law. *Duke Law Journal* 984–1077.

Senate Select Committee on Ministerial Discretion in Migration Matters. 2004. Report to the Parliament of Australia, Canberra.

Shapiro, M. 1981. *Courts: A comparative political analysis.* Chicago, IL: University of Chicago Press.

Shapiro, M., and A. Stone Sweet. 2002. *On law, politics and judicialization.* Oxford, UK: Oxford University Press.

Showler, P. 2006. *Refugee sandwich: Stories of exile and asylum.* Montreal: McGill University Press.

Showler, P. 2010. *Proposed refugee reforms may be a step towards a faster, fairer system.* News release by the Refugee Forum, Human Rights Education Centre, University of Ottawa, March 30.

Sicard, K. 1999. Section 601 of IIRIRA: A long road to a resolution of United States asylum policy regarding coercive methods of population control. *Georgetown Immigration Law Journal* 14:927–940.

Slaughter, A. 2000. Judicial globalization. *Virginia Journal of International Law* 40:1103–1124.

Slaughter, A. 2004. *A new world order.* Princeton: NJ. Princeton University Press.

Soennecken, D. 2008. The growing influence of the courts over the fate of refugees. *Review of European and Russian Affairs* 4 (2):55–88.

Sossin, L. 2004. The politics of soft law: How judicial decisions influence bureaucratic discretion in Canada. In *Judicial review and bureaucratic impact: International and interdisciplinary perspectives*, ed. M. Hertogh and S. Halliday, 129–160. Cambridge, UK: Cambridge University Press.

Soysal, Y. N. 1994. *Limits of citizenship: Migrants and postnational membership in Europe.* Chicago, IL: University of Chicago Press.

Spiro, P. 2007. *Beyond citizenship: American identity after globalization.* New York: Oxford University Press.

Steiner, N. 2000. *Arguing about asylum: The complexity of refugee debates in Europe.* New York: St. Martin's Press.

Stepputat, F. 1999. Dead horses? A response to Gaim Kibreab's "Revisiting the Debate on People, Place, Identity and Displacement." *Journal of Refugee Studies* 12 (4):416–419.

Stevens, C. A. 2002. Asylum seeking in Australia. *International Migration Review* 36 (2):864–893.

Stewart, R. B. 1975. The reformation of American administrative law. *Harvard Law Review* 88 (8):1667–1814.

Stewart, R. 2003. Administrative law in the twenty-first century. *New York University Law Review* 78 (3):437–460.

Stone Sweet, A. 1999. Judicialization and the construction of governance. *Comparative Political Studies* 32 (2):147–184.

Tate, C. N., and T. Vallinder. 1995. *The global expansion of judicial power.* New York: New York University Press.

Tavan, G. 2005. *The long slow death of white Australia.* Melbourne: Scribe Publications.

Taylor, S. 2003. The human rights of rejected asylum seekers being removed from Australia. In *The Refugee Convention 50 years on: Globalization and international law*, ed. S. Kneebone, 193–232. Surrey: UK. Ashgate Publishing.

Tichenor, D. J. 2002. *Dividing lines: The politics of immigration control in America.* Princeton, NJ: Princeton University Press.

Teitelbaum, M. S. 1980. Right versus Right: Immigration and refugee policy in the United States. *Foreign Affairs* 59 (1):21–59.

Teitelbaum, M. S. 1984. Immigration, refugees, and foreign policy. *International Organization* 38 (3):429–450.

Transactional Records Access Clearinghouse, 2012. *Immigration Judge Reports –Asylum.* Syracuse University. http://trac.syr.edu/immigration/reports/judgereports/.

Transactional Records Access Clearinghouse. 2006. *Denial Rankings of New York City Immigration Judges, FY 2000–FY 2005: Chinese versus Other Asylum Seekers.* Syracuse University. http://trac.syr.edu/immigration/reports/160/include/judge_denial_ch_vs_non.html.

UNHCR. 1980–2013. *Asylum levels and trends in industrialized countries: Statistical overview of asylum applications lodges in Europe and selected non-European countries.* Annual Report. Geneva: UNHCR.

UNHCR. 1991. *Guidelines on the protection of refugee women.* Executive Committee. Geneva: UNHCR, July 22.

UNHCR. 1993. *Refugee protection and sexual violence.* Executive Committee Conclusion 73, 1993. Geneva: UNHCR.

UNHCR. 1994. *Note on International Protection: A/AC.96/830.* Geneva: UNHCR, September 7.

UNHCR. 1999. *UNHCR guidelines on applicable criteria and standards relating to the detention of asylum seekers.* Geneva: UNHCR.

UNHCR. 2001. *Note on International Protection UN doc A/AC.96/951.* Geneva: UNHCR, September.

UNHCR. 2003. *UNHCR hails 10th anniversary of Canada's Guidelines on gender-related persecution.* Press release. Geneva: UNHCR, March 7.

UNHCR. 2005. *Executive Committee Conclusion no. 103 (LVI) 2005 section (q)).* Geneva: UNHCR.

UNHCR. 2009. *Thematic Compilation of Executive Committee Conclusions.* Geneva: UNHCR, August.

UNHCR. 2011. *Refugee Protection and Mixed Migration: The 10-Point Plan in Action.* Geneva: UNHCR, February.

UNHCR. 2013. *2012 Global Trends: Refugees, Asylees, Returnees, Internally Displaced and Stateless Persons.* UNHCR: Geneva.

UNHCR Statistical Online Population Database: http://www.unhcr.org/pages/4a013eb06.html.

United Nations. 1950. *UN General Assembly Resolution 428(v), December 14th, 1950: Statute of the Office of the United Nations High Commissioner for Refugees.* Geneva: United Nations.

United Nations Human Rights Committee. 2009. *Australia's compliance with the International Covenant on Civil and Political Rights.* Geneva: UN Human Rights Committee.

United Nations Population Fund. 2014. *Linking population, poverty, and development: A world on the move.* http://www.unfpa.org/pds/migration.html.

U.S. Coast Guard. 2014. *Alien migrant interdictions: Total interdictions, 1982 to the present.* http://www.uscg.mil/hq/cg5/cg531/AMIO/FlowStats/FY.asp.

U.S. Commission on Immigration Reform. 1997. *U.S. refugee policy: Taking leadership.* Report to Congress. Washington, D.C.: U.S. Commission on Immigration Reform.

U.S. Commission on International Religious Freedom. 2005. *Report on asylum seekers in expedited removal.* Washington, D.C.: U.S. Commission on International Religious Freedom.

U.S. Department of Homeland Security. 2007. *Fact sheet: Liberians provided Deferred Enforced Departure.* Washington, D.C.: U.S. Department of Homeland Security.

U.S. Department of Justice. 2002. *Board of Immigration Appeals: Final rule: Providing quality service through more expeditious review.* Washington, D.C.: U.S. Department of Justice fact sheet.

U.S. Department of Justice. 2006. *BIA restructuring and streamlining procedures.* Rev. Washington, D.C.: U.S. Department of Justice fact sheet.

United States Department of State. 1999–2013. *Country Report on Human Rights Practices: China.* Annual Report, Bureau of Democracy, Human Rights, and Labor. State Department: Washington, D.C.

U.S. Federal Courts. 2006. *Senate considers immigration litigation reform.* Newsletter 38 (4). Washington, D.C.: United States Courts.

Vital, D. 1967. *The inequality of states: A study of the small power in international relations.* Oxford, UK: Oxford University Press.

Vrachnas, J., K. Boyd, M. Bagaric, and P. Dimopoulos. 2005. *Migration and refugee law: Principles and practices in Australia.* Cambridge, UK: Cambridge University Press.

Walker, K. 2003. New uses of the Refugee Convention: Sexuality and refugee status. In *The Refugee Convention 50 years on: Globalization and international law*, ed. S. Kneebone, 251–278. Surrey: UK. Ashgate Publishing.

Wasem, R. E., and K. Ester. 2008. *Temporary protected status: Current immigration policy and issues.* Congressional Research Service report, Washington, D.C.

Williams, G. 1999. *Human rights under the Australian Constitution.* Melbourne: Oxford University Press.

Williams, G. 2000. *A Bill of Rights for Australia?* Sydney: University of New South Wales Press.

Williams, G. 2004. *The case for an Australian Bill of Rights: Freedom in the war on terror.* Sydney: University of New South Wales Press.

Wolgin, P. E. 2011. Beyond national origins: The development of modern immigration policy-making, 1948–1968. PhD diss., University of California, Berkeley.

Yarnold, B. M. 1990. The Refugee Act of 1980 and the depoliticization of refugee/asylum admissions: An example of failed policy implementation. *American Politics Research* 18:527–536.

Young, E. 2005. Foreign law and the denominator problem. *Harvard Law Review* 119:148–167.

Young, M. 1994. *Gender-related refugee claims.* Ottawa: Law and Government Division, Library of Parliament.

Young, M. 1997. *Canada's immigration program.* Background paper. Ottawa: Library of Parliament, Research Branch.

Zappala, G., and S. Castles. 2000. Citizenship and immigration in Australia. In *From migrants to citizens: Membership in a changing world,* ed. T. A. Aleinikoff and D. Klusmeyer, 32–81. Washington, D.C.: Carnegie Endowment for International Peace.

Zetter, R. 2007. More labels, fewer refugees: Remaking the refugee label in an era of globalization. *Journal of Refugee Studies* 20 (2):172–192.

Zhang, S. 2007. *Smuggling and trafficking in human beings: All roads lead to America.* Santa Barbara, CA: Greenwood Publishing.

Zolberg, A. R. 1992. Response to crisis: Refugee policy in the United States and Canada. In *Immigration, language and ethnicity: Canada and the United States,* ed. B. Chiswick, 55–112. Washington, D.C.: American Enterprise Institute Press.

Zolberg, A. 2009. *A nation by design: Immigration policy in the fashioning of America.* Cambridge, MA: Harvard University Press.

Zucker, N., and N. Zucker. 1987. *The guarded gate: The reality of American refugee policy.* San Diego, CA: Harcourt Brace Jovanovich.

Zucker, N., and N. Flink Zucker. 1991. The 1980 Refugee Act: A 1990 perspective. In *Refugee policy: Canada and the United States,* ed. H. Adelman, 224–252. Toronto: Center for Migration Studies.

Zucker, N., and N. Flink Zucker. 1992. From immigration to refugee redefinition: A history of refugee and asylum policy in the United States. *Journal of Policy History* 4 (1):54–70.

INDEX

Abbott, Tony, 57–58
administrative decision makers. *See* asylum
  adjudicators
Administrative Decisions (Judicial Review) Act
  (1977)—Australia (ADJR) 110–111,
  114, 190
adversarial legalism, 11, 19, 66, 77–78, 80,
  82–83, 87, 98, 103, 116–117, 148
Affirmance Without Opinion—United States
  (AWO), 73–74
*Al-Kateb v. Godwin and Minister for Immigration
  and Multicultural Affairs*, 116, 185
Alvarado, Rodi. See *Matter of R-A*
Amnesty International, 21, 39–40, 54, 129
*Applicant A v. Minister of Immigration and Ethnic
  Affairs* (MIEA), 140, 156–157
Ashcroft, John, 73, 134–135
Asylum Corps—United States, 39–40, 68, 90
asylum adjudicators, 6–9, 16, 19–23, 58–59,
  66–71, 77, 86, 90–98, 104, 107–109,
  124–141 146–159, 168–171, 183–184,
  189–191
  in Australia, 137–142, 155–159, 189–191
  in Canada, 126–130, 141–142,
    152–155, 158–159, 168–171,
    183–184
  and Chinese asylum seekers, 146
  and cultural bias, 22–23, 125
  and gender bias, 125, 133
  political pressure, 9, 11, 21–22, 33–34, 39,
    48, 53–54, 76, 88–89, 95–100, 103,
    108–110, 122, 126–127, 148, 159,
    172–173, 176, 187–188
  in the United States, 130–137, 141–142,
    148–152, 158–159
asylum seekers
  American, 46
  Central American, 39, 70, 131, 133–134,
    166

Chinese, 12, 49, 98, 104–105, 143–159, 185
cost of claims, 10, 15, 27–28, 40, 50, 87–89,
  93, 95, 100
Cuban, 26, 37–38, 41, 44
deterrence, 10, 24, 50, 163, 187
economic migrants, 3, 6, 12, 21, 24–25, 44,
  99, 105, 146, 183
fraudulent claims, 21, 24, 48–49, 51, 82,
  109, 147
Haitian, 37–41, 44, 48, 60, 76, 98, 167
homosexual, 99, 189
human smugglers, 21, 42, 48–49, 55–56,
  143, 149, 175
media coverage, 28–29, 35–36
Mexican, 8, 44, 96, 98–100, 155, 184, 187,
  189
as potential security threats, 3, 21, 32, 165,
  169–171
Vietnamese, 26, 38, 53
asylum seeker acceptance rates, 6–7,15, 24, 28,
  30, 69, 72, 99, 105, 147–149, 152, 158,
  163, 182, 187
Australia
  adversarial legalism, 103, 116–117
  administrative justice, 103, 106, 111,
    116–117, 138, 182
  asylum seeker acceptance rates, 6–7, 15, 59,
    105, 147
  asylum seeker advocates, 8–9 107–109
  boat arrivals, 35–37, 49, 53–59, 101
  bureaucratic adversarialism, 103, 116–117
  bureaucratic legalism, 109
  caseloads, 53–54, 93, 113, 191
  and Chinese asylum seekers, 104–105,
    147–148, 155–158, 185
  cost of asylum claims, 108, 111
  Convention Relating to the Status of
    Refugees (1951), 33–34, 176, 190
  Democrat Party, 174